COLD
WAR
RADIO

COLD WAR RADIO

The Russian Broadcasts of the
Voice of America and Radio
Free Europe/Radio Liberty

MARK G. POMAR

Potomac Books
An imprint of the University of Nebraska Press

Library of Congress Cataloging-in-Publication Data
Names: Pomar, Mark G., author.
Title: Cold War radio : the Russian broadcasts of the Voice of America and Radio Free Europe/Radio Liberty / Mark G. Pomar.
Description: Lincoln : Potomac Books, an imprint of the University of Nebraska Press, [2022] | Includes bibliographical references and index.
Identifiers: LCCN 2022003493
ISBN 9781640125148 (hardback)
ISBN 9781640125568 (epub)
ISBN 9781640125575 (pdf)
Subjects: LCSH: Radio Free Europe—History. | Radio Liberty—History. | International broadcasting—United States—History. | United States—Foreign relations—Soviet Union. | Soviet Union—Foreign relations—United States. | Cold War—Propaganda. | BISAC: HISTORY / Russia & the Former Soviet Union | SOCIAL SCIENCE / Media Studies
Classification: LCC HE8697.45.E852 P66 2022 | DDC 384.54094/09045—dc23/eng/20220127
LC record available at https://lccn.loc.gov/2022003493

Set in Lyon Text by Laura Buis.

CONTENTS

ILLUSTRATIONS

The Voice of America and Radio Free Europe/Radio Liberty are major international broadcasters, funded by the U.S. government through open congressional appropriations, and yet are virtually unknown even among the better educated and politically aware American public. Older Americans may recall the Crusade for Freedom and other media campaigns in the 1950s to solicit funding for Radio Free Europe, but in the 1980s when I would list RFE/RL or the Voice of America as my employer, I was usually met with sheer consternation. Even in Washington DC, few people seemed to know what those organizations were. When I was in Cavendish, Vermont, in 1984 to interview Alexandr Solzhenitsyn for VOA, the hotel clerk asked if I was a member of a national singing group.

Yet if one travels abroad, especially to Eastern Europe and the countries of the former Soviet Union, one quickly realizes that the two radio stations are popular American brands, loved and respected by tens of millions of dedicated listeners. Willis Conover, the legendary host of the VOA jazz program, was known throughout the world as the "voice of American music." When he traveled to Poland, he was mobbed as a superstar. He had fan clubs in China, Russia, and many other countries around the world. His broadcasts were the embodiment of U.S. cultural diplomacy, giving people in the farthest corners of the world a taste of American life.

The two radio stations, of course, offered much more than just music or entertainment. Alexandr Solzhenitsyn referred to VOA and RFE/RL as "the mighty non-military forces that reside in the airwaves and whose kindling power in the midst of darkness cannot even be grasped by the Western imagination."[1] The well-known Soviet dissident and Israeli politician Natan Sharansky credited VOA and RL with helping dissidents survive and keeping alive the spirit of Jewish *refuseniks*,

Soviet Jews not allowed to emigrate to Israel. By mentioning the names of human rights activists and telling their stories, the two radios often protected them from excessively harsh treatment by the KGB. Andrei Sakharov and his wife, Elena Bonner, told Western correspondents that they received most of their news about the world from the broadcasts of VOA and RL and considered them "their radios." In the 1990s I met a young man in Tatarstan, some four hundred miles east of Moscow, who, upon learning that I had worked at RFE/RL, hugged me and told me his parents had always listened to the Tatar-Bashkir Service of Radio Liberty and those broadcasts nurtured their culture. "You Americans," he said, "really cared about us."

VOA and RFE/RL lend themselves to serious study as part of U.S. public diplomacy, international journalism, or Cold War history. Books by Sig Mickelson, Arch Puddington, Alan Heil, Gene Parta, Michael Nelson, Nicholas Cull, and A. Ross Johnson have contributed significantly to our understanding of international broadcasting by examining how the radio stations developed into major institutions, their relationship to the U.S. government, and the composition of the audience. Memoirs by Gene Sosin, James Critchlow, George Urban, and Victor Franzusoff have given us a sense of what it was like to work at the radio stations and have sketched memorable portraits of the more eccentric personalities. My aim is different. I will tell the story of the radios by taking the reader inside Voice of America and Radio Liberty and examining the conception and development of the programs of the two Russian services and the impact those broadcasts had on the development of international broadcasting, U.S.-Soviet relations, Russian political and cultural history, and the end of the Cold War. My examination of the Russian-language broadcasts will give readers a deeper understanding of the multifaceted role the two radios played during the Cold War, ranging from instruments of Cold War policy to repositories of independent Russian culture, literature, philosophy, religion, and the arts. Among the questions I will address are the following: What subjects were most prominent in the broadcasts? Who were the broadcasters and their guest commentators? What tone did the broadcasters adopt, even in times of crisis? How did VOA and RFE/RL handle controversial issues, including Soviet disinformation campaigns? In what ways did the two radios nurture a "free and independent Russia" that could exist and flourish outside of the Soviet Union?

All too often VOA and RFE/RL have been painted with a broad brush, praised or excoriated by politicians, journalists, and academics on the basis of a superficial understanding of the actual programming. Given the difficulty of tuning in the shortwave broadcasts, as well as the challenges of parsing Russian politics, philosophy, and culture, both in their Soviet and émigré incarnations, many American foreign policy experts, journalists, and Soviet and East European scholars formed their judgments about VOA and RFE/RL based on English-language summaries of the broadcasts, official policy guidance, the occasional scandal, or Soviet publications that regularly lambasted the radios. These individuals quite often painted a distorted picture of VOA and RFE/RL. By analyzing a broad cross section of the Russian-language broadcasts, I will try to set the record straight and give readers an opportunity to draw their own conclusions about the two radios. I will supplement my examination of the programming with references to declassified U.S. government documents, interviews with former broadcasters, and my own notes and personal papers.

Although this study examines the entire Cold War, I focus primarily on the 1980s and early 1990s because this was a period of monumental political change that tested VOA and RFE/RL as they covered Gorbachev's policies of glasnost and perestroika, the collapse of communism in Eastern Europe, and the dissolution of the Soviet Union. The Reagan administration also made international broadcasting a high priority in the battle against communism. As Reagan said explicitly, "The West won't contain communism; it will transcend communism. . . . It will dismiss it as some bizarre chapter in human history whose last pages are even now being written."[2] And as VOA and RFE/RL helped to write those last pages, they received increased funding and played a more significant role in implementing U.S. foreign policy.

No less important was that, by the early 1980s, the Soviet Union had expelled many leading writers, thinkers, and artists. Alexandr Solzhenitsyn, Mstislav "Slava" Rostropovich, Galina Vishnevskaya,

Vladimir Voinovich, Vasily Aksyonov, and Sergei Dovlatov were among the many Russian artists and writers who were eager to lend their voices to the Russian broadcasts. They commanded authority and respect in their homeland, and their interviews and programs resonated throughout the Soviet Union, allowing the two radio stations to reach a mass audience.

During the Reagan and Bush administrations, I was involved in virtually every aspect of broadcasting to the USSR, first as the assistant director of the RL Russian Service and later as the chief of the VOA Russian Service, director of the VOA USSR Division, and executive director of the Board for International Broadcasting, the federal agency overseeing RFE/RL. I developed new programs and conducted interviews with prominent Russians; participated in high-level discussions of broadcast policy at the United States Information Agency (USIA), the Department of State, and the National Security Council (NSC); testified in Congress; took part in the first negotiations with Soviet authorities to end the jamming of RFE/RL; and opened an RFE/RL news bureau in Moscow. I had the privilege of working closely with Steve Forbes, Charles Wick, James Buckley, Gene Pell, Lane Kirkland, Kenneth Tomlinson, Michael Novak, and many other notable figures in international broadcasting. I also interviewed many prominent Russian writers, artists, and dissidents, including Alexandr Solzhenitsyn, Vasily Aksyonov, and Vladimir Voinovich, and became friends with Slava Rostropovich and his wife, the opera diva Galina Vishnevskaya. By drawing on my personal knowledge, I will be able to explain how broadcast policy was formulated, the way the Russian services of VOA and RL operated, and why the two broadcasters were greeted so positively in post-Communist Eastern Europe and Russia. On occasion, I will adopt a first-person narration when I draw on my personal experiences to elucidate the work of the radio stations.

Before 1980 VOA and RFE/RL were generally seen as separate organizations governed by distinct missions. VOA was part of the U.S. government, located in Washington DC, and staffed by federal employees. Like the British Broadcasting Corporation (BBC), Radio France Internationale, Deutsche Welle, Kol Israel, and many other government broadcasters, VOA was a national voice, charged with explaining U.S. government policies and telling America's story with the aim of gaining the respect and goodwill of its target audience. It operated under a charter (Public Law 94-350) that stated, "(1) VOA will serve as a consistently reliable and authoritative source of news; (2) VOA will represent America, not any single segment of American society; and (3) VOA will present the policies of the U.S. clearly and effectively, and will also present responsible discussion and opinion on those policies."[3] Until the 1980s many VOA Russian programs were translations from English sources, supplied either by the VOA Central News Division or taken from leading U.S. papers such as the *New York Times*, *Washington Post*, or the *Wall Street Journal*. Its management and staff were cautious in their treatment of controversial political subjects, especially concerning the internal politics of the USSR. The State Department paid close attention to the Russian broadcasts. Until the 1980s, the chief of the USSR Division was a senior foreign service officer; I was the first career civil servant to hold that position.

In contrast, RFE/RL was a grantee of the U.S. government and was located in Munich, before moving to Prague in the mid-1990s. It hired primarily émigrés and functioned as a "surrogate station"—in effect, a home service located abroad. Its Russian broadcasts did not speak for the United States and presented news, feature programming, and opinions that would have been part of daily political discourse if Russia had free media and the rule of law. For the VOA Russian broadcasters, the pronoun *we* meant the United States; for the RL Russian broadcasters, it meant Mother Russia. Most employees worked for only one broadcaster; books and articles were either about VOA or RFE/RL, but not both. This book breaks new ground, as I examine both broadcasters in the context of Cold War programming and the Reagan and Bush policies toward the Soviet Union.

Under the Reagan administration, the sharp divide between RFE/RL and VOA began to disappear. RFE/RL's past funding by the CIA (until 1971) was no longer taboo for VOA management and RL was eager to hire experienced VOA broadcasters. When I interviewed at VOA, I found that my RL experience was a great boon. The director, Kenneth

Tomlinson, told me that he wanted dynamic programs that addressed relevant issues in the Soviet Union, and if that upset the State Department, so be it. A case in point was Alexandr Solzhenitsyn. While his works were broadcast frequently on Radio Liberty, he was mostly kept off the air at VOA. Solzhenitsyn's nationalist views made him a controversial figure in the United States, while his adamant anticommunism angered Soviet authorities. To cautious U.S. policymakers, his presence on VOA was seen as unnecessarily provocative. When Tomlinson asked me if I would put Solzhenitsyn on the air, I said I certainly would. One could disagree with many of Solzhenitsyn's views, and some of his writings displayed authoritarian tendencies, but in the 1980s he was an iconic figure whose voice needed to be heard in Russia. That answer cemented the job offer.

In my examination of the programming, I do not ignore the different missions of VOA and RFE/RL, but my intention is to look at the overall impact of Russian-language broadcasts on Soviet domestic politics, Russian political culture, and U.S.-Soviet relations. As a general rule, Russian listeners did not care which station they tuned in, so long as the programs were relevant and interesting. Many Russians simply called all international broadcasters "voices," on occasion ironically referring to them with the Soviet cliché *vrazheskie golosa* (enemy voices).

ACKNOWLEDGMENTS

In conducting research for this book, I was able to discuss the Russian broadcasts with many old friends and former colleagues. Natalie Clarkson, Ludmila "Lucy" Obolensky Flam, Tatiana Retivov, Nik Sorokin, Vladimir Matlin, Marina Oeltjen, and the Rev. Victor Potapov helped me to gather materials about the VOA broadcasts and recreate the mood of the Russian Service in the 1980s. I also spent many hours discussing RFE/RL broadcasts with Ross Johnson, Gene Parta, and John Lindburg and am grateful to them for sharing their observations. Special thanks goes to Ivan Tolstoy, a senior editor at RFE/RL, who shared his thoughts on Radio Liberty programming and whose magisterial series featuring highlights from first half century of Russian broadcasts gave me a deeper understanding of the richness and diversity of Russian-language programming.

I would like to thank the Clements Center for National Security at the University of Texas, Austin, and its director, William Inboden, for giving me an intellectual home that allowed me to conduct research and share my views with colleagues. I also had the opportunity to teach a graduate course on U.S. international broadcasting at the Moody School of Journalism at the University of Texas. My UT students challenged my views and pushed me to see VOA and RFE/RL in a broader context of international media and public diplomacy. I am grateful to them, especially to Michelle Daniel and Audrius Justinas Rickus.

I would like to thank the Smith Richardson Foundation for providing me with a generous research grant.

Finally, and most important, I thank my wife, Susanne Sternthal, and my son, George, who gave me the time, space, encouragement, and support to complete this work. A gifted writer and a superb editor, Susanne read the text with a keen eye to detail and made many suggestions that improved the book. I am ever so grateful to her and dedicate this work to her, with all my love.

COLD
WAR
RADIO

Introduction

To understand the significance of the Russian broadcasts of VOA and Radio Liberty, one must realize that they were a direct outgrowth of the Cold War and were viewed by U.S. policymakers as important tools in confronting, and even defeating, a new and dangerous enemy. Although VOA had begun broadcasting shortly after the Japanese attack on Pearl Harbor in December 1941, out of deference to its Soviet ally, the U.S. government excluded Russian programming from its growing list of language services. Only in 1947, with the Cold War gaining traction, did VOA initiate Russian broadcasts that projected American policies and values and directly challenged the Soviet narrative of domestic and international affairs. In the case of surrogate broadcasting, it took until 1953 to establish Radio Liberty, with a prominent board of directors, a set of journalistic guidelines, shortwave transmitters, and a competent émigré staff. But as early as April 1948, George Kennan laid out the need and rationale for Radio Liberty's surrogate programming by employing the term *political warfare*, which he defined as "all means at a nation's command, short of war, to achieve its national objectives."[1] Responding to the Kremlin's growing foreign aggression, described as "the most refined and effective of any in history," Kennan argued for the creation of a toolkit that could counter the USSR on many different levels. In Kennan's words, these new operations would "range from such overt actions as political alliances, economic measures, and 'white' propaganda to such covert operations as clandestine support for 'friendly' foreign elements, 'black' psychological warfare and even the encouragement of underground resistance in hostile states."[2] Kennan viewed VOA and RFE/RL as the moral high ground of political warfare because their sources and activities were open and they were committed to presenting factually accurate news and feature programming. In today's political lexicon, he would probably have used the term *strategic narrative*, commonly defined as "promoting a country's interests, values, and aspirations for the international order and defining 'who we are' and what kind of world order we want." In the 1940s, however, words such as *propaganda* and *warfare* had not yet acquired their current negative connotations.[3] Only the initial covert funding of Radio Free Europe and Radio Liberty caused some officials to use the term *gray operations*, but *gray* changed to *white* in the early 1970s when the U.S. Congress started to fund RFE/RL through open congressional appropriations.

The raison d'être of Russian-language broadcasting was to confront the Soviet Union in a struggle that George Urban, RFE director in the 1980s, characterized as "unconventional warfare," fought not with tanks and artillery but with "words, ideas, perceptions, papal visits, arguments about shopping baskets and other soft means."[4] These new means of warfare required new weapons that would circumvent the Soviet regime's control of domestic media and address Russian listeners directly. U.S. policymakers believed that the free flow of verified and truthful information—so fundamental to any open society—posed a direct threat to the very survival of the USSR. "The intent of RFE and RL," Ross Johnson noted, "was to provide listeners with an intellectual bridge to Western Europe and the United States and a factual basis for comprehending their own lives and the world around them, so as to preserve the independent thinking that the controlled domestic media sought to prevent or suppress."[5] By broadcasting fact-based news about the world, and especially about the internal conditions in the USSR, U.S. policymakers believed the two radio stations could significantly weaken and even defeat communism. Their goal, as George Urban observed, "was to impart a sense of the 'right measure of things' to the communist world across the whole range of human activities . . . to make it easier for our audiences to distinguish reality from illusion, facts from fabrications, ideas consonant with a dignified and life enhancing conception of man and the human environment from ideas neutral or hostile to them."[6]

While the mission of VOA and RFE/RL was patriotic and aspirational, the formulation and development of the actual broadcasts proved to be complex and, at times, even contentious. Were current news broadcasts alone a sufficiently powerful weapon to challenge the USSR, or did VOA and RFE/RL need to target Soviet crimes, economic failures, and aggressive foreign policy? Should the two radios focus on life in the West, thereby exposing the shortcomings of the Soviet Union only indirectly, or should the broadcasts dwell on Soviet history and domestic problems? Did hard-hitting programming on economics, philosophy, or religion inevitably acquire aspects of propaganda?[7] And should the radios accept the label of propaganda or resist it? From the earliest days, these questions caused heated arguments among the broadcasters themselves, competing agendas among senior American management, direct and indirect involvement of the State Department and the White House, and bitter struggles over broadcast policy in Congress.

At the risk of simplification, I suggest that a useful way of making sense of the challenges facing the Russian broadcasts is to recognize the push and pull of two competing approaches to programming that emerged at the outset and, to varying degrees, coexisted throughout the Cold War years: strategic broadcasting and purist journalism. The strategic approach saw broadcasting as a weapon that could pierce the Iron Curtain and weaken Communist rule. "Our station has, above all, a fighting and political mission," noted Pavel Tigrid, an early editor at RFE. "Our offensive is directed against Communism."[8] That fighting spirit was echoed by other founders of RFE and RL as they justified the budgets and operations of the radios in terms of U.S. national security. John Foster Dulles, Frank Wisner, General Lucius Clay, among other early Cold Warriors, favored programming that exposed Soviet hypocrisy, gave voice to marginalized groups, fostered nationalism in different ethnic republics of the USSR, and reported on violations of human rights, Stalinist rule, and the gulag system. In the words of an early Cold War policy (National Security Policy Directive 68), radio programs "should foster a fundamental change in the Soviet system.... They should be designed to build and maintain confidence in our strength and resolution, and to wage overt psychological warfare calculated to encourage mass defections from Soviet allegiance."[9] For the strategists who tended to see programming in militarized terms,

Soviet censorship helped to set the daily agenda: issues that official Soviet media distorted or ignored became lead stories for VOA and RL. Every day there were new battlegrounds, and the strategists relished their role as warriors fighting for freedom.

In sharp contrast, advocates of the purist approach stressed high journalistic standards, disdained attempts at strategic narratives, favored the inclusion of nonpolitical and cultural topics, and argued that programming reflecting liberal values would attract a large and devoted audience that could be weaned away from Soviet propaganda. The purists were adamant that the news be straightforward and comprehensive, eschewing any rumors or hearsay and relying on the open two-source rule that allowed only publicly available news stories to be cited. From the outset, the purist view prevailed in news reporting. At VOA, the purists also advocated an American voice that reflected the diversity of American public opinion and did not shy away from addressing the problems facing American society. They favored John F. Kennedy's admonition that VOA, "as part of the cause of freedom, and the arm of freedom, is obliged to tell our story in a truthful way, painting us with all our blemishes and warts."[10] Purists at RL favored balanced, thoughtful discussions of important political issues supplemented by programming about culture, the arts, and literature. Most important, they advocated a calm and reasonable tone that avoided gratuitous criticism of the Soviet Union, convinced that communicating the creative freedom of the West, and especially the accomplishments of Russian émigrés, would be the most effective way to gain a large and dedicated audience. They emphatically rejected strident editorial commentary or direct appeals to the Soviet population to resist Communist rule.

No one, of course, was exclusively a strategist or purist. Everyone at VOA and RFE/RL recognized that with the exception of the newscast at the top of the hour, all feature programming fell somewhere along the continuum between the two approaches, combining fact-based reporting with a strategic purpose of informing listeners about events that Soviet media either distorted or ignored. But in my experience, broadcasters and radio executives inevitably leaned toward one approach or the other in their fundamental conception of the radio stations. As we will see in the ensuing chapters, these differing views created an underlying tension that fostered acrimonious editorial meetings, ideological debates, and uneasy compromises. I recall how the appearance of Soviet dissidents and human rights activists in the VOA studios, harshly criticizing Soviet actions, was greeted as a moment of triumph by many Russian broadcasters but seen as a selling-out of VOA's high-minded mission by some of the old-school American managers. RL programming about Russian nationalist traditions and conservative thought was enthusiastically heralded by some RFE/RL executives and older émigré broadcasters as the most effective strategy to defeat Communist rule but reviled by many recent Soviet émigrés as dangerous propaganda and a sop to Russian anti-Semites.

The fundamental divide between an aggressive stance and a neutral voice was further widened by overall U.S. policy toward the Soviet Union, which in the course of the Cold War first favored the radio strategists in the 1950s and then swung to the purists during the period of détente in the late 1960s and 1970s, only to return to the strategists in the Reagan years. These policy shifts principally affected official pronouncements about the radios, program-guidance documents, and the hiring and retention of key senior management. The actual broadcasts operated throughout the Cold War on a relatively even keel. In the 1950s and 1960s, when the strategists held the upper hand, Russian programs included sharp critiques of the Soviet Union, occasional diatribes by political émigrés, and even some direct appeals to the Soviet population by such luminary figures as Alexandra Tolstaya (the daughter of the novelist) and Natalia Sedova (Leon Trotsky's widow). But the bulk of the programming in those years featured straight news, cultural shows, popular and classical music, and many nonpolitical stories that would have been welcomed on any serious Western national radio. With the emergence of détente in the late 1960s and 1970s, the purists asserted that the rationale for the two radios was to promote the principles of democracy and to communicate American values through youth programming, cultural shows, and popular music. Reeling from attacks by Senator William Fulbright, who wanted to close Radio Liberty, U.S.

policymakers sought to bury earlier traces of aggressive programming and in their public pronouncements stressed VOA's and RFE/RL's commitment to a fair and balanced presentation of the news. But well-researched programs about the plight of Soviet dissidents, the travails of Jewish refuseniks, and Stalin's crimes continued to be broadcast on both VOA and RFE/RL, and elements of political warfare never went away. With the election of Ronald Reagan in 1980, official U.S. policy was once again redirected at defeating communism, and the strategists emerged triumphant, occupying many senior positions at both VOA and RFE/RL. The Reagan administration resurrected the original concept of the radios as weapons and gave broadcasters wide latitude in developing strategic broadcasts that exposed the fault lines of the Soviet regime. VOA was encouraged to invite prominent dissidents to the studios and to broadcast the works of Alexandr Solzhenitsyn; RL had a free hand in airing more programs on conservative philosophy and religion. These were major developments for both radio stations, but the core news and current-affairs programming remained true to the well-established precepts advocated by the purists and continued to live up to high journalistic standards.

When I joined the radios in the early 1980s, my principal task was to keep the strategists and the purists in a healthy and creative balance. These two approaches were instrumental in producing the kind of programming mix that proved to be relevant to Soviet listeners and helped to pave the way for glasnost and perestroika and the eventual demise of the regime. When the Soviet Union finally crumbled, both VOA and RFE/RL were universally acknowledged as heroes by both Mikhail Gorbachev and Boris Yeltsin and warmly welcomed in post-Communist Russia. The two radios were one of America's triumphs in the Cold War, and the key to their success lay in the programming that went on air.

A thorough examination of the Russian broadcasts of VOA and RFE/RL not only provides a deeper understanding of the Cold War itself and U.S.-Soviet relations but also sheds light on the multifaceted nature of Russian political culture. Since the Soviet Union controlled public debate on social, political, and ideological questions until the late

1980s, it in effect ceded to RFE/RL (and to a lesser extent, VOA) the all-important role of a public forum for the free and open discussion of Russian politics and culture. The eternal questions of Russian history—so vital to a free society—were discussed and debated in the hallways of the radios and, most important, in the broadcast studios: Is Russia part of Europe, or is it Asian? Or, perhaps, a separate civilization? Who was to blame for the February Revolution and the October 1917 coup d'état? Was Stalinism inevitable? Is the rise of Russian nationalism a positive development or a manifestation of age-old xenophobia? Is there a special path (*osoby put'*) for Russia, or is that policy just an excuse to maintain authoritarian rule? As a general rule, recent Soviet émigrés, many of them Jewish, favored a multicultural Russia that would evolve toward Western norms and practices. Given the legacy of pogroms and anti-Semitic policies, they were wary of Russian nationalism and the veneration of Tsarist Russia. Many older émigrés, especially at RL, saw nationalism as the key to a prosperous Russia and advocated Russian exceptionalism. There were even the occasional outliers, naive Socialists who were trying to find Leninist democracy and saw cooperatives as the surest path to a successful economy. To listen to the broadcasts was to be fully immersed in all the big issues as well as in the smaller byways of Russian politics and history. To work at the radios was to partake in the debates about the political, economic, and cultural values of a future non-Communist Russia.

1

Setting the Stage

The use of shortwave radio signals for long-distance transmission, pioneered by Guglielmo Marconi in the early 1920s, introduced a new tool of international relations that allowed states to communicate with their colonies and expatriate citizens, bolster national prestige, promote tourism and trade, and, most important, project their national values by telling their stories directly to people across the world. As early as 1926 the United Kingdom set up the Imperial Wireless Chain to carry radio broadcasts to Australia, India, South Africa, and Canada. A year later, the Dutch began broadcasting to their colonies in the West and East Indies and introduced foreign-language programming—in German, Spanish, and English—to reach influential international audiences. The Dutch even featured a purely entertainment program aired in Dutch, English, and Spanish—aptly named *The Happy Station Show*— that mixed music and light entertainment with lively discussions about Dutch life. In 1929 Radio Moscow began its first international broadcasting, initially in German and later in English and French. By the early 1930s Vatican Radio (1931); the Christian Missionary Service in Quito, Ecuador (1931); and German Auslandsrundfunk (Foreign Radio, 1933) were on the air. In 1932 the BBC started its worldwide English service to project a British narrative of world events and by 1938, with fascism on the rise, expanded its language services to include Arabic, Spanish, Portuguese, German, Italian, and French. "By September 1939," Holly Cowan Shulman noted, "every major power except the United States had its own international broadcasting service."[1]

Although preliminary discussions about creating an international U.S. government broadcaster began taking shape in the 1930s, President Roosevelt showed no interest in the project and eventually nixed those early efforts, siding with commercial broadcasters who had begun to develop their own overseas programs and resisted any form of competition. As early as 1925, NBC/RCA relayed its domestic programs to Europe, utilizing a 25,000-watt transmitter in Bound Brook, New Jersey. Shortly afterward, ABC and CBS began their international programs with a smaller, 10,000-watt station in Wayne, New Jersey. By the early 1930s Walter Lemon, a wealthy radio-technology inventor, took shortwave broadcasting to a new level, building a 150,000-watt transmitter in Scituate, Massachusetts, that could reach Europe, Asia, Africa, and Latin America.[2] In a sign of the growing potential of international broadcasting to shape perceptions of America, Lemon aired educational programs in Spanish and Portuguese with generous support from the Rockefeller Foundation.[3]

Only with the outbreak of World War II in 1939 did Roosevelt relent and allow his advisers to begin mapping a strategy for utilizing international broadcasting to bolster the Allies and to communicate America's values, policies, and moral resolve. On July 11, 1941, several months before the United States entered World War II, he authorized the creation of the Office of the Coordinator of Information (COI) at the recommendation of William J. Donovan, a prominent lawyer, and Robert Emmett Sherwood, who was Roosevelt's primary speechwriter on foreign affairs.[4] Initially, the COI combined both overt and covert information programs, but Sherwood believed the two activities were fundamentally different and persuaded Roosevelt to split the COI into two separate agencies: the Office of Strategic Services (the predecessor of the CIA), headed by Donovan, took on covert activities, while the overseas branch of the newly formed Office of War Information (OWI), headed by Sherwood, assumed responsibility for open public diplomacy and the VOA.

A scion of a distinguished American family, a noted playwright, and a popular intellectual with a national profile, Sherwood was at ease among intellectuals in Europe, artists and writers in New York, as well as political insiders in Washington. He had fought with the Royal Highlanders of Canada in World War I and had been wounded and decorated as a war hero, but upon returning home he became a pacifist. An original member of the Algonquin Round Table, he was a close friend of Dorothy Parker, Robert Benchley, and even Groucho Marx.

Sherwood authored several successful plays on Broadway, including *The Road to Rome* (1927), *Idiot's Delight* (1936), and, significantly, *There Shall Be No Night* (1940), a drama about the Soviet invasion of Finland in 1939. Sherwood was engaged in political issues and, by the late 1930s, cast aside his pacifism to adopt a public stance against the isolationist movement in America, even ridiculing Charles Lindbergh as "a Nazi with a Nazi's Olympian contempt for all democratic processes."[5] Sherwood, who was passionate in his opposition to the growing totalitarian threat in Europe, wrote the text of a full-page advertisement in the *New York Times* supporting American efforts to sustain Britain against Nazi Germany. Soon afterward, he was invited to join the Roosevelt administration as a speechwriter and close adviser. He penned some of Roosevelt's most stirring speeches, coining the phrase that America was the "arsenal of democracy," and brought a can-do spirit to the OWI and an undying commitment to the promotion of American values.[6]

In the introduction to his play *There Shall Be No Night*, Sherwood wrote that "we have within ourselves the power to conquer bestiality, not with our muscles and our swords, but with the power of the light that is in our minds."[7] In subsequent writings, he reiterated the power of truth, spoken boldly and forcefully. An American voice, he asserted, "should be the voice of news about America and America's war effort. . . . America's answers to the Axis propaganda should emerge from the power of truth."[8] For Roosevelt, as Shulman wryly noted, "Sherwood made a perfect choice for chief American propagandist: he was liberal, but not too left-wing; he had a national reputation and was well respected; he had no political enemies; and he was passionately committed to the president."[9] Sherwood also saw the role of the OWI as the worldwide disseminator of liberal democracy that would replace the discredited ideologies of totalitarian and autocratic rule. In his conception, the Voice of America would emerge as a new instrument of modern enlightenment.

Having received Roosevelt's blessing to build a U.S. broadcasting capability, Sherwood began by forming a team of experienced journalists who knew foreign affairs, had worked overseas, and "believed deeply and almost in their bones that wars are made in the minds of men and that wars are won in the minds of men."[10] To help understand how best to counter foreign propaganda, Sherwood turned to Edd Johnson, an experienced journalist who had run the CBS (Columbia Broadcasting System) monitoring service, and to James Warburg, a seventh-generation descendant of the international banking house of Warburg. In addition to having a wide professional network, Warburg, who was Jewish, had traveled frequently to Germany as a child and brought to the task a visceral aversion to fascism. The most colorful character in the group was Joseph F. Barnes. Reputed to be a child prodigy, Barnes had degrees from Harvard University and the London School of Economics and spent the 1930s as a foreign correspondent for the *New York Herald Tribune*, first in Moscow and later in Berlin. Fascinated by the Soviet Union, Barnes learned Russian, joined the American Socialist Party, and even translated several works of Soviet fiction. George Kennan, who knew Barnes from their time in Moscow, described him as "much more pro-Soviet than the rest of us—naively so, it seemed to me."[11] William Shirer, a colleague and friend, noted that up to 1939, when the Soviet Union and Nazi Germany signed the Molotov-Ribbentrop Pact of nonaggression, Barnes had been "very sympathetic to the Soviets and their aspirations and believed that World War II had been ignited by capitalist interests."[12] Although professing loyalty to the United States and championing Western democracy, Barnes brought a distinctly leftist political viewpoint to Sherwood's brain trust. He was adamant that the United States support not only Britain and the Allies but also European resistance movements and Socialist alternatives to capitalism, so prominent in the Popular Front campaigns of the 1930s. Barnes's Communist sympathies were later reflected in some of the personnel and policy decisions that the Voice of America made in the 1940s. As Ted Lipien, the former head of the VOA Polish Service and a historian of VOA, has pointed out, several early VOA managers and writers were sympathetic to communism, among them the first director of VOA, John Houseman, and Howard Fast, the American writer who was awarded the Stalin International Peace Prize in 1953.[13]

The task facing Sherwood and his advisers was daunting. As Shulman has shown, they "struggled to define their role, their aims, and their methods within a shifting and confusing environment. No authorized version of good, or even appropriate, propaganda existed. No department of the government or tradition of the government dictated what kind of message American propagandists should send to the world: friend, foe, or neutral. The task of 1941 and 1942 was to establish a propaganda agency and define its goals and methods."[14] Rather than spend months deliberating over strategy, in typical American fashion Sherwood began with dramatic action, hiring John Houseman. A Romanian-born, British American actor and producer of theater, film, and television, Houseman had worked closely with Orson Welles in the Federal Theatre Project, the Mercury Theatre, and the production of the infamous *War of the Worlds* (1938), whose dramatization of an alien invasion caused panic among American radio listeners. Later in his career, Houseman starred as Professor Charles Kingsfield in the popular film *The Paper Chase* (1973), for which he won the Academy Award for Best Actor in a Supporting Role.

Houseman believed that dramatic techniques, borrowed from commercial radio and theater, would give VOA a distinctive presence on the airwaves, different from what he considered to be the staid approach of the BBC and other international broadcasters. To accomplish the herculean task of fielding a new radio broadcasting in German, French, Italian, and English, Houseman brought on board professional U.S. broadcasters, including Virgil Thomson, Richard C. Hottelet, and Burgess Meredith. He also hired prominent European journalists, notably Pierre Lazareff, the editor of *Paris-Midi* and, later, *Paris-Soir*, who in turn hired such luminaries as the anthropologist Claude Lévi-Strauss, the surrealist writer André Breton, and the actor Yul Brynner. Not ones to sit by idly, Sherwood's executive team worked alongside the broadcasters in the VOA newsroom, producing scripts and commentaries. "I was very much impressed," recalled Leonard Miall, the BBC liaison officer to the OWI, "by the quiet efficiency with which Barnes managed to keep everything under control. Houseman turned out to be a tower of strength, and managed to reorganize all the transmitters and programs very smoothly and very fast.... Barnes and Johnson were writing scripts, Houseman was personally in the studio producing the shows,

Warburg was writing the leads for the German section. . . . This was the first time that I had seen people at this level so close to the microphone."[15] Within months, Houseman's enterprise was broadcasting hundreds of hours of programming a week. As Walter Roberts, the head of the VOA Austrian Service and years later the executive director of the Board for International Broadcasting, recalled, Houseman was a natural leader "with his royal voice, his regal stride. . . . He walked up and down Madison Avenue [where VOA was initially located] as if he owned it."[16]

Dramatic radio techniques aside, the fledgling VOA understood that its principal task was a new type of warfare that called for defeating the enemy on the battlefield of ideas, supporting the Allies in their combat, and providing aid and comfort to the civilian populations under siege. An early VOA policy report referred to this type of warfare as "not merely a battle of words, but a battle for people's minds and through their minds their physical actions."[17] From the outset, VOA chose straightforward reporting of the facts as its main weapon to defeat the Axis powers. "We ruled out the technique of falsehood," Barnes stated bluntly. "The task of U.S. radio would be to 'tell the truth,' the simple truth in a friendly spirit."[18] His reasoning was that fact-based broadcasting embodied deeply held American values and would immediately set VOA apart from the Axis broadcasts, thereby helping to win the trust of people living under Nazi rule. "We bring you Voices from America," the very first broadcast stated in German. "Today, and daily from now on, we shall speak to you about America and the war. The news may be good for us. The news may be bad. But we shall tell you the truth."[19]

Houseman later recalled that "the news that VOA would carry to the world in the first half of 1942 was almost all bad. As Japanese invasions followed one after another with sickening regularity and the Nazi armies moved ever deeper into Russia and the Near East, we would have to report our reverses without weaseling. Only thus could we establish a reputation for honesty that we hoped would pay off on that distant but inevitable day when we would start reporting our own invasions and victories."[20] The critical decision to "play it straight" became a VOA trademark and laid the foundation for three programming pillars that were to govern all subsequent U.S. international broadcasting. The first was broadcasting the latest news quickly and accurately. During World War II, this was vital for establishing VOA's reputation. When, for example, General Joseph "Vinegar Joe" Stilwell commented that his units "took a hell of a beating" by the Japanese, VOA broadcast his words in full. After the war, German, Italian, and Japanese officials testified that Stilwell's statement, as well as many other reports acknowledging American defeats, convinced them that VOA was indeed a source of truthful information.[21] The second pillar supported inchoate surrogate broadcasting. To aid the civilian population, VOA editors realized that they had to monitor conditions on the ground and, to the extent possible, create a credible "local" radio station. In her examination of VOA French broadcasts, Shulman showed how VOA's granular analysis of political developments in Vichy France made its broadcasts a daily staple for the French audience. The third pillar was an unvarnished presentation of the United States—its policies, institutions, aspirations, as well as the struggles to live up to its lofty ideals. Together, these principles shaped VOA's political warfare during WWII and established the framework of future broadcasts.

The emphasis on truthful information that animated the founders of VOA had its roots in New Deal liberalism that Reinhold Niebuhr, Henry Wallace, and the readers of *The Nation* would have recognized as a two-front battle: the fight for democracy on foreign soil and the corollary battle to realize full democracy at home. For Sherwood, Barnes, Johnson, and Houseman, it was not enough to simply defeat Hitler and then go back to business as usual. Rather, they saw military victory as a unique opportunity to make the world safe for democracy by fully realizing Roosevelt's New Deal. In their conception, VOA would propagate the principles of liberal democracy not only in its news reporting but also through creative radio plays and feature programs that showed how democracy functioned and why foreign societies should adopt democratic norms. As Warburg wrote in *The Isolationist Illusion and World Peace*, the goal of the OWI was a new world order "permeated with justice that demands that all those who are affected by the exercise of any power—political, social, or economic—must have a voice in deciding to whom that power is delegated and how it is exercised."[22] Above all, Sherwood and his team wanted VOA to be the promoter of universal democracy as embodied in Roosevelt's famous Four Freedoms: "We look forward to a world founded upon four essential human freedoms: (1) freedom of speech and expression—everywhere in the world; (2) freedom of every person to worship God in his way—everywhere in the world; (3) freedom from want—economic understandings which will secure to every nation a healthy peacetime life for its inhabitants— everywhere in the world; and (4) freedom from fear and aggression— anywhere in the world."[23]

Despite the technical creativity of the early broadcasts and the enthusiasm of its founders, VOA was engulfed in the inevitable bureaucratic infighting between journalistic independence and the exigencies of government policy, especially during a time of war. VOA's freewheeling advocacy of democratic liberalism rankled the military, especially when the broadcasts ran counter to the actual prosecution of the war. A striking example was Eisenhower's controversial decision to appoint the Vichy minister of the navy, Jean Darlan, as the head of the postliberation government of French North Africa in the aftermath of Operation Torch, the successful Allied invasion. The Roosevelt administration felt justified in making this appointment for tactical military reasons, but for the antifascist forces in Europe Darlan was simply a French version of a Gestapo leader. So strong were the ties between the French resistance and Sherwood's team that VOA even balked at airing programs that supported the Darlan appointment, seeing it as a violation of its liberal democratic messianism. Warburg went so far as to declare that the Darlan agreement "indicates to the world that when we liberate a country, we shall make a practice of putting our friends in jail and turning the liberated country over to the enemies of democracy."[24] Rather than compromising their long-held liberal principles for the expediency of military victory, the founders of VOA clung to their belief that the overarching goal of VOA was the destruction of National Socialism as a political system and the creation of a new world order based on democracy.

Many officials in the State Department saw the founders of VOA as leftist radicals who placed their ideology above government policy and for this reason had to be restrained through bureaucratic means. Some treated Joseph Barnes as a Stalinist and called his wife an out-and-out Communist.[25] Others went so far as to use the passport office to deny John Houseman the right to travel abroad to inspect growing VOA field operations, convinced that he was a politically unreliable figure. As the Roosevelt government stepped back from universal democracy as the ultimate goal of the war and pursued military victory at all costs, the idealistic Popular Front liberals who had created VOA found themselves isolated and subjected to increased criticism. This tension came to a head when VOA refused to treat the resignation of Benito Mussolini as a major positive step in the prosecution of the war. Warburg even commissioned a commentary from Samuel Grafton of the *New York Post* that stated that "the moronic little King [Victor Emmanuel III of Italy] who has stood behind Mussolini's shoulders for 21 years has now moved forward one pace. This is political minuet, not the revolution we have been waiting for."[26] This statement was picked up by the *New York Times* and later broadcast on VOA, causing a diplomatic scandal. This forced Roosevelt to state at a press conference that he did not approve of this characterization of Victor Emmanuel and that the VOA was not speaking for the administration. Several months later, Sherwood was transferred to the OWI office in London, while the other members of his team were fired. "Only after Sherwood, Barnes, Warburg, and Johnson had left," Shulman observed, and "the new, more politically accommodating leaders of the Overseas Branch withdrew propaganda from controversial liberal political positions and moved the Voice toward 'straight' news and information could the OWI and the State Department begin to work together smoothly."[27] The new team of Lou Cowan, Edward Barrett, and Wallace Carroll accepted the fundamental premise that American foreign policy had to be reflected in VOA broadcasts, even when they personally disagreed with it.[28]

Although ultimately defeated, Sherwood and his colleagues left an indelible mark on all subsequent U.S. international broadcasting. Their clarion call for individual freedom and democracy would be repeated in hundreds of U.S. policy guidelines during the Cold War and is imbedded in the current mission of the U.S. Agency for Global Media that oversees all U.S. broadcasting: "to inform, engage, and connect people around the world in support of freedom and democracy."[29] Their intuitive sense that, to be relevant, international broadcasters had to study and understand the target countries to which they were broadcasting would lay the groundwork for the concept of surrogate broadcasting and the creation of Radio Free Europe and Radio Liberty in the early 1950s. Their clear-eyed presentation of the ills of America and fervent belief in the reform agenda of the New Deal would temper boosterism in VOA broadcasts and lead to programs about the Watergate scandal, racism, and other problems of American society. Their willingness to resist encroachments from the State Department and the White House that violated the broadcasting mission would necessitate the enactment of the VOA Charter. And their principled support of liberal values would be repeated when VOA and RFE/RL shed the burdens of diplomacy to practice sound and professional journalism.

In 1945, with military victory over the Axis powers in reach, VOA's future hung in the balance. So strong was its association with the war effort that the Roosevelt administration had not even drawn up plans about a peacetime mission. Some officials advocated placing VOA within the State Department, simply as an information service. Others suggested creating a new information agency, while a third group thought it best to leave international broadcasting to the private sector. Among the senior officials at VOA, the predominant sentiment was for the U.S. government to bow out gracefully. "During the war," Sherwood wrote, "there had been a moral (but tangible) legitimacy of the term—Voice of America—but with the war ended in Europe I feel it would be patently dishonest to describe as the Voice of America broadcasts that are subject to rigid control by the State Department. . . . [These officials] could not in peacetime be qualified to interpret the real voice of America, which is, eternally, many voices."[30] Having fought his share of bureaucratic battles, Sherwood was skeptical that a federal agency could muster the creativity necessary to reflect the diversity of American life and culture. His parting words raised one of the perennial questions facing

VOA: How could it be an independent broadcaster within a political and bureaucratic structure? As we will see in our examination of the Russian broadcasts, VOA occasionally fell victim to tight policy control, producing weak programming and avoiding politically charged issues of the day. Under more dynamic leadership, however, it rose above the bureaucratic fray and lived up to the best traditions set forth by Sherwood and the founders.

VOA Russian Broadcasts: The Early Years

On August 31, 1945, President Truman signed an executive order abolishing the OWI, transferring responsibility for its functions, including VOA, to the State Department and renaming the new unit the Interim International Information Service (IIIS). An unwanted stepchild, the IIIS was generally ignored by senior State Department officials and subject to deep budget cuts by Congress. More conservative members of Congress long suspected OWI and VOA of harboring dangerous Communists who were useful during the war but would be prone to using the resources of the U.S. government to spread leftist ideology and trumpet the New Deal as a model for the world. Liberal members were skeptical that truthful media could ever be produced within a government bureaucracy and preferred to have private broadcasters take up the task of broadcasting to foreign audiences. Prominent journalists such as Arthur Sulzberger of the *New York Times* also weighed in against VOA, accusing it of distorting the news "in order to create specific impressions abroad about a specific situation in which we have specific interests."[31] By early 1946 the future of VOA looked bleak, and the State Department started planning its shutdown.

VOA survived primarily through the efforts of William Benton, who became the director of the IIIS in May 1946. A dynamic businessman, educator, and aspiring politician, Benton rallied support for VOA by seizing on Truman's words that "the nature of present-day foreign relations makes it essential for the United States to maintain informational activities abroad as an integral part of the conduct of our foreign affairs."[32] Mindful of congressional attacks on government broadcasting, Benton stressed that under his watch VOA would adopt a "purist" approach, eschewing any form of propaganda. In justifying the broadcasts, he noted, "We try to present as objective a news report as is humanly possible. . . . We present the unfavorable, the good about America, and the bad."[33] During his two-year tenure, Benton lobbied Congress for adequate funding, kept transmitter leases alive, and established an influential advisory committee, headed by the legendary journalist Edward R. Murrow. Most important, he understood that VOA could serve as an indispensable counterweight to the Soviet Union's aggressive policies in the area of information and propaganda. He commissioned an analysis from one of the leading U.S. social scientists of the day, Harold Lasswell. "The dominant structure of world politics," Lasswell posited, "is the two-power system. America and Russia will confront one another on practically every question throughout the globe. This multiplies opportunities for friction and for anxiety neuroses on both sides."[34] Lasswell understood that the battle for the hearts and minds of people across the world would be a defining element of the postwar international order and recommended that the United States develop effective means of communication to combat the Soviet Union and to present a full and truthful picture of life in the United States.

Benton's domestic lobbying to save the VOA was abetted by Soviet words and actions. With victory over Germany achieved, the uneasy alliance between an aggressive USSR and its Western allies began to fray rapidly, and the Soviet Union started adopting a warlike stance. On February 9, 1946, Stalin declared that a fundamental ideological chasm existed between "two centers of world significance: a socialist center, drawing to itself the countries which tend toward socialism, and a capitalist center, drawing to itself the countries that incline toward capitalism. Battle between these two centers for command of the world economy will decide the fate of capitalism and communism in the entire world."[35] These words unleashed an all-out propaganda campaign, accompanied by tightening Soviet control over Central and Eastern Europe. "Totalitarian regimes now rule," noted a British intelligence report in 1946, "not only in the Soviet Union but [also] throughout Eastern Europe: in Yugoslavia we have a fully-fledged Communist regime on the Soviet model. . . . In Romania, all legal opposition has now been eliminated. . . . In Bulgaria, the only legal Opposition party and the Opposition press have now been suppressed. . . . In Hungary, Communists control the Ministry of the Interior and its machinery."[36] This sober assessment of Soviet actions was in line with George Kennan's famous long telegram (February 22, 1946), urging the United States to stand firm against a "political force committed fanatically to the belief that with the U.S. there can be no permanent modus vivendi, that it is desirable and necessary that the internal harmony of our society be disrupted, our traditional way of life be destroyed, the international authority of our State be broken, if Soviet power is to be secure. . . . The problem of how to cope with this force is undoubtedly the greatest task our diplomacy has ever faced."[37] Kennan's dire warnings were further echoed on March 5, when Churchill told an audience in Fulton, Missouri, that "from Stettin in the Baltic to Trieste in the Adriatic, an Iron Curtain has descended across the continent. Behind that line lie all the capitals of the ancient states of Central and Eastern Europe: Warsaw, Berlin, Prague, Vienna, Budapest, Belgrade, Bucharest, and Sofia."[38]

These pronouncements, along with growing evidence of Stalin's belligerent actions in Greece and Italy, triggered a government reappraisal of the tools of WWII that could be repurposed for the looming confrontation. Significantly, Kennan noted that unlike Nazi Germany, the Soviet Union would likely not pursue a military struggle if it encountered robust resistance but would opt for a war of words and ideology. The emerging Cold War, he posited, would be fought on a rhetorical plane. In this changing international environment, the strategies developed by international broadcasters during World War II suddenly gained new relevance. As the historian Alban Webb pointed out, the Western allies believed that "the Second World War had demonstrated the influence and importance of broadcasting abroad, both in its own right and as an adjunct to wider government strategies. It had also shown the value of building credibility with audiences through objective and truthful reporting."[39]

In March 1946 the Joint Intelligence Committee (JIC), the coordinating and analytical body of British intelligence, concluded that the Soviet

Union's long-range strategic aim "was to build up the Soviet Union into a position of strength and greatness commensurate with its vast size and resources. Part of its strategy would be to use all weapons, short of a major war . . . to weaken foreign countries, key among which was the full use of propaganda, including radio broadcasts."[40] To counter Soviet propaganda, the British Foreign Office created the Committee on Russian Policy with the task of developing new forms of political warfare. Its main recommendation was to create a Russian-language broadcasting service.

Until March 1946, when the BBC initiated its Russian programming, VOA and BBC had refrained from broadcasting in Russian in deference to its wartime ally.[41] Western powers understood that the Soviet Union practiced draconian censorship and maintained a firm grip over its media. Above all, it feared any outside voice that it could not control and for that reason would have strenuously opposed any Western-funded Russian-language programming. Mindful of these sensitivities, the BBC approached Russian broadcasts with utmost caution. As the British Foreign Office reported, the first Russian broadcasts "were almost entirely non-political, consciously avoiding the kind of critical engagement that had become such a marked characteristic of its regional counterparts."[42] The BBC official in charge of the Russian broadcasts, Hugh Carleton Greene, saw Eastern Europe as occupied lands where "Russian rule may be shaken off" but insisted, quite erroneously from today's perspective, that "no one in his senses could believe that it should be any part of our objective to contribute to the overthrow of the Soviet regime or to liberate the Soviet people, who probably had no desire to be liberated."[43] BBC officials further convinced themselves that the typical Soviet listener was tired of Soviet propaganda and hence not interested in an outsider's critical assessment of Soviet politics. That reasoning led them to favor building "a large and friendly audience by presenting listeners with a straightforward, honest News Bulletin, a comprehensive review of Britain, Parliament, and other British institutions, scientific and cultural achievements, and sporting events (particularly football and chess); and to elucidate in a varied manner and form as many fields as possible of the British way of life."[44] According to Webb, BBC avoided controversial topics, and that resulted in programming that projected Britain's role in the world.[45] So innocuous and irrelevant were these early broadcasts that a delegation of the Supreme Soviet of the USSR visiting Britain called them an "admirable projection of Anglo-Russian friendship."[46]

As the Cold War grew in intensity, the BBC Russian broadcasts began to acquire some bite, but they lagged far behind the BBC broadcasts to Central and Eastern Europe that adopted a strident tone in confronting communist regimes. By mid-1948 the British Embassy in Moscow was recommending more robust programming about current political issues, and the Russian Service responded with reviews of the British press that acknowledged the growing rift between East and West. Even Anatol Goldberg, a longtime commentator, began to address Soviet policies directly, though he avoided reproaching the Soviet government and steered clear of outright criticism of the Soviet system, preferring a tone of regret over the strained relations between the Soviet Union and the West. But with growing political pressure to respond to Soviet rhetoric, Russian broadcasts of BBC began to question Marxist-Leninist ideology, Soviet foreign policy, and the political structure of the Soviet regime. The fundamental shift toward critical programming, however, came only in the spring of 1949 when the Russian Service featured a series of talks by Grigori Tokaev, a colonel in the Red Army who had defected in late 1947. An internal BBC review concluded that "cautious methods . . . have been abandoned, and have, it would seem, given place to undisguised political warfare."[47] On April 25, 1949, the Soviet Union responded to the new BBC tone by initiating systematic jamming, the sending of radio signals on the same frequencies that would disrupt the broadcasts and frequently render the programs virtually incomprehensible.

With BBC Russian broadcasts on air, the U.S. Embassy in Moscow called for an analogous Russian Service for VOA that could challenge Soviet propaganda, explain U.S. policies, and tell America's story to the Soviet people.[48] Recalling Lasswell's warning about an emerging global "informational war," Benton realized that the Russian broadcasts could not only promote the virtues of U.S. democracy but also challenge Soviet ideology and expose the crimes of the regime. Russian programming had the potential to become a powerful tool of psychological warfare because it bypassed Soviet control of the media and spoke directly to the citizens of the USSR. With his usual alacrity, Benton negotiated for the use of European transmitters aimed at the Soviet Union and brought on board an experienced diplomat, Charles Thayer, to build the Russian Service. "Early plans," Nicholas Cull noted, "called for such luminaries as Brooks Atkinson of the *New York Times* to advise VOA and for George Kennan himself to deliver a regular broadcast commentary. Atkinson declined ... whereas Kennan tried a microphone test, but alarmed by his exaggerated accent, recommended that Benton look elsewhere for a vibrant Russian voice."[49] Heeding Kennan's advice, VOA chose two prominent members of the Russian emigration, Victor Franzusoff and Helen Yakobson, to voice the first broadcasts on February 17, 1947.

Benton justified his vision of a robust VOA Russian Service by arguing that the Soviet Union had chosen a belligerent stance and was becoming a major adversary, if not an outright enemy of the West. He noted that an earlier presidential commission, headed by Truman's special counsel, Clark Clifford, had concluded that "Soviet propaganda denounced U.S. aid programs as imperialism and called for a determined effort to expose the fallacies of such propaganda."[50] The report had also advocated "the distribution of books, magazines, newspapers, and films to the Soviet Union, as well as radio broadcasts to the USSR to correct the misinformation being fed to the masses by their Communist rulers."[51] Similar assessments were echoed in U.S. Embassy reports that regularly cited anti-American rhetoric voiced by Soviet leaders that was disseminated both domestically and internationally by Soviet media. Typical was a cable to H. Freeman Matthews, the director of European affairs (January 16, 1947), in which Ambassador Walter Bedell Smith recounted his private meeting with Andrei Vyshinsky, first deputy minister of foreign affairs. Smith's main point was that American goodwill toward the Soviet Union exhibited at the end of World War II had now been fully spent. "I sat in session after session in Paris," Smith told Vyshinsky, "and heard Mr. Molotov, Mr. Manuilski, yourself, and other representatives of the Soviet Union give speech after speech which can only be characterized as antagonistic, violent, and unjustified attacks on the United States, its representatives, and its institutions."[52] These attacks grew into a steady drumbeat through the spring and summer of 1947 and led the newly established National Security Council (September 1947) to conclude "that the USSR had declared psychological warfare against the United States."[53]

With the U.S.-Soviet relationship deteriorating rapidly, Benton advocated a confrontational approach toward the USSR, but most senior officials preferred to weaken Soviet rule indirectly by addressing East Europeans and nurturing their hopes for freedom and liberation from Communist rule. Realizing the deep historical antagonism of East Europeans toward Russia, State Department officials were certain that programming in Polish, Czech, Hungarian, and other languages of the region would attract a large audience and would give Soviet authorities a taste of their own medicine. General Eisenhower made this view explicit: "The United States must intensify the will for freedom in the satellite countries.... These countries are in the Soviet backyard and only as their people are reminded that the outside world has not forgotten them ... do they remain potential deterrents to Soviet aggression."[54]

As the date of the first Russian broadcast approached, senior State Department officials opted for a cautious approach, more in line with BBC's early broadcasts. While agreeing with Benton that there was no need to notify the Soviet government or to invite the Soviet ambassador to the United States to participate in the first broadcast, a gesture that BBC had extended to the Soviet ambassador, the State Department nonetheless thought it wise "to find a spontaneous opportunity" to inform Soviet officials about the impending broadcasts and allay any fears they may have.[55] In the spirit of conciliation, the U.S. Embassy even issued a "friendly statement" two days before the inaugural broadcast:

> The American Ambassador takes pleasure in announcing that beginning on February 17, 1947 American Government's radio program

Voice of America will include daily broadcasts in the Russian language beamed to the USSR. These broadcasts will consist of music, news about America, world affairs, and special features. The Ambassador believes that these broadcasts, which are in line with the desire frequently expressed by representatives of the governments of both countries for wider exchange of information of a cultural and scientific character, will help to broaden the base of understanding and friendship between the peoples of the Soviet Union and the United States.[56]

Although the ambassador's announcement was intended primarily for the Soviet press, and even included the times and frequencies of the broadcasts, there was neither an official response from the Soviet government nor any mention of VOA in the Soviet press.

The State Department documents of 1947 reveal a keen interest on the part of the U.S. policymakers in the nascent Russian broadcasts. Immediately after the first broadcast, the U.S. Embassy gathered a group of Russian listeners, American journalists working in Moscow, and embassy staff to analyze the programming. Marked "Personal for Benton," their report noted that the "accent, pronunciation, and use of modern Russian were excellent ... at least as good as the BBC," but the programs were "a little too cultured in the Russian sense of the word. A fifteen-minute talk on the structure of American government was rather ponderous, particularly as Soviets are rather bored with long-winded discussions of political conditions." What was needed, the report suggested, was less political content: "Russian people are starved for humor, bright music, folk songs, and any form of entertainment which offers an escape from the grim reality of daily existence.... We must strive for a happy medium between what the Soviet audience would consider uncultured ... and the ponderous political polemics with which the Soviet radio audience is saturated. Carefully selected cowboy songs, negro spirituals, light music seem to us to be the type of program which will have the greatest appeal."[57] Although the Russian broadcasters did not eschew serious news stories, they followed the advice of the U.S. Embassy and began to include musical interludes amid reports on American politics, economics, and society.

Meanwhile, the U.S. Embassy in Moscow continued to monitor the content of the Russian broadcasts on a regular basis, assess the quality of the radio signal, solicit suggestions from its small circle of informal Russian contacts, and send critiques of content and tone. The embassy wanted to fine-tune the Russian programming so it could accomplish three major goals: to present U.S. policies and the American way of life by adhering to fundamental principles of fairness and truth, to develop the necessary context for stories about the West that would make them understandable to Soviet listeners, and to select issues of relevance to the United States that would serve as a corrective to the lies in the Soviet press. Of particular concern to the embassy was the presentation of negative news about the U.S. The ambassador noted:

> We should not try to hide our problems from the Russians, nor should we indulge in a guilt complex by making a point of our faults. The Russian press already does that. Our aim should be to emphasize what we as a democratic people are doing to solve these problems. . . . We should show no hesitation in discussing our problems whenever we can do so in a way as to put them in a proper perspective and show that the American people are concerned and working for their solution. If we cannot present American news in such a way and still be honest, then we have no business broadcasting to Russians at all.[58]

As an example, the embassy cited the case of lynching. "If the story [of a lynching] is grisly enough, TASS will cover it in full detail. We [however] must wait until we can carry a more comprehensive story that American public opinion has been aroused, that newspapers throughout the country are demanding action, and that Federal officers have made arrests in accordance with the President's orders. . . . We will not enhance our reputation for credibility merely by confirming accounts in the Soviet press."[59]

Although the Russian broadcasts were still in their infancy, the embassy reports identified one of the perennial challenges facing VOA throughout the Cold War—namely, how to find the right balance between the American tendency to dwell on social, political, and economic problems and the strategic imperative to gain the goodwill of an audience that was woefully ignorant of Western institutions and practices and subjected to ceaseless criticism of America. As our examination of the broadcasts will show, VOA always covered major political problems in America, from the race riots of the 1960s to the Iran-Contra Affair and the antinuclear demonstrations of the 1980s, but in every case, we sought to provide a much-needed context for these events that illustrated how American institutions functioned and explained the corrective mechanisms of democracy.

Not all the advice proffered by the embassy dealt with serious subjects. Concerned that VOA was veering toward a "highbrow sound" directed to a small group of Moscow intellectuals, embassy officials suggested less talk and more music: "The following program structure is recommended: 15 minutes of news to be followed by 15 minutes of light music; during the next 20 minutes there should be news commentary or a talk on a topic of general interest, followed by a musical break and then a radio play, dialogue, interviews, sports, or other entertainment, with news repeated and a good snappy tune at the ending.... Music must be gay and tuneful, with an accent on melodic jazz, but also operettas, popular music like '[There Is a] Tavern in the Town.'"[60] Although it's not clear how quickly the Russian Service incorporated the embassy suggestions, several weeks later the embassy informed Benton that it had noted a "distinct improvement" in the programming and a growing interest in VOA broadcasts among Russians "in Moscow and in outlying provincial cities." The embassy report also pointed out that the Russian broadcasts were reaching "thousands of listeners in the satellite states on the Soviet periphery . . . [who] are even more receptive to learn of America" and that reaching the non-Russian republics of the Soviet Union should be an important element of overall U.S. strategy.[61]

The embassy's initial preoccupation with the format of the programming and the quality of its entertainment gave way to more serious discussions of strategy as ever more aggressive Soviet propaganda aimed its fire on America. In May the embassy was alarmed by Ilya Ehrenburg's article "The Law of Nature" in *Pravda* (May 1, 1947) that "unleashed the most virulent attack yet to appear in the Soviet press on new American foreign policy, likening Americans to hypocrites carrying a bomb in one pocket and an Easter egg in the other."[62] This was accompanied by a half-page *Pravda* cartoon, with verses by Samuil Marshak, showing "Churchill and Uncle Sam in provocative poses behind 'optical illusions of democracy': Churchill waving a firebrand and Uncle Sam with pockets full of atom bombs strangling a chained Negro on whose back he is riding."[63] Several days later, the embassy reported on Konstantin Simonov's anti-American play *The Russian Question*, whose central message was that the U.S. press, together with reactionary forces and monopoly capitalists, were systematically "distorting Soviet motives and policies in an effort to wean Americans from their natural sympathy, understanding, and admiration of the Soviet Union."[64] The first performance of *The Russian Question* was attended by Stalin, and that ensured its official status as a must-see play. Staged throughout the country, *The Russian Question* received many accolades for its portrayal of America as a wellspring of anti-Soviet vituperation. These crude, frontal attacks on the United States led the embassy to assert that the "intensity and widespread nature of the Soviet campaign" to discredit a factual picture of world events and a frank discussion of Soviet motives "constitutes the most pungent argument why it is essential for the U.S. to continue objective and factual reporting to the USSR by the Voice of America."[65] By June 10, as the attacks continued to escalate, the embassy reports projected a tougher stance toward the Soviet Union, specifically calling for U.S. newspapers to insert the word *censored* above every story sent from the USSR, to publish captured German documents in toto showing Soviet aggressive intentions in collaboration with Hitler, and, most important, to use VOA to describe positive American policies and, where appropriate, the realities of Soviet policies and life.[66] This was the embassy's retaliatory shot at the Soviet Union, and it supported Benton's view of the Russian broadcasts as effective tools of psychological warfare.

The cavalcade of Soviet attacks grew to such a fevered pitch by September that Ambassador Bedell Smith felt compelled to send an official letter to Molotov:

During the year and a half that I have resided in the Soviet Union, I have been obliged with the deepest regret to witness in the Soviet press an increasing flood of half-truths, distortions of truth, and utter falsehoods about my country and my government. I have tried to overlook this incendiary press campaign, feeling that to take issue with a myriad of false or incorrect statements would simply be adding fuel to the flame of hatred toward my country, which the Soviet press has apparently undertaken to kindle in the hearts of the Soviet people. However, an occasion has now arisen when I must break this self-imposed rule. An article by Boris Gorbatov, just published in *The Literary Gazette*, No. 39, is so wantonly libelous in its personal attack on the President of the United States that I cannot permit it to pass without the strongest protest.... I cannot recall that Goebbels, at the height of our common struggle against Nazi Germany, ever stooped to greater ridicule and vituperation against the head of an enemy country than has Mr. Gorbatov against the chief executive of a friendly and allied state.[67]

In his response, Molotov brushed aside Smith's points, going so far as to claim that "Soviet government cannot bear responsibility for Gorbatov's article," even though all Soviet press was in the hands of the government and the author was a high ranking member of the Communist Party and the Secretary of the Union of Soviet Writers.[68] Significantly, Molotov ignored Smith's contention that the United States was a "friendly and allied" country and thus, through his silence, acknowledged that the wartime alliance was dead. Given the growing tide of Stalinist aggression, Smith's letter had no discernible impact on the steady anti-American drumbeat. By the fall, the Soviet Union unleashed a worldwide campaign "to discredit any kind of opposition to Soviet aspirations" and to "identify American capitalism with Fascist imperialism."[69] This engendered the first attack on VOA in the Soviet press. On October 24, 1947, *Gudok*, a "literary publication" of the Ministry of Transportation, lambasted the Russian Service for its rosy picture of America and promotion of Western values. At roughly the same time, the embassy learned through informal channels that the Soviet authorities were drawing up plans to jam VOA Russian broadcasts. Systematic jamming began several months later.[70]

With the Cold War settling in, the U.S. Embassy's intense interest in VOA broadcasts started to wane as it became clear that the Soviet authorities did not welcome any independent voices communicating with their citizens and had no desire to build better ties with the West. Indeed, so hostile was the Soviet stance toward VOA that one of its most trusted ideologues, Boris Lavrenev (1891–1959), even wrote a play in 1949, entitled *Golos Ameriki* (Voice of America), that described Russian broadcasts as frontline weapons of Western imperialism aimed at destroying the Soviet Union. Given its timely political message, Lavrenev's play was performed in all the major Soviet theaters, and in 1950 the author received the coveted Stalin Prize. The play also signaled the start of Soviet press attacks on the VOA, giving birth to a cottage industry that would flourish until the late 1980s when Gorbachev's policies of glasnost and perestroika finally acknowledged the need for open and free communication.

The public vilification of VOA, however, did not prevent U.S. Embassy officials from continuing to raise the question of jamming as a violation of international law. Though initially sporadic, Soviet jamming was gradually causing more distortion of VOA radio signals, and the embassy would regularly commission studies to determine the level and origin of the interference. Jamming also created an unequal playing field because the United States and other Western powers adhered to international legal norms and would not interfere with the broadcasts of Radio Moscow, despite their aggressive tone and dubious news sources. Soviet jamming, however, offered the U.S. government a useful diplomatic hook to raise this issue of illegality at every appropriate meeting with Soviet officials and even at international gatherings.[71] So concerned was the embassy about jamming that in his first meeting with Stalin on August 15, 1949, Ambassador Alan Kirk raised only two major issues—Lend-Lease and the jamming of VOA. While Stalin was ready to discuss Lend-Lease, he did not utter a single word about VOA, leading Kirk to conclude that the politburo had taken a firm decision to block Western broadcasts.[72]

The certainty of an open-ended Cold War with the Soviet Union forced Washington to begin developing a comprehensive, multifaceted foreign policy apparatus that would be geared to projecting American values and confronting Soviet propaganda. What was needed were institutions that could implement a variety of programs and respond quickly and effectively to changing priorities. As early as the spring of 1946, William Benton had proposed the creation of an independent Voice of America under a new International Broadcasting Foundation, which would be governed by a board comprising fourteen private U.S. citizens and the Secretary of State or his designee. The broadcasts would operate under a charter that defined the voa's role as "disseminating information pertaining to American life, policy, industry, techniques, culture, and customs."[73] As U.S. intelligence learned more about ambitious Soviet plans to create a new propaganda agency—Cominform—and catalogued the increasing Soviet attacks on voa, Benton realized that the U.S. information offensive should repay the USSR in kind. In a memorandum to Secretary of State George Marshall, he proposed that voa include a direct counterattack on Soviet psychological warfare. Notably, there was pushback from the State Department. "The use of propaganda," Marshall noted, "is contrary to our generally accepted precepts of democracy. Our sole aim in our overseas information program must be to present nothing but the truth, in a completely factual and unbiased manner. Only by these means can we justify the procedure and establish a reputation before the world for integrity of action."[74]

Undeterred, Benton continued to make his case for a more robust voa, even drafting legislation that would set up an independent voa, but when he left the State Department in September 1947, his ambitious plans were abandoned. His legacy, however, remained strong, and upon his departure, the voa staff presented Benton with a large screen on which they had pasted some of the twenty-five thousand monthly letters from voa listeners. The inscription read, "To Bill Benton without whose valiant fight there would be no Voice of America."[75] Although Benton was a strong proponent of a worldwide voa, years later, he admitted that his proudest achievement had been the launching of the Russian Service.[76]

Benton's belief in challenging the Soviet Union had strong support among many senior policymakers. Only three months after his departure, the newly formed National Security Council issued a directive (NSC 4) outlining the steps "required to strengthen and coordinate all foreign information measures of the U.S. government in furtherance of the attainment of U.S. national objectives."[77] Of central concern was the Soviet "intensive propaganda campaign directed primarily against the U.S. and employing coordinated psychological, political, and economic measures designed to undermine non-Communist elements in all countries. The ultimate objective is not merely to undermine the prestige of the U.S. and the effectiveness of its national policy, but to weaken and divide world opinion to a point where effective opposition to Soviet designs is no longer attainable."[78] Since the NSC determined that the United States lacked a strong information policy, it recommended that the president empower an assistant secretary of state for public affairs to begin building an effective communications policy. This was a "major milestone in the development of U.S. propaganda," Nicholas Cull noted. "It meant the end of both the old concept of U.S. cultural diplomacy as a conversation between countries and the 'full and fair' policy enunciated by Truman in 1945. The Truman administration now saw such overseas information activities as a one-way sales pitch. No one doubted that the U.S. was now engaged in a propaganda war."[79] The institutional home for this strategic mission was created just weeks later when the U.S. Congress passed the U.S. Information and Educational Exchange Act of 1948 (Public Law 80-402), commonly known as the Smith-Mundt Act. The aim of the legislation—to raise the quality and output of U.S. overseas information programs—drew high-level support. George Marshall, Dwight Eisenhower, Dean Acheson, Averell Harriman, and Walter Bedell Smith were among the many statesmen who testified in support of this law. The Smith-Mundt Act identified six key principles: tell the truth; explain the motives of the United States; bolster morale and extend hope; give a true and convincing picture of American life, methods, and ideals; combat misrepresentation and distortion; and aggressively interpret and support American foreign policy. It formed the basis of the new United States Information Agency, the home of VOA during the Cold War.

The hardening confrontation between the United States and USSR had a profound impact on VOA Russian broadcasts. The naive attempts to forge mutual understanding through radio broadcasts were abandoned as the U.S. Embassy focused primarily on seeking ways to overcome jamming of the Russian broadcasts. Gone as well were the embassy reports on the contents of the programming, as VOA management began to take full responsibility for the actual programming.

The Russian broadcasts, however, found themselves increasingly buffeted by strong political winds. A telling example was Truman's Campaign for Truth (1950–51) that directed VOA to focus on the UN actions against North Korean aggression, the consolidation of the North Atlantic community, the mobilization of the United States for the defense of peace, the advancement of American democracy, and the exposure of the Soviet "peace campaign" and its expansionist foreign policy.[80] For the Russian Service, this meant challenging Soviet propaganda head-on and exposing the hypocrisy of Soviet peace overtures. On rare occasions, however, the Truman administration would reverse course and extend an olive branch to the Soviet Union. This occurred when the McMahon-Ribicoff Concurrent Resolution of Congress (June 1951), endorsed by Truman, declared that the "American people deeply regret the artificial barriers which separate them from the peoples of the Soviet Union" and called on the "Soviet government to advance the cause of peace immeasurably by removing those artificial barriers, thus permitting the free exchange of information between our peoples."[81] In his transmission of the resolution on July 6, 1951, to the president of the Presidium of the Supreme Soviet of the USSR, Nikolai Shvernik, Truman asked that the text be shared with the Russian people in the spirit of future cooperation with the USSR. At the same time, the VOA Russian Service was instructed to broadcast Truman's communication to Shvernik and the enclosed congressional resolution twice an hour, twenty-four hours a day, for three full days. One week later, when the State Department realized that the Soviet Union had ignored the resolution, the Russian Service was then told to inform its listeners of the failure of the Soviet government to share Truman's letter and the accompanying resolution with its people, exposing once more Soviet hypocrisy and antagonism toward the West. In these crosscurrents of U.S.-Soviet relations, the VOA Russian Service would inevitably find itself enmeshed in high-stakes politics.

Throughout the turbulent 1950s, however, the VOA Russian Service stood its ground, trying to adhere to a balanced approach to the Soviet Union. Its news and current-affairs programming retained a purist approach, and much of its feature programming included music and apolitical entertainment shows. If pressured to become more politically aggressive, the Russian Service would push back. In a memo to the VOA director, for example, Alexander Frenkley, the codirector of the Russian Service, insisted that VOA Russian broadcasts were committed to "an objective presentation of the news without editorializing . . . [because] to start on the path of editorializing news would affect our reputation for objectivity, and therefore our credibility."[82] These views were generally supported by senior management, which in its public presentations stressed VOA's commitment to mutual understanding between the United States and the Soviet Union and its comprehensive presentation of American life, including political, social, and economic problems. Moreover, VOA management stressed caution in treating any subject connected with the Soviet Union, even spelling out how to do this in a policy guidance: "It is imperative that every reference to Soviet internal affairs be scrupulously accurate. For balance, VOA output should contain some acknowledgement of the aspects of Soviet life considered favorably by Soviet citizens (e.g., education, science, theatre)." In addition, "materials dealing with Soviet internal affairs shall constitute no more than a minor portion of programming."[83]

In its feature programming, the Russian Service cast a wide net that included political and nonpolitical programs. In addition to the ten-minute news summary at the top of the hour, it reported on culture, the arts, and everyday American life, as well as on Soviet crimes, Stalinism, the plight of human rights, and the suppression of religion. From its earliest days, the Russian Service broadcast Orthodox liturgies, talks about religion, as well as "small stories" that poked holes in the Soviet presentation of life. In 1948, for example, a visiting Soviet schoolteacher leapt from the third floor of the Soviet consulate in New York and sought asylum. VOA covered this story in detail, and it resounded immediately in the USSR. Two months later, two Soviet pilots crash-landed in the American zone in Austria seeking asylum, claiming that VOA stories about America had prompted them to take this daring step.[84] In March 1951 a State Department report called for VOA broadcasts to expose the "vast gaps between Soviet propaganda promises and reality."

Some of the feature programs on Russian history, culture, and religion provided political bite, resorting to Benton's strategy of "getting tough on the Soviet Union." VOA even set up the Munich Radio Center to prepare more hard-hitting reports about the USSR. Its location in Europe gave the Russian staff the opportunity to interview former Soviet citizens living in displaced-persons camps in Germany who were eager to expose Soviet brutality. The Munich location also allowed VOA staff to monitor taped dictations of the daily *Pravda* editorials, intended for replication in outlying Soviet regions. They would listen to a long litany of heroic Socialist achievements until the fateful words came, "However, not everything yet—" and the tidbit of official criticism that would follow those key words would serve as the basis for a VOA editorial on the inadequacies of the Soviet system. VOA reports, especially about the political infighting among the collective Soviet leadership in the 1950s, didn't mince words about the lies perpetrated by Soviet media.[85] The head of the Munich office, Charles Malamuth, on occasion even carried his emotional anti-Soviet tirades so far as to accuse John Foster Dulles of moral turpitude for shaking hands with "that henchman, Vyshinsky."[86] Despite official VOA policies requiring a balanced approach to U.S.-Soviet relations, the Munich staff was given a free hand during the early 1950s to produce political programs, including a daily fifteen-minute program, *Pages of History*, that examined Stalin's rule, the collectivization of the peasantry in the 1930s, and the gulag system. By directly challenging official Soviet historiography, the Munich office functioned as the front line of Cold War broadcasting until the mid-1950s when Radio Liberation (Liberty) was established.

While the core programming of the VOA Russian Service remained constant over the decades, official policy guidelines governing those broadcasts were subject to the vicissitudes of U.S.-Soviet relations as well as to the seemingly endless bureaucratic battles endemic to government institutions. Over her four decades as a senior broadcaster at VOA, Ludmila Obolensky Flam recalled that "the pendulum swung a number of times, from being strident and openly hostile towards the Soviet regime to being more moderate, to downright subservient to the politics of détente."[87]

Yet despite State Department control over VOA policy and occasional White House interference, the Russian Service enjoyed a degree of freedom to forge its own programs to the Soviet Union as it saw fit. In his memoirs, Victor Franzusoff, the longtime head of the VOA Russian Service, recounted that during the late 1940s and 1950s, the Russian Service had a distinctly "Russian sound" with its exclusively Russia-born staff and its hard-charging director, Alexander Barmine.[88] A Soviet general who had defected to the Americans in Athens, Barmine considered himself an expert on the Soviet Union and was loathe to follow policy guidelines or programming proposals from American management. As Alan Heil recalls, Barmine "would sit in the morning editorial meeting with the *New York Times* in front of his face, and the leadership of the Voice across from him on a raised platform, just ignoring them until they said something that he didn't agree with. And then, he'd put down the paper and say: 'Nonsense' or 'Ridiculous.'"[89] When I joined VOA, Barmine was long gone, but stories about him still circulated. He had been feared by many of the old timers but also deeply admired for the way he stood up to American management and supported an independently minded Russian Service.

The Russian "sound" changed in the 1960s with the appointment of Terence Catherman, a legendary, though controversial, figure at VOA. "Catherman signaled a change in VOA's approach to broadcasting," Franzusoff noted in his memoirs. "Unlike Barmine, who had been an outspoken, passionate crusader against communism and the Soviet system, Catherman was dispassionate and strict about following official government policy toward all foreign nations, including the Soviet Union."[90] In keeping with the spirit of the 1960s, he encouraged a shift in programming from extolling life in the United States to examining the "warts"—the antiwar protests, the slaying of Martin Luther King

Jr. and Robert F. Kennedy, and the Vietnam War. VOA's extensive and objective coverage of the Watergate hearings proved to be a sensation in Russia. As older listeners recounted to me, the fact that VOA would expose the misdeeds of the Nixon administration so openly proved that the VOA was committed to telling the truth, no matter the subject.

Catherman's major innovation was to seek a youthful audience and to reorient Russian broadcasts toward culture, music, religion, literature, and the arts. He entrusted the new programming to a senior Russian editor, Vladimir Mansvetov, a noted Russian poet who had grown up in Prague. After visiting the Soviet Union in the 1960s on a diplomatic passport, Mansvetov was convinced that VOA would never reach the Stalinist generation but felt that the Khrushchev thaw offered an opportunity to attract younger Russians who no longer lived in fear of the KGB. He began his transformation by hiring Americans who had learned Russian in school, at home, through language programs in the Soviet Union, or as guides at the U.S. exhibits in the USSR. They spoke Russian exceptionally well but were not native speakers, which occasionally caused tension when their scripts were edited. But the divide between the older Russians, many of whom had escaped from the Soviet Union, and the young Americans ran deeper than language. "The Americans wanted to share the vibrancy of American culture with Russians," recalled Nik Sorokin, a senior correspondent at VOA who had grown up in Syracuse, New York. "No one in our service—old or young—was positively disposed toward the Soviet system even in the slightest way, but the 'Americans' thought that the way to oppose the Soviet system was to show what America had to offer and allow the listeners to draw their own conclusions about which system was better."[91] This new American approach fit the political climate of the late 1960s and 1970s, especially as Nixon's policy of détente with the Soviet Union gained momentum. Catherman also encouraged staff to adlib during live shows and introduced American pop culture and rock 'n' roll. The lighter fare of fashion, sports, and travel appealed to new Russian audiences and communicated a vibrant American spirit.

The new "American sound" did not go unnoticed by the guardians of Soviet orthodoxy. "By aiming its poisoned ideological arrows at Soviet youth," Ya. A. Mayorov wrote in a Soviet media journal, "imperialism expects to succeed in softening the Communist party and lowering its fighting power. . . . VOA's purpose is to inoculate Soviet youth with indifference to the fate of socialism and imbue them with admiration for the western way of life and dissatisfaction with Soviet reality."[92] Similar comments appeared often in the Soviet press and strengthened the hand of the new Russian Service managers as they argued that the old strategic approach of criticizing Soviet policies and practice was spent. In the freer spirit of the 1960s and 1970s, VOA would be far more effective if it held to straight news, critical stories about the United States, and plenty of popular cultural programs. This would lead to a larger audience and a greater impact on Soviet society as a whole.

While Soviet officials saw the VOA as a dangerous tool for corrupting youth, recent Soviet émigrés, many of them human rights activists and Jewish refuseniks, saw VOA as spineless, capitulating to the Soviet Union in the war of ideas and depicting a rosy picture of Soviet life. In their view, VOA was not paying sufficient attention to Soviet crimes, persecution of dissidents, samizdat, and aggressive foreign policy. VOA management discouraged citing émigré journals, such as *Kontinent*, and even considered an interview with the poet Joseph Brodsky as unnecessarily provocative. The Nixon administration even tried to shape the contents of the VOA Russian broadcasts. Shortly before Nixon's visit to the USSR, Alexander Haig, then the national security adviser, instructed VOA to "continue eschewing polemics, not seeking quarrels and not attempting to magnify small incidents in your broadcasts to the Soviet Union."[93] More troubling still was the fear on the part of the U.S. government that VOA Russian broadcasts would offend Soviet officials. While VOA was allowed to report on the publication of Solzhenitsyn's *The Gulag Archipelago* by citing Western sources, the Russian Service was prohibited from interviewing the author or broadcasting readings from the book. A series developed by the VOA Europe bureau about corruption in various Communist countries was nixed because, in the words of the USIA European area office, "if the series had been honest and accurate, it would have seemed gratuitous and ideologically polemical."[94] Such kowtowing to Soviet authorities was "rewarded" with a temporary suspension of jamming in the 1970s, but what VOA gained in audibility it lost in credibility. As Kirill Khenkin, a prominent Soviet journalist who had emigrated to Israel, wryly noted, "Something that is inoffensive to the Soviet government isn't likely to be worth tuning in."[95]

VOA coverage of human rights in the Soviet Union was especially problematic since Soviet violations exposed the weakness of détente as a governing policy of the U.S. government. Such prominent dissidents as Lyudmila Alexeyeva, Alexander Ginzburg, Yuri Orlov, and Valentin Turchin voiced their concerns that the Moscow Helsinki Group received short shrift in VOA programming and that the *Chronicle of Current Events*, a major samizdat publication, was not rebroadcast on VOA. Even U.S.-based organizations dealing with human rights issues, such as Khronika Press and Chalidze Publications, were rarely, if ever, mentioned.[96] Criticism of VOA Russian broadcasts was most succinctly expressed by Alexandr Solzhenitsyn. "The Russian Section of the Voice of America," he wrote, "poorly serves American interests and at times directly does damage to them. Except for late news and the most acute political commentary, many hours of daily broadcasts are filled with vulgar junk, which causes only irritation among millions of hungry, repressed listeners. . . . Hours of broadcasts are filled with insignificant stories of the pleasures of sea cruises, lifestyle of modern singers, much about sports, jazz and no less useful stories on how Jewish émigrés have established themselves after leaving the Soviet Union. The latter do nothing but give rise to anti-Semitism in the Soviet Union."[97]

Although this blanket criticism was undeserved, Solzhenitsyn raised essential questions about VOA's mission during détente. Was VOA's aim simply to acquaint Russian audiences with American life in the hope that knowledge about Western life and U.S. policies would have a positive impact on Soviet policies? Or should VOA complement its lighter fare with news about Soviet repression and the state of human rights? Was VOA to be the home station for Russians who opposed the Soviet Union or just an American radio station that happened to broadcast in the Russian language? These fundamental questions split the Russian

Service and caused confusion among senior American executives. When I arrived at VOA in the early 1980s, the purists and the strategists had formed opposing factions, and my task was to bridge the differences and to help revitalize the programming.

Radio Liberty: The Early Years

The architects of post-WWII U.S. foreign policy, including George Kennan, John Foster Dulles, and Frank Wisner, understood that the Cold War would be an epic struggle requiring a varied arsenal. VOA offered an effective set of weapons, but as part of the federal government, it would be subject to prevailing political winds, and its programs would have to conform, to some degree, to the foreign policy overtures of any given administration. Why not, they reasoned, create a complementary radio voice that would remain at arm's length from the U.S. government and would be capable of striking at the vulnerabilities of Communist regimes? As General Lucius Clay, commanding general of the U.S. occupation forces in Europe, noted, "When I left Germany, I came home with a very firm conviction that we needed in addition to the Voice of America a different, broader voice—a voice of the free people—a radio that would speak to each country behind the Iron Curtain in its own language, and from the throats of its own people who fled for their lives because of their beliefs in freedom."[98] In a memo on waging political warfare, Kennan pointed to the tens of thousands of displaced persons from Eastern Europe and the Soviet Union who could be a potent force for the liberation of their homelands through well-coordinated, diaspora-led committees. These committees could "form centers of national hope and revive a sense of purpose among political refugees from the Soviet world; provide an inspiration for continuing popular resistance within the countries of the soviet world; and provide a potential nucleus for all-out liberation movements."[99] His memo led to the creation of the Soviet émigré project, which "envisaged a central organization in Germany, with branches in New York and Paris, controlled and funded by the OPC [Office of Policy Coordination] and focused initially on émigré welfare until the operation could become effective enough to be used for political warfare."[100]

Kennan's recommendations were greeted positively by the Truman administration, and that led to the creation of two separate entities: one for the recently Sovietized Eastern European countries—the National Committee for a Free Europe—and the other for the Soviet Union itself—the American Committee for Liberation for the Peoples of Russia (AMCOMLIB). Their common objective was to employ the displaced persons in West German camps and put their voices on air, addressing their people in their own language.[101] The refugees had escaped Communist takeovers in Central and Eastern Europe, knew firsthand how Soviet agents had overthrown democratically elected governments, and formed a willing army to combat the Soviet Union. Among the émigrés were former cabinet members, parliamentarians, editors, writers, and public intellectuals. The first director of the Czechoslovak Service was Ferdinand Peroutka, a legendary figure in Czech intellectual life and a close associate of Tomas Masaryk, the father of democratic Czechoslovakia. An editor and historian, Peroutka had been imprisoned by the Nazis and later exiled by the Communists. Other prominent émigrés had been political leaders before the war or members of governments in exile during WWII, working closely with Allied forces. Jan Nowak Jezioranski, the director of the RFE Polish Service, had fought in the Polish Underground and served as a wartime courier traveling between Warsaw and London. A much-revered figure, Nowak returned to post-Communist Poland as a national hero. These refugees had a following in their home countries. Setting up the radios and employing them was an effective way to advance U.S. interests and continue wartime collaboration.

Radio Free Europe and Radio Liberation—the latter renamed Radio Liberty in 1959—became the instruments of choice. Rather than justifying the funding of VOA and two additional international radio stations to the U.S. Congress and the American public, the Truman administration decided to support the surrogate stations covertly through the recently established Central Intelligence Agency. With Soviet military buildup and the establishment of an Iron Curtain, the Truman administration saw the need to contain communism and perhaps, over time, even roll it back from Eastern Europe. In his private papers, Truman noted, "Russia intends an invasion of Turkey and the seizure of the Black Sea Straits. Unless Russia is faced with an iron fist and strong language, another war is in the making."[102] Further Soviet efforts to destabilize Europe—from the 1948 coup in Czechoslovakia to the Communist-inspired strikes in Italy and France—galvanized strategic efforts to combat the Soviet Union. According to Paul Henze, a CIA official instrumental in the establishment of RFE, the invasion of South Korea by North Korea was the key factor that made RFE a round-the-clock home-service broadcaster. The Soviet threat was clear and apparent to all.[103]

One of the policies for containing communism was to broadcast news, history, politics, culture, and religion directly to captive populations under Soviet domination. In his speech to the American Society of Newspaper Editors (April 20, 1950), President Truman laid out the essence of surrogate broadcasting:

> This is a struggle, above all else, for the minds of men. Propaganda is one of the most powerful weapons that the Communists have in this struggle. Deceit, distortion and lies are systematically used by them as a matter of deliberate policy. . . . Communist propaganda is so false, so crude, so blatant that we wonder how men can be swayed by it. We forget that most of the people to whom it is directed do not have free access to accurate information. . . . In many parts of the world where men must choose between freedom and Communism, the true story is going untold. We cannot run the risk that nations may be lost to the cause of freedom because their people do not know the facts. . . . We must use every means at our command, private as well as governmental, to get the truth to other peoples.[104]

Truman's belief that *truth was power*—spelled out earlier by Robert Sherwood—was imbedded in RFE/RL broadcasts that nurtured the cultures of Eastern Europe and the Soviet Union and bolstered resistance to Soviet rule. An early CIA policy paper stated that "the overall objective of the radio broadcasts to the Soviet Union should be to deepen and widen the gulf between the peoples of the Soviet Union and its

Communist rulers. With this end in view, the broadcasts should seek to increase the stress and strain and the tensions which exist in the Soviet Union."[105] One of the founders of RFE/RL went so far as to declare the mission of the radios as "psychological warfare intended to keep hope alive among our friends behind the Iron Curtain and to sow dissension among our enemies. . . . We enter this fight with bare fists."[106]

The general consensus was that the most effective way to liberate Russians living under Communist rule was by creating an independent "Russian voice" that Soviet citizens would recognize as their own.[107] Early RL policy guidelines made that explicit: "RL broadcasts are to be Russian broadcasts—not American broadcasts; they are to serve the interests of the Russian liberation movement—not the interests of the U.S. Consequently, they will not explain or defend American policies, propagate American ideas, extol the American way of life, build up American prestige, play American jazz, or otherwise encroach upon the field of activity of VOA."[108] Subsequent policy guidelines elaborated on the notion of "liberation," noting in passing that "liberation had a richness of variation—liberation from Soviet tyranny, liberation from police rule, liberation from hunger and fear."[109]

The early Cold Warriors adopted a two-pronged approach: VOA would assume the role of carrying the message of the U.S. government and presenting American life, with only occasional programming about internal Soviet developments, while RFE and RL would become the voices of free Poland, free Russia, free Bulgaria, and so forth. To accomplish their task and build credibility, RFE and RL had to empower émigré broadcasters with the editorial authority to determine what stories would go on the air and what tone to adopt. While senior American management assumed responsibility for the overall programming and operations, they had to form a partnership with émigré broadcasters and trust their judgment regarding the programming. An early memo from the Office of Policy Coordination noted that RL would be "a program of Russians speaking to Russians, not the U.S. government speaking to the Russians and other nationalities of the Soviet Union."[110] With boldness born of war, the Truman administration translated these fundamental principles into a unique network of national broadcast services that challenged Communist control of all media and offered its listeners an alternative vision of the future.[111]

Although sharing the same basic mission, Radio Free Europe and Radio Liberation (Liberty) faced different challenges. RFE had several distinct advantages in developing its broadcast services. Its overall policy of "liberating" the captive nations of Central and Eastern Europe had the explicit support of the U.S. Congress and the executive branch. RFE could also draw on a highly educated class of journalists, thinkers, and politicians who had recently fled the imposed Communist regimes. They understood their home countries and, in some cases, personally knew the leaders that the Soviet regime had placed in power. RFE broadcasters also shared the same culture as their listeners, and they all considered themselves European victims of Soviet aggression. In some cases, principally Poland, RFE broadcasters could count on their compatriots in the United States, who fervently championed their cause and also knew how to exert pressure on the U.S. government officials when that would further RFE's goals.

For RL, "the Soviet Union offered a far more complex set of problems," Sig Mickelson noted, "both in the composition of its exiles and diversity of its land areas. . . . There were few cultural similarities or affinities with the West. Few exiles knew English. Maintaining cover was regarded as an important element. Assigning AMCOMLIB the same high visibility group that directed Free Europe could . . . give away the whole game. It was decided to operate the venture on a low key, in contrast to Free Europe's razzle dazzle."[112] More troubling was the notion of liberation: Was AMCOMLIB advocating the liberation of a multiethnic Soviet Union from communism or from Russian imperialism? The CIA initially sought to create a political organization that would unite Soviet exiles living in displaced-persons camps in Germany by establishing the American Committee for Freedom for the Peoples of the USSR to distribute funds and oversee the broadcasts. But under pressure from Russian émigré groups that saw the territory of the USSR as coterminous with greater Russia, the CIA changed the name to the American Committee for the Liberation of the Peoples of Russia. After various Soviet nationality groups protested that the new name was an insult, the CIA settled on a compromise: The American Committee for Liberation from Bolshevism (AMCOMLIB).[113]

To build an effective radio operation, Kennan recruited a prestigious board of directors with Eugene Lyons, a former Moscow correspondent and an editor of *Reader's Digest*, as the president of AMCOMLIB. Rounding out the board were William Henry Chamberlin of the *Wall Street Journal*, Allen Grover of *Time* magazine, William Y. Elliot of Harvard, and the Russian-born journalist Isaac Don Levine.[114] One of the many contentious issues facing the committee was the potential breakup of the Soviet Union, especially since the CIA ended up establishing separate nationality services to broadcast in Ukrainian, Belorussian, Georgian, Armenian, and other languages of the Soviet Union. The key question was, Did RL envision a non-Communist country occupying the territory of the USSR but under democratic rule, or was the intention to break up the USSR into its constituent republics? For the Russian Service, and especially the more nationalist broadcasters, the territory of the USSR was "greater Russia" and hence inviolable. Indeed, some broadcasters considered Ukraine, Belarus, and northern Kazakhstan as historic Russian lands. The nationality services, in contrast, promoted their separate cultures, and many advocated independent nations. "With the first RL broadcasts on the air," Ross Johnson noted, "the policy dispute about the role of émigré organizations in RL broadcasting came to a head. AMCOMLIB president staunchly defended the original concept of the broadcasts as the voice of the Soviet emigration, while the Soviet Russia Division and other CIA units concluded that the Russian emigration—let alone the Ukrainian and other Soviet nationalities—would never be united enough to take responsibility for the broadcasts."[115] Even Isaac Don Levine, who had been active in trying to unite Soviet émigrés, was despairing: "First, the quest for a fairly broad political front in the emigration is a delusion. Second, the chasm between the majority of the Great Russians and the non-Russian nationalities is beyond bridging."[116] Wisely, RL management sidestepped the question of the breakup of the USSR, preferring a hazy policy that left hard decisions to future generations. In 1956 RL even changed its corporate name to the American Committee for Liberation, explaining that it was "less cumbersome, more understandable by more people."[117] In January 1964 it became simply the Radio Liberty Committee.

In its inaugural broadcast on March 1, 1953, Radio Liberation set forth its basic principles. Speaking on behalf of the Coordinating Center of the Anti-Bolshevik Struggle, RL proclaimed,

> We who are living abroad clearly see the terrible danger threatening Russia and all of humanity because of the aggressive foreign policy of Bolshevism . . . that Communism and the Russian people are not one and the same, that the Russian people are secretly inimical to Communism.
>
> The Coordinating Center will always struggle for the liquidation of the Soviet Union's aggressive foreign policy . . . and we can achieve this only by means of the overthrow of the Soviet regime and the liquidation of Bolshevism. Our task is to tell you about what you will never hear in the Soviet Union, provide you with truthful information, and help liberate you from that web with which Soviet propaganda is enveloping your souls.[118]

Dramatic in tone and strategic in purpose, the first broadcast set in motion RL programming for the following decades. Above all, it sought to establish a kinship between the broadcasters and the listeners, implying that age-old Russian culture united the émigrés with the Russian population in the Soviet Union, while communism was a recent and alien force. The programming also signaled a hopeful future, a Russia without Communist rule, and it made a big promise to its listeners— that RL would provide truthful information. But the first broadcast also included several words that would bedevil American managers who were fearful that RL programs would actually call for the "overthrow of the Soviet regime." As the subsequent examination of the broadcasts will show, RL would occasionally come close to that red line, even implying the need for eventual regime change, but would never explicitly cross it, staying within the broad guidelines set out at the start.

While VOA was continually buffeted by shifting political winds, evolving U.S. policy toward the Soviet Union, and the introduction of an American radio "sound," Radio Liberty was able to stay true to its surrogate mission and remained deeply entrenched in its Russo-centric world. Whereas English was the preferred language for meetings, memoranda, and brainstorming sessions in the Russian Service of VOA, Russian was the primary language used at RL. The VOA Central News reports and the American press—mostly the *New York Times*, *Washington Post*, and the *Wall Street Journal*—had a major impact on the way the VOA Russian Service would cover news about the Soviet Union. In contrast, RL drew heavily on the European press, the monitoring of the Soviet press, academic publications, and the output of its research department. Significantly, RL had a proud tradition of scholarly analysis and meticulous research. As early as 1955 it organized a two-day conference for its editors with leading experts on the Soviet Union at Harvard and MIT, including Merle Fainsod, Alex Inkeles, Richard Pipes, and Walt Rostow.[119] Throughout the Cold War, RL would hold regular conferences with the participation of leading Soviet experts and would draw on the academic work of communications experts. It would also send randomly selected broadcasts to outside academic experts for review and evaluation, making sure that the language services adhered to journalistic guidelines. Radio Liberty broadcasters closely followed the latest cultural and political developments in the Soviet Union and would debate for hours the merits of the latest Soviet novel or film. In a word, Radio Liberty was a thoroughly Russian radio station that just happened to be located in Munich.

Despite its clearly articulated mission, Radio Liberty was also riven by conflicts that at times escalated into ideological standoffs. The point of contention was not U.S. policy or even U.S.-Soviet relations but the past and especially the future of Russia. RL was a microcosm of the Russian emigration, reflecting myriad different political strands. There was a saying at RL that all émigrés agreed that the Soviet Union was a failure, but few could agree on the exact date when the country went awry. For the monarchists, February 1917 spelled the death knell of true Russia; for the liberal intelligentsia, the crucial date was the October 1917 coup d'état. Leftist intellectuals, primarily Mensheviks and Social Revolutionaries (SRs), believed that Stalin and the show trials of the 1930s destroyed the democratic potential of Leninist rule. Some RL broadcasters rejected the Soviet Union in its entirety, seeking a non-Communist Russia that would embrace its tsarist past. Others saw the Soviet Union as a legitimate world power that simply needed to be reformed to make it more open and prosperous.[120]

To complicate matters, RL drew on three distinct waves of emigration to staff the Russian Service, each with its own set of values and interpretation of Russia's historical role. The first wave referred to a diverse group of Russians who had fled the country after the 1917 Revolution. They included monarchists, White Russian army officers and soldiers, liberals, Socialists, and apolitical Russians who rejected the new Soviet system. Some became world famous, notably Igor Stravinsky, Sergei Rachmaninov, Igor Sikorsky, and Vladimir Zworykin. In 1922 Lenin even drew up a list of 160 "undesirable" intellectuals—mostly philosophers, academics, scientists, and journalists—who were to be deported. "We're going to cleanse Russia once and for all," Lenin wrote to Stalin who was to oversee the deportation. Two of the intellectuals expelled by Lenin became editors of the Russian Service. Many others were frequent radio guests.

The first emigration—both the immigrants themselves as well as their children who had grown up in the West—had a profound impact on the creation of RL. These White Russians, as they were often called, spoke several European languages, were highly educated, and understood Western norms and culture but continued to consider themselves Russian and sought ways to preserve true Russian culture so that someday it could be transplanted back to its native soil. Capitalizing on their in-depth knowledge of Russian life, RL undertook a major project in the early 1960s: conducting extensive interviews with sixty-nine prominent members of the first emigration who had witnessed the 1917 February Revolution and October coup d'état. These interviews spanned the political landscape, from monarchists to Social Revolutionaries, and provided a nuanced and detailed picture of everyday life in Russia during the critical years of 1917 and 1918.[121] In their totality these interviews showcased the worldly sophistication of the first emigration, their use of an older, more refined Russian language, and their understanding of Russian history, philosophy, and literature. Although these early

Russian émigrés had not lived under Communist rule and had had little personal contact with ordinary Soviet citizens, they personified an independent Russian culture and were instrumental in setting the basic foundation of RL broadcasting.

The driving force behind the creation of Russian broadcasts was Boris Shub, the American-born son of the first emigration. His father, David Shub, was a well-known Russian socialist writer and publicist, who had personally known Lenin, Trotsky, Bukharin, and other pre-revolutionary Marxist leaders. Not only was Shub well versed in the byways of Russian politics, but he also had the right temperament and experience to launch RL. Before joining RL, he had worked as the programming director of Radio in the American Sector (RIAS), the Berlin-based radio station broadcasting to East Germany that had served as the first U.S.-funded surrogate broadcaster. Through his family ties, he knew the first emigration well, including conservatives, liberals, and socialists. He recruited talented journalists, among them Victor Frank, the chief of the BBC Russian-language service; Roman Gul, the editor of the most respected émigré publication, *Novy Zhurnal* (The new review); and two former Soviet journalists who had defected to the West: Mikhail Koriakov and Vladimir Yurasov. Among the regular freelancers was the Reverend Alexander Schmemann, a Russian Orthodox priest and the dean of the St. Vladimir's Orthodox Theological Seminary in Crestwood, New York. "Together with Boris Shub," Gene Sosin, a longtime RL executive, recalled, "Schmemann conceived a weekly 'Sunday Talk' aimed not only at secret believers but also at people who were dissatisfied with the Marxist-Leninist atheistic *Weltanschauung* and were seeking spiritual inspiration to fill the void in their lives."[122] Born in Estonia in 1921 to Russian parents, Schmemann personified the urbane and cosmopolitan first emigration. He was fluent in several languages, educated at the Sorbonne, a scholar of Eastern Orthodoxy, and an adjunct professor at Columbia University and the Union Theological Seminary. His *Sunday Talk* was broadcast for over thirty years. It avoided sermonizing and focused on ethical and religious issues of interest to Soviet believers and receptive nonbelievers. His talks attracted a wide following, especially among the Russian intelligentsia. In an interview with Western reporters in the early 1970s, Solzhenitsyn declared that Schmemann's talks were the "temple in which I worship."[123] And Schmemann was among the first people Solzhenitsyn sought out when he came to the United States.

Shub's enduring contribution to RL was his conception of the Russian programming. He felt that RL had to distinguish itself from Soviet media by being bold and exhibiting dramatic flair. He proposed to start the inaugural show with a ticking clock, followed by a solemn voice intoning, "Today, Josef Vissarionovich Stalin is 73 years, 2 months and 9 days old. . . . [pause and more ticking] . . . The time of Stalin is drawing to a close." Shub's idea was to remind listeners of Stalin's mortality every day. Although catchy, this intro was nixed when the Russian editors felt that Stalin, as a Georgian, could go on living for many more years and these words would become laughable. Ironically, Stalin died two days after RL went on the air.

More important, Shub believed that the Russian broadcasts had to be hard-hitting, exposing Soviet crimes and injustices and filling in the blank spots of history, but at the same time they shouldn't denigrate Russian listeners or imply that they were responsible for the actions of Soviet authorities. For Shub and many RL broadcasters, Russians were victims of a brutal regime, no less so than Poles, Czechs, or the Balts. In her memoirs, Natalie Clarkson, the director of the VOA Russian Service in the late 1980s, expressed the prevailing attitude of the first emigration toward the Soviet regime: "What must be understood is that the archenemy of my family and others who had fled Russia after the October Revolution was the Soviet regime which had exterminated millions of Russians. . . . Whole social classes were decimated: the aristocracy, the landed nobility, the merchants, the priests, monks and nuns, the so-called kulaks. . . . For Russian émigrés 'The Russians Are Coming' was not the title of an American film but a death sentence."[124] The firmly held conviction that the Soviet regime was an alien force destroying Russia defined the first emigration's attitude toward the USSR, and it elicited a sense of responsibility to preserve and nurture independent Russian culture. Therefore, the RL broadcasts sought to reassure listeners that they were not alone, that émigrés in the West loved Mother Russia and viewed Communism as the enemy, not the Russian people.

The second wave of emigration commonly referred to Soviet prisoners of war and millions of ordinary citizens who had been taken captive by the invading Nazi army and brought back to Germany to toil in factories or labor camps. The vast majority of these Soviet citizens dreaded the Communist regime and did not want to be repatriated, knowing that they would face either execution or long sentences in the gulag camps. Initially, the victorious Western Allies did not understand their fear of Stalinist Russia and ended up committing one of the heinous crimes of WWII—forcibly repatriating tens of thousands of prisoners and displaced persons to the Soviet Union. The most horrific incident occurred on May 28, 1945, in Lienz, Austria, where the British forces transported over five thousand Cossacks and former Soviet soldiers to the Soviet authorities. Knowing the fate that awaited them in the USSR, some killed their own children and then committed suicide; others tried to escape.[125] An early RL document acknowledged the tragedy that had befallen many Soviet citizens: "RL will make an explanation of the forced repatriation of former Soviet citizens following WWII in the light that the West misread the heroic struggle of the Soviet peoples against Hitler as a sign of their support for the Stalin regime. . . . The West failed to recognize the fate awaiting those to be repatriated."[126] Fortunately, some former Soviet citizens were able to escape repatriation and eventually found employment at Radio Liberty and the Voice of America.

The second wave of emigration included a diverse group of former Soviet citizens. Some became leading cultural figures. Herman Ermolaev, Olga Raevsky Hughes, and Vladimir Markov were outstanding scholars of Russian literature. George Shevelev, a proud Ukrainian, was one of the world's preeminent scholars of Slavic languages. Juri Jelagin became the concertmaster of the Houston Symphony and a major émigré writer. Nikolai Marchenko (pen name Nikolai Morshen) and Ivan Matveyev (pen name, Ivan Elagin) were popular Russian poets.[127] Many members of the second emigration, however, were not well educated and had ended up in war-torn Germany as forced laborers. Few had been writers or journalists in the Soviet Union, but they knew Soviet reality first hand in a way that the older émigrés did not. Several broadcasters had spent time in the gulag in the 1920s and

1930s and were able to share their experience with listeners, including popular "gulag songs." Others explained why they had defected to the West and what it was like to live as a free person. On May 1, 1953, while the USSR was celebrating the workers' holiday, RL broadcast interviews with several former Soviet citizens who had toiled in mine shafts, factories, and kolkhozes (collective farms). Their unvarnished description of Soviet labor must have struck listeners as a discordant note of truth that shattered a chorus of Soviet platitudes. Listening to these broadcasts some thirty years after the fall of communism, one is struck by their simplistic approach, the harshness of tone, and the absolute rejection of Stalin and Communist rule. But given their life experience, including years of hardship under both Stalinist and Nazi rule, it is remarkable how patriotic these former workers sounded and how deeply committed they were to a free Russia.[128]

One of the reasons why the second emigration has received short shrift in Russian studies and has often been unfairly maligned is the stark fact that a sizable number of Soviet POWs, along with some members of the first emigration, had taken up arms against the Soviet Union as part of General Andrei Vlasov's Russian Liberation Army. A Soviet general who had surrendered near Leningrad, Vlasov made a pact with the Nazis to field an army of Russian volunteers who would fight for the liberation of their homeland. The Nazis never trusted Vlasov, and his army saw little action on the battlefield. Vlasov was eventually captured by the Soviet forces and later executed as a traitor.

A highly controversial figure, Vlasov caused deep rifts in the Russian emigration and hence within Radio Liberty. For older émigrés such as Alexandra Tolstaya and for many members in the second wave, Vlasov was a hero, and his army represented a glorious liberation movement.[129] The conservative Russian Orthodox Church Abroad has even memorialized Vlasov as a major Russian patriot. One of its revered sites, the Novo-Diveevo Convent in Nanuet, New York, honors members of the Romanov family, the White Army soldiers, General Vlasov, and his troops.[130] Twice annually, on the anniversary of Vlasov's execution and on the Sunday following Orthodox Easter, the convent church holds a memorial service for Vlasov and members of the Russian Liberation Army.

For Soviet authorities, however, Vlasov was a despised traitor and even worse, a Nazi collaborator. The presence of "Vlasovites" at Radio Liberty was often cited by Soviet journalists as "proof" that RFE/RL was a bastion of fascists. Vlasovites also posed problems for Americans, especially Jews, who saw them as Nazi sympathizers. "The hiring of former collaborators with the Nazis," Gene Sosin wrote in his memoirs, "not only made the radios vulnerable to Soviet attacks but also turned away some potential émigré contributors to our broadcasts and disturbed segments of the American public. In my many contacts with former Vlasovites on the Munich staff, I felt uncomfortable that Cold War politics had thrown me together with such strange bedfellows."[131] For the CIA, however, the Vlasovites were hardened anti-Soviet forces that were committed to fighting the Soviet Union. Their official organization, the Armed Forces of the Committee for the Liberation of the Peoples of Russia, served as the basis for the first committee to establish Radio Liberty. Most important, unlike the first emigration, Vlasovites shared the same culture as the general Soviet population and could be especially effective in producing broadcasts that would be receptive to the Soviet military forces in Eastern Europe, a prime target of early RL broadcasts.[132]

Despite its association with prisoner-of-war camps and Vlasov's army, the second emigration formed a sizable part of the Radio Liberty and VOA Russian Service staffs until the early 1970s, when the Soviet Union, under great pressure from the West, began to allow the emigration of Soviet citizens, primarily Soviet Jews. Prior to this third wave, the staffs at RL and VOA generally reflected the ethnic and religious mix of the old Russian empire. The editors and broadcasters were Jewish, Orthodox, Muslim, or simply atheist, but Russian culture, in the broadest sense, united them. There was a general understanding that the intended audience identified itself as ethnically Russian and culturally Orthodox, and that created a "radio culture" that celebrated prerevolutionary holidays and traditions such as Christmas and Easter but ignored Soviet holidays and practices. Gene Sosin recalled that his "eagerness to think and feel like a Russian went to such an extreme that once, on the Monday after Russian Orthodox Easter, when Mikhail

Koriakov came to work and greeted everyone with three kisses on their cheeks and a solemn 'Khristos voskrese' (Christ is risen), I joined in, despite my Jewish heritage."[133] That Russian spirit, so defiant in its opposition to all things Soviet and so righteous in its historical role as the crucible of Russian culture, fully expressed itself in RL's programming on literature, Orthodoxy, history, and national traditions.

The third wave of emigration challenged that Russian spirit. The new émigrés were well educated, had occupied important positions in Soviet science and culture, spoke and wrote a refined contemporary Russian, and, most important, knew and understood current conditions in the Soviet Union. Some were former dissidents who had fought Soviet authorities and wanted to continue that struggle at the radios. They expected to be the leaders of the radios and were disdainful of the Russian staff from the second emigration, considering them poorly educated and hopelessly out of touch with current politics in the Soviet Union. "In the VOA Russian Service," Lyudmila Alexeyeva noted, "the conflict [between the emigrations] was exacerbated by the undeniable superiority of the newer generation in terms of professional formation, knowledge of the audience, and good Russian language.... The chief argument used by those with longer service to defend their higher grades was that the 'third wave' consisted of people of Soviet mentality."[134]

At times, differing attitudes among the émigrés led to personnel conflicts. Early in my tenure at VOA, for instance, I was drawn into a lawsuit filed by a recent émigré who had been a lawyer in the Soviet Union and was outraged when his scripts were edited by longtime VOA editors who, in his words, were just "stupid Russian housewives." That case went all the way to District Court in Washington DC. At the hearing, I explained that the federal personnel system rewarded successful tenure and that recent émigrés could not assume the top editorial positions simply on the basis of their fresh knowledge of the Soviet Union. As expected, the former Soviet lawyer lost his case in court, but his argument damaged morale and split the Russian Service into distinct camps. I tried to find ways of bringing the two sides together and even invited prominent Russian writers and scholars to help us sort out linguistic and cultural issues, but the divisions ran deep. For the older Russian staff and for many of the younger Americans, some members of the third wave brought with them a Soviet work culture that resulted in anonymous denunciations and formal complaints about colleagues. As one VOA veteran told me, the Russian staff had always been contentious, and arguments would periodically erupt, but they would be resolved within the service. During my tenure at VOA, grievances, denunciations, and threats of lawsuits became so frequent that I even met with USIA security officers to discuss the likelihood of Soviet agents operating at VOA with the intention of disrupting our programming. No agents were identified, but someday, declassified KGB files may put that question to rest.

The Russian Service at Radio Liberty was also riven by conflicts among the different waves of emigration. In the late 1970s a longtime radio producer from the second emigration wrote an open letter, accusing recent Soviet émigrés of destroying true Russian culture by ignoring its Orthodox roots. In her mind, Jewish émigrés were not sufficiently Russian, and the programs they were producing did not have "a Russian spirit or Great Russian Culture." And by *spirit* she meant one based on Orthodoxy that could serve as an alternative to Soviet existence.[135] Her volley caused an outburst of acrimony with counteraccusations of anti-Semitism. Although she received little support from the staff and RFE/RL management immediately reprimanded her, the point she raised caused still further splintering of the Russian Service.

At RL the conflict between the emigrations was also exacerbated by KGB agents working through staff members. We always suspected that the KGB had infiltrated RFE/RL but were never sure exactly who was on the Soviet payroll. The most egregious incident concerned a senior editor, Oleg Tumanov, who appeared to be an upstanding employee. But in February 1986 he suddenly turned up at a press conference in Moscow, where he denounced the work of Radio Liberty as a CIA operation and claimed he had always been a KGB agent assigned to infiltrate the operation. "Tumanov's control agent," Arch Puddington wrote, "whom he met regularly in East Berlin, had a detailed knowledge of RL's Russian staffers and gave explicit instructions on how Tumanov should deal with various personalities in Munich . . . and send reports of political divisions."[136] Tumanov claimed that he was an agent who used RL as a cover to do espionage in Europe. His account, however, was disputed by Oleg Kalugin, a high-ranking KBG defector, who claimed that Tumanov was a low-level agent who mostly copied reports and unclassified documents and occasionally posted fake anti-Semitic letters on the RL bulletin board that further heightened tensions in the Russian Service.[137]

Soviet interference aside, the serious personnel conflicts in the Russian Service centered on a set of beliefs about Russia and its destiny. For the overwhelming part of the first and second emigrations, the most effective way of defeating communism and reintegrating Russia into the community of free nations was by resurrecting the nobler traditions of prerevolutionary Russia. The liberally minded émigrés looked to the Westernizers as the more prudent ones to follow; the conservative émigrés turned to the Slavophiles. But in each case, there was deep pride in being part of Russian national culture and a firm belief that Russian nationalism was fundamentally a positive force. This approach was also shared by several contemporary Russian writers and cultural figures, including Alexandr Solzhenitsyn, Vladimir Maximov, and Slava Rostropovich. They were fervent anti-Communists and dismissed the notion that the USSR could evolve into a normal European country.

At Radio Liberty, many members of the third emigration rejected that belief. Early in my tenure at RL, I met with several senior editors and tried to explain the Reagan administration policy of encouraging Russian nationalism and religion as effective weapons to defeat communism. By appealing to nationalist sentiments, I explained, the United States could strike at the vulnerable underbelly of the USSR. They listened to me in horror. Communism, they asserted, was a dying ideology that Soviet citizens no longer believed in and certainly were not willing to die for. But Russian nationalism, they claimed, with its endemic xenophobia, militancy, and residual anti-Semitism, was growing in the Soviet Union and one day would pose a grave threat to the West. Presciently, they stated that the West would rue the day when Russian nationalism and Soviet practice would come together to confront the West. As an American, I appreciated their intellectual reasoning and deep insight into the workings of late Brezhnevite USSR but thought naively that Russians would be able to harness national pride in pursuit of a modern society integrated with the West. Looking back, I can admire how perceptive these RL editors were in predicting Putin's Russia. For a sizable part of the RL staff in the 1980s, however, the editors' assertions were exploding grenades that threatened the staff members' identity and undercut their personal mission. So much of Solzhenitsyn's disdain and utter rejection of the Western orientation of the third wave was rooted in his belief that Russian nationalism was the one and only healthy path for Russia.[138] In my years at VOA and RFE/RL, I spent considerable time talking with both camps in an attempt to find common ground, but splits among staff were deeply imbedded in the unresolved issues of Russian history.

Impact of Détente

With the advent of détente in the 1960s, the future of U.S. broadcasting to the Soviet Union, and especially Radio Liberty, was called into question. If the "liberation" of the Soviet Union was no longer the ostensible mission of U.S. policy, why support a radio station that was created to fight communism and help usher in a new form of government in the USSR? If the aim of the U.S. government was to have a stable and productive relationship with the USSR, why should VOA, the national voice of the United States, air programming in five Soviet nationality languages: Ukrainian, Georgian, Armenian, Azeri, and Uzbek? Weren't these broadcasts attempting to dismember the country? If normalization of relations was the chief goal of détente, how should the U.S. government respond to official Soviet démarches about the deleterious effect of VOA and RL on overall U.S.-Soviet relations? As Soviet ambassador Anatoly Dobrynin noted, Radio Liberty (and other CIA funded émigré radio stations) "are in manifest contradiction with the task of normalization and development of relations between the USSR and the USA and it is time to put an end to such activities."[139] As the policy of détente gained traction, the Soviet Union called for the closure of RFE/RL and for curbing VOA programming about domestic

Soviet issues, citing the radio stations as serious obstacles to the general improvement of relations with the United States. Soviet media intensified its attacks on the radios, while Soviet and East European security services instituted clandestine campaigns against the radios and even their personnel.

In late 1968, with the policy of détente on his agenda, President Richard Nixon signaled his intention to close Radio Liberty, notionally on budgetary grounds, even though RL's budget of $15 million was but a tiny fraction of the total U.S. federal budget. This impending decision spurred the CIA to form an interagency committee to study the impact of RL. In February 1969 the committee presented its recommendations for continued funding to Henry Kissinger, then the NSC adviser, noting in particular that Radio Liberty served as a catalyst for Soviet dissidents striving to change their society. The committee stressed that Soviet émigrés could influence Soviet leaders toward making their government a more constructive and responsible member of the world community. Relying on this report, Kissinger recommended funding but only for eight months "in an effort to determine what quid pro quo might be obtainable from the USSR and/or the West German governments should it be considered desirable to terminate RL."[140]

Apparently, the Nixon administration did not receive an adequate quid pro quo, and RFE/RL continued to operate, but under the sword of Damocles. Indeed, shortly after escaping termination by the White House, RFE/RL came under direct attack in the Senate. Although there had been reports in various publications that RFE and RL were funded covertly by the CIA, they had been spared public scrutiny. But on January 25, 1971, Senator Clifford Case publicly acknowledged CIA funding and accused RFE and RL of deceiving their listeners and impeding progress toward more normal U.S.-Soviet relations. He was especially angry that the Congress had not been "asked or permitted to carry out its constitutional role of approving the expenditures."[141]

Not to be outdone, Senator J. William Fulbright, the powerful chairman of the Senate Foreign Relations Committee, joined the fray with fire and fury, stating that "RFE and RL were surely a part of a pattern of falsehood and deception; a pattern of conspiracy to mislead. The radios are an anachronism. . . . They have outlived any usefulness they once may have had . . . and should be given an opportunity to take their rightful place in the graveyard of war relics."[142]

Case and Fulbright, along with Senators Stuart Symington and Frank Church, unleashed a protracted bureaucratic struggle in Washington over the fate of the radios. Case favored placing the radios under the State Department, but senior officials at the State Department were wary of assuming responsibility for radio broadcasts that could run counter to short-term diplomatic goals. Congress was equally hesitant to approve open-ended authorization and expenditures by RFE and RL—legally nongovernmental entities—without clearly defined lines of accountability. This bureaucratic dilemma led to endless meetings, reports and backroom maneuvering in Congress until a compromise was reached: RFE and RL would be merged into one organization, and a small federal agency, the Board for International Broadcasting, would be established to oversee their operations. The BIB would consist of part-time directors, nominated by the president on a bipartisan basis and confirmed by the Senate. The chair would be of the party of the president; day-to-day operations would be administered by a senior staff of career federal employees.

Although the bureaucratic organization of the radios was settled, Congress and the executive branch continued to question the mission of the radios. Despite studies by the State Department, the Congressional Research Office, and the CIA that highlighted the positive impact of the broadcasts and noted their growing audiences, the Senate Foreign Relations Committee continued to be ambivalent about the future funding of the radios. Typical of this attitude was a statement by Senator Claiborne Pell, who supported Radio Free Europe programming but gave short shrift to Radio Liberty: "There is a difference when it comes to Radio Liberty. This is a program that I believe is more questionable as its basic objective is the removal of an indigenous, stable and apparently permanent regime."[143] Pell echoed the views of several senators and many Western kremlinologists who assumed that Eastern Europe could someday break free of Soviet domination and evolve into a quasi-market economy, but the USSR, at its core, would remain Soviet forever. If that was the case, then the raison d'être of Radio Liberty was highly questionable. A *New York Times* editorial (February 21, 1972) captured this prevailing attitude:

> If the deadlock kills Radio Free Europe and Radio Liberty, the chief gainers will be the Soviet bloc's hard liners who hate the two radio stations as allies of the liberal and progressive elements in the Communist world. We believe the work of these two stations has a lasting validity and importance, but even those of a different view must realize that the existence of these organizations provides potential bargaining counters for President Nixon's Moscow visit next May. At the least, all concerned should be able to agree that a final decision on the future of Radio Free Europe and Radio Liberty cannot be made until Mr. Nixon has returned from the Kremlin and Congress can take a hard look at the post-Moscow situation of American foreign policy.[144]

The editorial raised two critical points that were to haunt Radio Liberty until the advent of the Reagan administration. The first noted that because RL was despised and feared by the Soviet authorities, more liberally minded Americans saw it as an impediment to normal U.S.-Soviet relations. This made it relatively easy for Nixon and Kissinger to use RL as a bargaining chip in their deliberations with Soviet officials. That RL was not terminated in the early 1970s indicated that most likely the Nixon administration demanded too large a quid pro quo for its closure. The second point in the editorial was more troubling for the radios, namely that they should be supported because they were allies of the liberal and progressive elements in the Communist world. Put simply, to survive, the two radios needed to show they were friends of détente and be seen as a positive force in the peaceful evolution of communism.

Stung by Fulbright's mocking criticism, as well as by Nixon's and Kissinger's indifference, the management of RFE/RL publicly hewed to this new mission as a way to protect the radio operations. Gene Sosin took up the public-relations mantle, serving as a liaison with U.S. media and the university community. On the university lecture circuit, Sosin would generally speak about RL as an educational tool promoting an evolutionary process toward democracy in the Soviet world. At Princeton University, for example, he stated that "Radio Liberty rejects the politics of confrontation and directs its energies toward developing rational thought among its listeners, on the assumption that the Soviet citizen has within himself the natural capability of eventually shaping his country's destiny."[145] Sosin's views were echoed in a report by Joseph Whelan, a Russia specialist at the Library of Congress, who went even further, noting that "RL politics are attuned to the most refined thinking in the Western community of Soviet specialists from which it draws for counsel in programming and policy formation. Its philosophical orientation, reformist, idealistic, and pacifistic, is in the tradition of American Jeffersonian-Wilsonian democratic liberalism."[146]

As important as Sosin's and Whelan's statements were in helping Radio Liberty to survive, their assessments bore only a tangential connection to the programs themselves. As our subsequent analysis of the broadcasts will show, RL editors and broadcasters were deeply skeptical of détente. They questioned some of the underlying principles of Western liberalism and did not see themselves as embodying Jeffersonian democracy. Hardly any RL editors or writers would express the view that the Soviet system could be transformed into a democracy or even evolve into a benign power. At VOA, management had the bureaucratic tools to exert tight editorial control and curb what it considered provocative programming, but RL, true to its independence, continued its hard-hitting broadcasts. Despite the policies of détente, RL broadcast the entire text of Solzhenitsyn's *The Gulag Archipelago*, reported extensively on the trials of dissidents and refuseniks, and interviewed critics of the Soviet regime.

Was Anyone Listening?
The overriding questions facing VOA and RFE/RL from the outset were, Was anyone listening? And if they were, what was the practical effect of the broadcasts? Trying to answer these questions was difficult not only because the target area was off limits to audience researchers but also because the very act of listening to a foreign broadcast was

considered treasonous. To compound the problem, the Soviet Union jammed both VOA and RL, although monitoring reports indicated that the radio signals did get through and there was a steadily growing audience for international broadcasting.[147]

As a government entity, VOA based its audience size and impact primarily on U.S. Embassy reports and studies conducted by the USIA Office of Research. In addition, it would draw on audience surveys conducted by the BBC, the CIA's Foreign Broadcast Information Service, and Radio Free Europe/Radio Liberty analysis of listenership. But during the Cold War, VOA never invested the necessary resources to develop a full-fledged audience research operation. There was even a common saying at VOA that if you compare the BBC and VOA you would find only two things bigger at the BBC—the audience and the Audience Research Department.[148]

In contrast, Radio Free Europe/Radio Liberty took audience research seriously and devoted significant resources to analyzing the listenership. In the summer of 1953 RFE set up a small audience analysis section that included the study of East European and Soviet media, as well as reports from defectors, travelers, journalists, and businessmen. In 1956 RL established an Audience Research Department, headed by Max Ralis, a Russian-born social scientist, that analyzed not only media attacks on RFE and RL but also letters from listeners that were sent to *accommodation addresses*—post office boxes in various European cities. Ralis trained Russian speakers to discreetly interview Soviet visitors in Europe. "At the Brussels World's Fair in 1958," Gene Sosin recalled, "our representatives interviewed three hundred Soviet tourists and discovered that sixty-five were RL listeners."[149] Although the samples were small and the letters infrequent, anecdotal evidence slowly built up to indicate that RL was indeed being heard and appreciated by more critically minded Soviet citizens.

Audience research was especially important for RL because it helped to shape the programs and identify key subject areas. Starting in the mid 1960s, RL began working with Western specialists in communications theory. A key contributor to RL's research was Ithiel de Sola Pool, who directed the Project on Communist Communications at MIT's Center for International Studies. Based on an analysis of interviews with over two thousand Soviet citizens, Pool and his colleagues recommended that RL avoid making long-term projections of how Soviet society would evolve and, to maintain credibility, occasionally take a stand different from that of the U.S. government. The goal of the radio broadcasts was to be treated as a "welcomed guest in the living room."

In 1981 RFE/RL established the Soviet Area Audience and Opinion Research division, under the leadership of R. Eugene Parta. By the mid-1980s RL was analyzing several thousand interviews a year with Soviet travelers. By 1991 RL audience research had conducted fifty-one thousand interviews. Since the travelers were mostly members of the Communist Party, RL relied on MIT's simulation model to adjust for the skewed demographic group.[150] In addition, RL interviewed legal émigrés from the Soviet Union who provided in-depth responses to the programming and were useful for cross-checking data from other sources. Parta and his team carried out serious research and tried to construct an accurate picture of the audience size and its composition, but they never claimed that their work produced results that would have been as accurate as surveys conducted within the USSR using state-of-the-art methodology. But when the Cold War ended and Western-style research could be conducted in Russia and the successor states, RL discovered that its earlier measurements and assessment of the audience had been on target and did not require major reassessments. Subsequent surveys conducted inside Russia, Gene Parta noted, "bore out the finding of widespread listening to foreign radio stations during the Cold War period and the importance of Western broadcasts to the Soviet people."[151]

The question of audience size and impact was an important issue in the 1980s when both VOA and RFE/RL sought increased funding. Congressional staff and officials in the White House Office of Management and Budget asked for hard data, and the BIB would not only cite the numbers and reports produced by RL audience research but would also argue that Soviet media attacks on VOA and RL and the jamming of the broadcasts were significant indicators of impact. Before Gorbachev's policy of glasnost made jamming futile, the Soviet Union was employing roughly seventeen hundred transmitters generating an output of 45 megawatts at a cost of approximately $48 million in electricity alone.[152] That the USSR would expend such precious resources to blot out factual news and commentary testified to its sense of vulnerability and inordinate fear of independent media.

Since the fall of communism, we have learned in greater detail that Soviet authorities considered foreign radio broadcasts to be a serious threat. As Elena Bashkirova, a Russian sociologist formerly at the Academy of Science, noted, "The USSR ideological services were interested in getting information about listeners to foreign radio stations to help them undertake appropriate counterpropaganda measures."[153] The research of the Academy of Science showed that by the end of the 1970s, roughly half of the Russian urban population listened to foreign broadcasting on a regular basis. Although dissidents and refuseniks were avid listeners, the vast majority of the audience consisted of predominantly young people (under thirty-five) who preferred music and contemporary cultural programs. Foreign broadcasts were the forbidden fruit, and that made them especially attractive.

Recently, scholars have also begun studying the impact foreign broadcasts had on the ruling elite in the Soviet Union. During Stalin's rule, TASS set up a special division—OZP (Osobye zakrytye pis'ma—special classified documents)—to monitor foreign-press articles and to prepare summaries of foreign radio broadcasts. These documents were intended for the Central Committee of the Communist Party of the Soviet Union (CPSU) and the Council of Ministers, but in the early 1950s they went only to the top leadership. They provided an uncensored picture of how the West viewed Soviet leaders and the political situation in the country as a whole. When Stalin died, for example, the four addressees of these reports—Georgy Malenkov, Lavrenty Beria, Vyacheslav Molotov, and Nikita Khrushchev—relied on VOA broadcasts to understand how the West might view the impending power struggle. A secret Soviet report, dated March 5, 1953, stated,

The Voice of America asserted in a program for Communist countries a few hours after Georgy Malenkov came to power in Russia that this moment signifies only the beginning of a power struggle.

His appointment does not signify that the serious problems of succession in the Soviet Union have come to a final resolution. . . . 'The definitive transfer of power may be decided only after a drawn-out fight among the supreme representatives. . . . It remains unclear whether Malenkov will be able to hold on to power. . . . The Voice of America insists that the truth of this statement is supported by the fact that Marshal Stalin's death was initially kept secret in order to prepare a semblance of unity.[154]

Declassified Soviet documents have shown that the Soviet leadership used the reports of BBC, VOA, and RFE/RL to help shape their domestic and international policies. In typical Soviet fashion, the KGB, which monitored all the radio broadcasts, also used these reports to collect *kompromat* (compromising materials) on important Soviet figures without informing the individual in question. In a telling example, the KGB compiled an extensive *kompromat* file on Marshal Georgy Zhukov but sent it only to the other members of the ruling elite. However, Zhukov, along with sixteen high-ranking leaders, received detailed summaries of RFE/RL and BBC broadcasts that highlighted Khrushchev's drunken statements at various diplomatic receptions.[155]

By the 1960s, radio summaries were an important source of information for Soviet officials. "Being a regular recipient of OZP in its full edition," a senior RL researcher noted, "doubtless signified that one had attained the highest level of the Soviet hierarchy. By the same token, exclusion from the lists, or reduction in the amount of data received, would be a sign of diminishing significance in the party and State and in some cases banishment from political life."[156] Although the goal of VOA, RL, and the other foreign broadcasters was to reach the Soviet population directly, over the heads of State, their broadcasts ended up being an integral part of the leadership's knowledge of itself and the world as a whole. In a totalitarian system, where all media had to conform to political censorship and control, foreign radio broadcasts not only provided vital information to a broad swath of the population but also were an indispensable breath of freedom, necessary for the sustenance of civic life.

2

The Reagan Revolution

In 1955 a young Ronald Reagan lent his voice to the Crusade for Freedom, a national campaign organized by the Free Europe Committee to raise public funding for Radio Free Europe and garner broad public support for Cold War policies. Already a popular host of *General Electric Theater*, appearing on national television every Sunday evening, Reagan was becoming a genial and trusted spokesman for the values of personal liberty and individual responsibility that GE hoped would project its image of corporate patriotism and keep Socialist policies at bay.[1] It was one small step for Reagan from the GE platform to the Crusade for Freedom that embodied many of the same core principles of liberty but cast them in an international setting with Soviet communism as the main enemy. The crusade was closely associated with one of Reagan's heroes, Dwight David Eisenhower, for whom he voted twice for president despite being a registered Democrat.

During his presidential campaign, on September 4, 1952, Eisenhower stated that "to destroy human liberty the Communists use every conceivable weapon. . . . None is more insidious than propaganda. I speak tonight about the Crusade for Freedom, a campaign sponsored by private American citizens to fight the big lie with the big truth. . . . You and I have a definite part to play. Each of us will have the opportunity to sign the Freedom Scroll . . . our faith in freedom and our belief in the dignity of the individual."[2] Several months later, after his election as the thirty-fourth president of the United States, Eisenhower recorded another message on behalf of the third Crusade for Freedom campaign, noting that "the only way to frustrate the evil manipulation of human minds and emotions is to supply the truth which gives oppressed people a measuring stick to lay against each lie that is told to them."[3] In the same spirit of patriotism, his rival, Governor Adlai Stevenson, also recorded a message in support of Radio Free Europe, adding that "the programs have a spontaneity and freshness, which no official information agency can have. Freedom speaks most clearly between man and man, when its voice is neither muffled nor amplified by government intervention. . . . There are mounting indications of the effectiveness of free radio broadcasts. . . . One of the best tests is the shrill violence of the attacks upon them by Radio Moscow."[4] These messages were broadcast by all four major radio networks—CBS, ABC, NBC, and MBS (Mutual Broadcast System)—leading Henry Ford II, the chair of the Crusade for Freedom, to note that "the joint statement of the two political rivals showed this nation is strongly united in the cause of freedom."[5] Eisenhower's continuing support of the mission of RFE was evident throughout his years in office as he made periodic statements about the radio broadcasts and hosted gala dinners at the White House for large corporate donors to the Crusade for Freedom.

Eisenhower's endorsement of RFE broadcasts reinforced Reagan's growing fear of communism and his determination to join the good fight. What better way was there to complement his work as a GE spokesman than to propound the values of freedom and individual enterprise in a setting that brought together the U.S. government, major corporations, and American communities throughout the country? After all, the aim of the Crusade for Freedom was to "win the hearts and minds of Americans" as the Cold War struggle gathered strength and to rally Americans around a radio voice that could pierce the Iron Curtain, weaken communist regimes, and project American values abroad. As Richard Cummings has aptly described, "from 1950 to 1960 millions of Americans throughout the United States willingly and enthusiastically signed 'Freedom Scrolls' and 'Freedom-Grams,' participated in fund-raising dinners and lunches, attended 'Crusader' meetings, marched in parades, launched large balloons filled with leaflets, participated in writing contests, bowled in tournaments, and otherwise were active in the belief that they were individually and collectively supporting Radio Free Europe in the battle against Communist aggression in Europe. . . . Thousands of local volunteer 'Crusaders' used their imagination, creativity, and willpower to keep the campaigns moving for ten years."[6] Because the funding for Radio Free Europe and Radio

Liberty came from the CIA, the Crusade for Freedom was needed not so much for the dollars it brought in as for the façade it provided that allowed the U.S. government to maintain an arms-length distance from the radio broadcasts and promote the work of émigré groups beaming the voice of freedom to the captive nations of Eastern Europe. The Crusade for Freedom also helped to build a national constituency for surrogate broadcasting that ensured a more aggressive stance toward the Soviet Union.

Whether Reagan knew of the CIA link to RFE is unclear, but the core mission of surrogate broadcasting resonated with his deeply held personal and political beliefs. With his mellifluous voice and engaging style, he became an effective spokesman for the Crusade for Freedom, addressing the American people through public service announcements. In one of his television clips, he appealed directly to the audience:

> Last year the contributions of 16 million Americans to the Crusade for Freedom made possible the World Freedom Bell, symbol of hope and freedom to the Communist-dominated peoples of Eastern Europe and built this powerful 135,000-watt Radio Free Europe transmitter in Western Germany. This station daily pierces the Iron Curtain with the truth, answering the lies of the Kremlin and bringing a message of hope to millions trapped behind the Iron Curtain. Grateful letters from listeners smuggled past the secret police expressed thanks to Radio Free Europe for identifying Communist quislings and informers by name. The Crusade for Freedom is your chance, and mine, to fight Communism.[7]

Reagan's support of the Crusade for Freedom embodied many aspects of his character: a fervent belief in freedom and individual enterprise, abhorrence of communism, recognition of the power of a free voice to engender political change, and an uncanny ability to communicate his message directly to the American public through the medium of television. These core principles came to full fruition as Reagan entered politics in his own right and was able to translate his long-held beliefs into concrete policies that condemned Soviet rule on moral grounds, expressed empathy for the victims of communism, and confronted Soviet aggression without resorting to arms.

Foremost on Reagan's agenda in the 1970s was the rejection of détente as the governing approach to the Soviet Union, a policy that had practically led to the closing of Radio Free Europe and Radio Liberty and to the toning down of VOA's Russian broadcasts. In challenging Gerald Ford for the Republican nomination in 1976, Reagan called détente a failed strategy and asserted the need to confront Soviet aggression. "Last year and this," he noted in 1976, "the Soviet Union intervened decisively in the Angola civil war and routed the pro-Western forces, yet Messrs Ford and Kissinger continue to tell us that we must not let this interfere with détente. . . . We have given the Soviets our trade and our technology . . . and at Kissinger's insistence, Mr. Ford snubbed Aleksandr Solzhenitsyn, one of the great moral heroes of our time. . . . What has the U.S. gotten in return, other than Soviet belligerence in the Middle East, Soviet duplicity in Southeast Asia and Soviet imperialism in South Central Africa?"[8] Later, Reagan opposed Carter's détente policies, characterizing them as "having to beg the Soviets to negotiate seriously with an appeal to their better nature."[9] During the 1980 Presidential campaign and in the early days of his administration, Reagan made it clear that détente was not a goal of U.S. policy, calling it "a one-way street that the Soviet Union has used to pursue its own aims."[10] Later, he characterized détente as a policy for Russians to engage in subversion, aggression, and expansionism anywhere in the world.[11]

Along with his criticism of détente, Reagan rejected the notion that Soviet communism had become a lifeless ideology. In the view of most American kremlinologists, the driving force of Soviet foreign policy was great power politics and age-old Russian territorial ambitions. Rather than seeking global domination, the experts argued, the post-Stalin USSR wanted to preserve its superpower status and protect its national interests. Hence, most experts concluded, the most effective way of influencing Soviet behavior was by negotiating international agreements and participating in cooperative programs that dispelled Soviet fears of Western aggression.

To the shock of the academic establishment and some quarters in the State Department, Reagan and his advisers rejected the prevailing view of the Soviet Union, unambiguously pointing to Communist ideology as the driving force of Soviet behavior both abroad and at home. Reagan even went so far as to campaign on a platform of confronting and defeating Soviet communism. Echoing the main precepts of the Crusade for Freedom, the 1980 Republican Party platform, largely written by Reagan's staff, stated that one of the administration's goals would be to "pursue positive, non-military means to roll back the growth of communism."[12] Reagan's stark assessment of communism and Soviet rule was greeted positively not only by American conservatives and foreign policy hawks but also by many prominent Russian dissidents and émigrés. Alexandr Solzhenitsyn and Slava Rostropovich forged a personal relationship with Reagan and publicly endorsed his foreign policies. Many Russian dissidents, religious figures, and Jewish refuseniks, including Lyudmila Alexeyeva and Avital Sharansky, respected Reagan for his principled stand in support of human rights. Even Joseph Brodsky, lionized by the New York liberal literati, felt honored to attend Reagan's last state dinner honoring Margaret Thatcher and acknowledged the important role Reagan had played in confronting the Soviet Union.[13] Most Russian broadcasters at VOA and Radio Liberty were strong supporters of Reagan's approach to the Soviet Union, even if many disagreed with him on economic or social issues. Russian émigrés of different political views felt that Reagan cared deeply about human rights in the Communist world, tried to help individual Russians suffering under Soviet rule, and offered hope to millions that someday they would live as free citizens. That message had always been at the core of VOA and RL Russian broadcasts. By proclaiming it boldly, Reagan reaffirmed the fundamental mission of international broadcasting and raised the morale of the broadcasters.

Reagan believed that one of the most effective ways to accomplish his goal of defeating communism was through the power of media and mass communication. Writing in *Foreign Affairs* (Spring 1981), Kenneth Adelman noted that Reagan was "a gifted professional communicator who has spent much of his life in radio, on the lecture circuit, in syndicated column writing, or along the campaign trail. Public diplomacy is the component of international broadcasting he knows best and does best."[14] Drawing on his association with the Crusade for Freedom, Reagan felt comfortable referencing RFE/RL or VOA in his speeches and professed a belief in projecting U.S. policy through international broadcasting. At a Lincoln Day dinner in Worcester, Massachusetts, in February 1980, for instance, he stated that "it's time to expand dramatically the Voice of America, Radio Free Europe and Radio Liberty. We have a message of peace and hope and nothing to be ashamed of in the examples we set for the world. Millions upon millions of people look to us as a beacon of freedom in a world that is fast losing freedom."[15] Unlike his immediate predecessors, Reagan would acknowledge the two radio stations in his public pronouncements. In his opening campaign speech at Liberty State Park (September 1, 1980), he noted "that more than anything I've ever wanted [is] to have an administration that will, through its actions, at home and in the international arena, let millions of people know that Miss Liberty still 'Lifts her lamp beside the golden door.' Through our international broadcasting stations—the Voice of America, Radio Free Europe, and the others—let us send, loud and clear, the message that this generation of Americans intends to keep that lamp shining."[16]

Even though VOA and RFE/RL had no discernible domestic constituency and were not well known to the general public, Reagan continued to invoke their critical role throughout the campaign. On October 19, 1980, in a televised address rebutting Carter's foreign policy, he pledged to strengthen VOA and RFE/RL, adding "what we need most is conviction, the conviction that in carrying the American message abroad we strengthen the foundations of peace."[17] Reagan's words underscored how the rhetoric about the radios had changed from the early 1970s when Fulbright, Case, and other senators saw RFE/RL as an anachronism, while Nixon and Kissinger considered them bargaining chips. By challenging détente, Reagan recast the public dialogue about international radio broadcasting, asserting that VOA and RFE/RL were necessary and effective tools in implementing his policy toward the Soviet Union. "The Reagan administration," Nicholas Cull concluded, "arrived with a zeal and ideological self-confidence not seen since the days of Kennedy."[18]

Shortly after his election, Reagan's campaign rhetoric and core beliefs were translated into the language of policy. One of the early formulations of U.S. policy toward the Soviet Union, NSDD (National Security Decision Directive) 11-82, encapsulated the essence of Reagan's approach to the Soviet Union:

> Communist ideology is the main source of the regime's legitimacy. It explains why there is only one political party, which controls the state administration and all spheres of society, why the media are subject to censorship, and why the party Politburo dominates political life. This ideology also serves to buttress and rationalize the privileged position of the ruling elite (nomenklatura) in Soviet society.
>
> U.S. policy toward the Soviet Union must have an ideological thrust which clearly demonstrates the superiority of U.S. and Western values of individual dignity and freedom, a free press, free trade unions, free enterprise, and political democracy over the repressive character of Soviet communism. We should state openly our belief that people in Communist countries have the right to democratic systems.
>
> To break the mental habits these ideas have fostered, it is essential that the United States take the offensive in exposing the bankruptcy of the Communist system, its failure to provide adequately for the basic needs of its peoples, and its dependence on the force of arms for the seizure and retention of political power. The U.S. should stress that, 65 years after the October Revolution, the Soviet regime continues to deny its people fundamental human rights. . . . In short, the U.S. must make clear to the world that democracy, not Communism, is mankind's future.[19]

Since the Reagan administration believed that communism dominated all spheres of life in the USSR, it advocated the public promotion of democratic Western values. Reagan's views were expressed most cogently in his speech to the British Parliament in June 1982 when he called on the West "to foster the infrastructure of democracy—the system of free press, unions, political parties, universities—which allow a people to choose their own way, to develop their own culture, to reconcile their own differences through peaceful means."[20] As Carnes Lord, an official in the Reagan administration, added, "By openly, publicly, and officially committing itself to spreading democracy, the Reagan administration expressed a faith in the principles of liberal democracy and a confidence in the democratic future that had a profound influence on the Soviet elites as well as the general population behind the Iron Curtain."[21]

The Reagan administration believed that Russians and other nationalities in the Soviet Union could understand Western values and intentions better if they were presented *in their own language* and in the context *of their own culture*. Implicit in this strategy was the notion that the language services of VOA and RFE/RL were unique tools for communicating the fundamental message of democracy in ways that were *culturally understandable* to their audiences. This was especially true in the 1980s when VOA and RFE/RL could draw on many of the better-known Russian writers, thinkers, philosophers, religious leaders, and artists who were living in the West and were eager to participate in the broadcasts. Their credibility and conviction carried weight that no American could muster. Their presence on the airwaves could expand the size of the VOA and RFE/RL listenership, and, most important, their words could have political consequences.

The new policy of empowering émigrés had the full support of senior management, though it was considered provocative by many old timers at VOA. Before the Reagan administration, the general policy at VOA had been to require language services to rely primarily on translations of VOA English-language scripts. In the Reagan years the situation changed dramatically, and language services were given the freedom to be strategic in developing their feature programming. In a direct way, the Reagan administration called upon the Russian broadcasts of VOA and RFE/RL to return to their foundational mission of challenging the Communist regimes and reaching Russians with messages of hope, democracy, and a brighter future. The NSDD 11-82 explicitly named VOA and RFE/RL as major tools of U.S. policy, ensuring additional resources that were needed to expand programming and overcome jamming. It also established an international task force that included experts from BBC and Deutsche Welle to help coordinate technical issues. Most important, NSDD 11-82 called for the inclusion of RFE/RL in the distribution of U.S. government information on events in the Soviet Union and Eastern Europe, thereby acknowledging its fundamental role in supporting U.S. foreign policy.[22]

Voice of America

Reagan's strategy of confronting and defeating communism was such a radical departure from established norms that it inevitably caused turmoil at VOA and RFE/RL. Alan Heil, a senior VOA executive, reflected the apprehension of many longtime broadcasters when he stated that the struggle over the basic philosophy of the VOA "centered on the question: would the Voice continue to focus principally on the free flow of information—accurate, objective, and comprehensive programming consistent with the Charter—or would it be redirected toward what Carnes Lord of the NSC later termed an ideological struggle with the Soviet Union?"[23] Since VOA was capable of broadcasting news in an accurate and objective way and, at the same time, of airing hard-hitting programs about Soviet human rights abuses, Heil and many veteran managers focused most of their criticism on the VOA editorials that were intended to communicate the official U.S. government position on international issues. In their attempt to project American values as seen by the Reagan administration, these editorials would occasionally resort to crude advertising techniques that made them convenient targets for Reagan's critics. The first editorial denounced the hypocrisy of the Soviet position on the eve of the UN session on disarmament. As Heil noted, subsequent

> editorials included such titles as "By Hook or Crook" (an attack on the Kremlin's industrial and economic espionage in the West); "Shave Closer, Sleep Better" (on the shortage of razors and other consumer goods in the Soviet Union); and "Comrade, can you spare a dime" (a scathing denunciation of an American citizen who was

visiting the USSR and lionized for criticizing capitalism in the United States). What made the editorials especially irksome to many VOA journalists was the requirement to run them daily, whether or not they were relevant to their listeners. Each editorial, moreover, was labelled as "reflecting the views of the United States government."[24]

For the VOA establishment—American journalists, managers, and career foreign service personnel—the editorials, along with programming critical of the Soviet Union, represented a major break with VOA practice and a reversion to an earlier, more aggressive journalistic style. During détente, VOA strived to be a public broadcaster, taking as its model the PBS NewsHour, the BBC World Service, or NPR's *All Things Considered*. This was especially true for the VOA English Service that recruited broadcasters from leading schools of journalism in the United States and commercial media. In the spirit of détente, the VOA saw itself as an independent journalistic voice that was "above the fray" of the Cold War and treated the Soviet Union as just another country. Its English-language broadcasts sought common ground with ordinary Soviet listeners, and that meant more apolitical programs and fewer broadcasts that exposed the Soviet regime's lies, crimes, or suppression of human rights. For the VOA establishment, the Reagan administration's intention to use the radios as tools in political warfare was not just a throwback to an earlier era, but a downright travesty and a violation of the highest ideals.

The appointment of Reaganites at VOA, ready to implement the NSC "battle plan," caused additional internecine warfare. The lightening rod in the early years was a VOA policy adviser, Philip Nicolaides, whose previous professional experience had been in commercial advertising. "His burning desire," Alan Heil noted, "was to destabilize the Soviet Union by using VOA to win what he called the 'war of ideas.'"[25] In an infamous memo, dated September 21, 1981, to James B. Conkling, director of VOA, Nicolaides wrote, "The only convincing *raison d'etre* for the VOA is to counter USSR propaganda by portraying it as the last great predatory empire on earth. . . . We should seek to drive wedges of resentment and suspicion between the leadership of the various Communist bloc nations. . . . News should be factually accurate. Credibility is all-important. But we need not expatiate endlessly on stories which tend to put us or our allies in a bad light while glossing over stories which discredit the leadership of the communist nations."[26]

Nicolaides's call to arms caused a maelstrom that resulted in bureaucratic bloodletting. Nicolaides himself was soon relieved of his duties, as was the first director of the VOA under Reagan, James Conkling, but the liberal establishment also suffered sizable losses. As Heil noted, "In just three months [after the Nicolaides memo], at least ten senior and midlevel managers at the Voice had retired, been removed, or been transferred. . . . Wick demanded the removal of VOA USSR Division chief Barbara Allen, a foreign service officer . . . to placate an ultraconservative congressman who considered VOA Russian broadcasts 'too soft' and accused VOA of downplaying the views of Alexandr Solzhenitsyn."[27]

The pitched battles between the VOA establishment and the Reagan appointees had subsided by the summer of 1983, when I joined VOA as director of the Russian Service. Two professional journalists—Kenneth Tomlinson and Gene Pell—headed VOA and pledged to uphold high journalistic standards. They hired new managers in the English Service and declared a fresh start at VOA.

What I discovered very quickly was that the Russian broadcasters (along with their colleagues in other foreign-language services at VOA) were generally pleased with the Reagan administration approach. While they mocked the VOA editorials for their simplistic approach and frequently disagreed with Reagan's domestic policies, they relished their new journalistic freedom and a renewed sense of mission. The staff shared Reagan's aversion to communism and reviled the Soviet system. For a long time, the foreign-language broadcasters felt hemmed in by the strictures of détente, which often meant avoiding such topics as the gulag, dissidents, or émigré critics of the Soviet regime. What the VOA establishment saw as nonideological, purist programming, the Russian Service viewed as capitulation to Soviet demands. The most egregious example was the prohibition to interview Russian dissidents in the West and to limit reports about them to citations in Western media. When I raised this issue with Tomlinson and Pell, recommending that such prohibitions be lifted, they readily acquiesced. As we will see in the examination of the broadcasts, the Russian Service now had the freedom to invite such prominent critics of the Soviet system as Solzhenitsyn, Rostropovich, Vishnevskaya, Aksyonov, and Alexeyeva and allow them to have their say. Rather than strictly adhering to English-language sources, VOA was now able to cite émigré publications. Instead of limiting its current-affairs programming to the news lineup prepared by the VOA Central News bureau, the Russian Service could use reports filed by its own journalists and select news stories from a broad range of media sources, including the European press. The Russian Service could also devote airtime to subjects the Soviet media avoided or purposefully distorted, such as news about religion or achievements of Russian émigrés.

Our aim was to make the news and feature programs of interest and relevance to a critical, politically aware audience. We were strategic, but this did not mean that we slanted the news or avoided material that shed a negative light on the United States or the Reagan administration. A notable example was Reagan's infamous, off-the-record "joke." On August 11, 1984, Reagan was asked to make a prebroadcast microphone check and obliged by declaring, "My fellow Americans. I'm pleased to tell you today that I've signed legislation that will outlaw the Soviet Union forever. We begin bombing in five minutes." Those remarks were leaked to the U.S. media and caused an uproar. Reagan's "joke" was the lead story on all the news networks and was quickly picked up by media in other countries. When the VOA Russian news desk called me, frantic over whether we should broadcast this item in Russian to the Soviet Union, I made the decision—yes. We needed to provide context and explain how this tasteless "joke" arose, but we absolutely had to air the story if we wanted to retain credibility with our audience. When I called Tomlinson at home to tell him how the Russian Service was treating the story, he assured me that we had made the right decision.

After initial turmoil at VOA in the first two years of the Reagan administration, Tomlinson and his management team brought much needed stability and professionalism. The Reagan administration settled on the right approach to the foreign-language services of VOA: it trusted the services to know how to develop relevant programming that was bold and occasionally hard-hitting and, at the same time, did not violate the core principles of the VOA Charter. As we will see in subsequent chapters, the Russian Service was given the freedom and resources to create exciting programming that has led some observers to refer to the 1980s as "the golden age of Russian broadcasting."

Radio Free Europe/Radio Liberty

The policy of détente in the 1970s had a profound impact on the programming of RFE/RL. With the merger of RFE and RL, the Board for International Broadcasting and the senior American management began to assert more active supervision of the broadcasts. That entailed daily reviews of program content, the preparation of short English summaries of the broadcasts, and occasional back translations of the broadcasts themselves. In 1976 the Board for International Broadcasting issued a mission statement that tried to communicate a less confrontational approach:

> RFE and RL seek to encourage a constructive dialogue with the peoples of Eastern Europe and the Soviet Union by enhancing their knowledge of developments in the world at large and in their own countries. In openly communicating information and ideas to peoples restricted by censorship, RFE and RL help to maintain an informed public opinion in the USSR and Eastern Europe. . . . They seek to create neither "American radio" . . . nor "exile radio" in the sense of organized political opposition, but international radio. It is international in the breadth of its coverage, its freedom from national or sectarian bias, its dedication to open communication of accurate information and a broad range of democratic ideas.[28]

After the attacks on the radios in the Congress, the BIB and RFE/RL shied away from using such words as *fighting communism* in their public statements. Like VOA, RFE/RL preferred to be known as an international public broadcaster, even if the editors and writers remained deeply skeptical of détente and continued to produce many hard-hitting programs.

This bifurcation between public image and the actual programming resulted in conflicts, as senior management tried to protect RFE/RL funding by stressing its apolitical stance and the broadcasters sought to continue to expose Soviet injustice and suppression of human rights.

In an effort to strengthen control over the broadcasts, the newly formed BIB commissioned outside evaluations of the broadcasts by leading American historians, journalists, and political scientists. Typically, the BIB senior staff would randomly select several weeks of programs and send cassette recordings to outside evaluators who would produce a detailed report, citing any violations of the broadcast code and making recommendations for improvements. Most reviewers were American professors, who advocated a less aggressive approach to the Soviet government and encouraged the radios to reach new listeners, not just disgruntled Soviet citizens. One reviewer even recommended that RL programs be addressed to loyal Soviet citizens and "specifically to the frame of reference and potential curiosity of the Soviet officialdom, the higher the better."[29] Most reviews recommended the greater use of Western books about Russia and the Soviet Union and discouraged focusing primarily on dissidents and human rights. In an effort to persuade the Soviet authorities that RL had turned a new leaf, the BIB chair in the 1970s, John Gronouski, a former ambassador to Poland and dean of the LBJ School of Public Affairs at the University of Texas, even proposed that RFE/RL grant Soviet officials the right of reply to any broadcasts that they found to be demonstrably false or defamatory.[30] The broadcasters at RFE/RL were stunned by what they considered incredible American naivete, if not downright foolishness. The mission of the radios was to give a truthful view of political and economic events, not to give Soviet propagandists another platform to showcase their disinformation. Fortunately, the Soviet authorities ignored Gronouski's proposal, claiming that the broadcasts were provocations, slander, and interference in their internal affairs. But the fact that the chair of the BIB would make such an offer indicated how deeply entrenched détente had become in the mindset of senior management.

In his memoirs, George Urban argued that détente stripped away the fundamental mission of RFE/RL by promoting the notion that Communist regimes could be reformed if they were treated as stable, normal countries. "Legitimacy building," Urban stated, "required supporting any initiative within the ruling communist parties that promised to smooth away the hard edges of the party-state dictatorship."[31] To achieve this goal, RFE/RL would have to treat Communist leaders as legitimate representatives of their nations and encourage their listeners to support them. They would have to acknowledge that the Soviet Union was a coherent and purposefully led superpower and that through its broadcasts, the radios could help shape "communism with a human face." Although this approach had advocates among senior RFE/RL management in the 1970s, editors in the language services strenuously opposed the approach, viewing it as abject appeasement.

Determined to reestablish the radios as the frontline in the war against communism, the Reagan administration began with major staff changes. Shortly after assuming office, the Reagan administration eliminated a separate RFE/RL corporate board and vested all authority in a new board of directors, headed by Frank Shakespeare as the BIB chair. The new members included several prominent journalists and public figures, among them Steve Forbes, Lane Kirkland, Michael Novak, Ben Wattenberg, and James Michener. Although the BIB was bipartisan by law, all the new appointees shared Reagan's fundamental anti-Soviet stance. "Wattenberg was a champion of the American system," Arch Puddington recalled, "and unabashed in his contempt for those who contended that American capitalism and Soviet communism were equally flawed. Novak was prominent among a small group of writers who identified capitalism as not only more efficient than other arrangements but also as virtuous."[32] Lane Kirkland, as the head of the AFL-CIO, provided material support for Poland's Solidarity movement and was adamant in his anti-Communist views. All directors believed deeply in the fundamental mission of the radios—to help facilitate democratic change in the USSR—and worked tirelessly to accomplish it.

As was the case at VOA, the initial personnel changes and the early outbursts of anti-Communist zeal set off fireworks at RFE/RL. Much of that had to do with the character and actions of the first BIB Chair.

A passionate conservative and an outspoken Cold Warrior, Shakespeare had served in the Nixon administration as the director of the U.S. Information Agency (USIA) but had never felt comfortable in the world of transactional diplomacy. In a 1990 interview he recalled his days at USIA: "I didn't agree in my deeper private self with some of the things that were being undertaken. The root of it was this. I have always believed that communism as it existed as an idea linked to states and power was evil. I thought it represented a mortal threat, that coexistence or convergence was nonsense. You don't converge or coexist with evil."[33]

A former president of CBS television, Shakespeare was a decisive leader who immediately started forming a new senior management team at RFE/RL, convinced that the old executives had become too soft on communism and unwilling to embrace Reagan's policy toward the Soviet Union. In short order, he named former U.S. Senator James Buckley as the new president of RFE/RL and brought on board two veteran Cold Warriors, George Urban, as the new director of RFE, and George Bailey, as the director of RL. Shakespeare was deeply engaged as chair of the BIB and on occasion would visit Munich to address the staff and explain the new Reagan approach to broadcasting. I attended such a meeting in the summer of 1983 and recall the enthusiasm with which Shakespeare spoke about the radio broadcasts. He recounted the historical role RFE/RL had played and vowed to provide more funding and resources for the critical battle with the Soviet Union. What struck me then was how differently staff at RFE/RL reacted to the new Reagan policies. The Russian broadcasters with whom I spoke afterwards were enthusiastic about Shakespeare's approach. Finally, they told me, Americans were beginning to understand the challenges ahead and would not burden the language services with irrelevant Western studies of the Soviet economy or the Communist Party structure. We would be free, they exclaimed, to develop programs that resonated with the Russian people and would help them defeat their Communist rulers. They were even more pleased when Reagan gave an unprecedented RFE/RL interview to James Buckley that boldly expressed his anti-Communist views. "While we were waiting for the tape recorder to be plugged in," Buckley reminisced, "Reagan muttered that it was indeed an Evil Empire and proceeded [to tell] the people of the Soviet Union and Eastern Europe that America intended by its example to show the captive nations that resisting totalitarianism is possible, while cautioning listeners that what the people choose to do to achieve freedom is their own business."[34] So sharp were Reagan's words that some critics in Washington even questioned if Reagan had violated RFE/RL guidelines by encouraging regime change.

In contrast, the hold-over American management was aghast by Shakespeare's words and felt that the Reagan administration was not only taking RFE and RL back to the past but was blithely unaware of the many political changes that were taking place in the East bloc. James F. Brown, who served as RFE director for many years and was a distinguished specialist on Eastern Europe, captured the typical reaction of the old guard at RFE/RL: "None of them [on the BIB] knows anything about Eastern Europe. . . . Shakespeare is an innocent fanatic, who is more concerned with spreading the gospel according to St Ronald than with serving an audience of millions that has come to regard RFE/RL as their domestic radio in exile."[35] Combative and impatient, Shakespeare did not last long as chair and left to take the position of U.S. ambassador to the Vatican. He was replaced by Steve Forbes, whose congenial personality and quiet wisdom brought much-needed calm to the management of the radios. He remained as chair until 1993, providing steady leadership through a dynamic and tumultuous political period. I served as his executive director and came to admire his clarity of vision, commitment to the core mission of the radios, and self-effacing style of leadership. He always knew he would have to make the tough decisions, but he tried to empower the senior radio management and the BIB staff and supported us in our role as leaders.

Implementation of Reagan Policy

Although the Reagan revolution at VOA and RFE/RL began with senior management turnover and bureaucratic turmoil, it quickly redeemed itself, even in the eyes of its critics, by its public support for the radio stations and concomitant budget increases. "In budget after budget,"

Arch Puddington noted, "Reagan raised the appropriations for both the VOA and RFE/RL, even as he hacked away at the spending levels of a long list of domestic programs. The radios were able to overhaul antiquated equipment, hire new staff, add correspondents to cover the war in Afghanistan, and launch a new service, Radio Free Afghanistan."[36] The VOA Russian Service was allotted more personnel slots to fill and had a generous travel budget to cover the most important political developments. In a break from past practice, the Russian Service could send its own correspondents to cover the Olympics; the Conference on Security and Cooperation in Europe (CSCE) in Madrid, a follow-on to the Helsinki Final Act; and major world events. It also had the resources to recruit broadcasters in Europe and Israel and hire freelance writers. But the most important result of the Reagan revolution was a new conception of programming. For the VOA Russian Service and its sister services—Ukrainian, Georgian, Armenian, Uzbek, and Azeri—the Reagan years meant greater creative freedom to shape programs that were relevant to their audiences. We had a free hand in developing our own programs on religion, both Orthodoxy and Judaism, as well as discussions of books and cultural developments banned in the Soviet Union. In a bold decision, I signed off on readings from recent novels even though some contained Russian four-letter words and descriptions of sex. Though concerned about how conservative members of Congress might react, I nonetheless was proud that VOA had taken a major step in broadcasting significant literary works without censorship. With some exceptions, we could now ignore cables from the U.S. Embassy Moscow questioning why we had broadcast a story that demeaned Lenin or cast aspersions on Soviet actions. Most important, VOA and USIA senior management were committed to protecting journalistic independence with a much-needed firewall.

At RL the Reagan revolution played out differently. While RFE/RL management publicly adhered to détente in the 1970s, the actual RL programs continued along traditional lines. Solzhenitsyn was frequently interviewed, his *Gulag Archipelago* was broadcast in full, and the plight of human rights activists and Jewish refuseniks was covered every day. What did change in the Reagan years was the loosening of controls over highly controversial subjects, principally antidemocratic nationalist philosophy, the role of resistance groups fighting Soviet authorities, anti-Semitism, Russian-Ukrainian relations, and the political role of the Orthodox Church. As we will see in subsequent chapters, more conservatively minded broadcasters felt empowered to air programs that questioned liberal values and Western democracy. To cite just two examples, in December 1982, the Russian Service broadcast Solzhenitsyn's Taiwan speech, in which he accused the West of demanding that Taiwan establish "democracy bordering on chaos, on state treason, on the right to freely destroy one's own country the way Western countries allow it at home."[37] Another broadcast in June 1983 quoted Vladimir Maximov, a prominent émigré writer, who contended that former Soviet citizens in the West "had the opportunity to become convinced that democracy in its traditional meaning was slowly but steadily beginning to outlive itself."[38] Excerpts from these and other similar programs—often taken out of context—found their way to the U.S. press and Congress, causing innumerable problems for RFE/RL. In a *Washington Post* essay, Josef Joffe and Dmitri Simes opined, "Which American radio station airs lengthy speeches portraying the United States as a decadent power and an unreliable ally? Which American station employs commentators openly contemptuous of Western democratic ideals? The name of the station is Radio Liberty."[39] However hyperbolic their rhetoric, Joffe and Simes pointed to a critical problem facing RL: if you were going to empower Russian broadcasters to fight communism and reach a critical audience in the Soviet Union, you could not expect them to act and sound like proper East Coast liberals. As our examination of the actual broadcasts will show, the Reagan revolution opened the door to a stream of creative programs at VOA and RFE/RL that resonated with the Russian audience and had a positive impact on political developments in the Soviet Union but, on occasion, caused political controversy.

3

Human Rights

Emblazoned on the wall in the front vestibule of the RFE/RL head-quarters in Munich, greeting all entering staff and visitors, were the words of the Universal Declaration of Human Rights: "freedom to seek, receive and impart information and ideas through any media and regardless of frontiers" (Article 19). The fundamental concepts of human rights, explicit in Article 19 and imbedded in the other twenty-nine articles, formed the bedrock of RFE/RL and VOA programming. Whether setting the daily news lineup, reporting on debates in the U.S. Congress or in European parliaments, or selecting works of literature for extended readings, the Russian broadcasters were guided by the basic concept that individuals were "born free and equal in dignity and rights" (Article 1). All programming embodied the basic tenet that "everyone is entitled to all rights and freedoms, without distinc-tion of any kind, such as race, color, sex, language, religion, political or other opinion, national or social origin, property, birth, or other status" (Article 2). Indeed, so central was the Universal Declaration of Human Rights to the work of VOA and RFE/RL that separate articles formed the basis of specific programs. Notably, Article 13—"the right to freely leave any country"—was the raison d'être for programming about Jewish refuseniks, and Article 18—"freedom of thought, con-science and religion"—laid the groundwork for programming about history, political philosophy, and religion. Adopted by forty-eight of the fifty-eight member states of the United Nations on December 10, 1948, with the USSR and its Eastern European allies abstaining, the Universal Declaration of Human Rights became a core document of democratic values and gave VOA and RFE/RL the imprimatur and tools to challenge the Soviet version of events and inform their listeners of the chasm between Soviet words and actions.

From its first days on air to the 1960s, Radio Liberty reported on human rights abuses in the USSR by drawing on Western news sources, émigré literature, scholarly studies, and especially publications by Soviet defectors. Works such as Victor Kravchenko's *I Chose Freedom: The Personal and Political Life of a Soviet Official* (1946), Vladimir Petrov's *It Happens in Russia: Seven Years of Forced Labor in the Siberian Gold-fields* (1951), and Isaac Don Levine's studies of Lenin, Stalin, and the gulag system exposed the horrors of Communist rule, including the Ukrainian famine. But broadcasts about these works, together with Western accounts of Soviet atrocities, engendered a never-ending fusillade of counterattacks. Soviet officials denounced defectors as traitors, waged relentless media campaigns against VOA and RL broadcasters, cast aspersions on Western journalists and scholars, and asserted that any *outside* criticism of Soviet life was a frontal attack on the motherland. Caricatures of VOA and RL broadcasters appeared in satirical publications such as *Krokodil*, and the KGB regularly published books and articles that denounced the radio broadcasts. With no independent public voices within the USSR raising the issue of human rights, Soviet media could whitewash its history and label the radio broadcasters as simply "enemy voices," always harping on supposed Soviet crimes and projecting a hatred of socialism. The savvy urban listener would likely see through the Soviet propaganda and understand the true state of human rights in the Soviet bloc, but for the less sophisticated radio listener, questions of human rights were likely lost in the din of cacophonous voices.

By the 1960s, the discourse about human rights in the Soviet Union began to change. In his path-breaking essay *Will the Soviet Union Survive until 1984?*, Andrei Amalrik posited the notion that "the fish" (Soviet citizens) were beginning to voice their views openly, thereby giving ichthyologists (Western observers) a truer and more nuanced picture of society.[1] The roughly ten years of Khrushchev's "thaw" that followed Stalin's death in 1953 had indeed left a deep mark on Soviet life. With the general easing of censorship, the release of millions of political prisoners from the gulag, Khrushchev's formal condemnation of Stalin's cult of personality, and the ever-so-slight opening of Soviet society through international festivals, cultural events, and educational exchanges, Soviet citizens had the confidence to stand up and be heard. The publication of Solzhenitsyn's short novel *One Day in the Life of Ivan Denisovich* (1962) in an official Soviet journal, *Novy Mir*, caused a sensation, as it openly described Stalinist repression. Fear, the controlling element of Communist rule, was receding, and Soviet citizens began to gather independently to exchange privately produced materials, which in time came to be known as *samizdat*. This new phenomenon of "self-publishing" was a daring personal act that Vladimir Bukovsky aptly described as "I write it myself; edit it myself; censor it myself; publish it myself; distribute it myself; and spend jail time for it myself."[2]

Initially, samizdat materials consisted primarily of poetry, unofficial songs, and an occasional novel, such as Boris Pasternak's *Doctor Zhivago*. But by the mid-1960s, samizdat acquired more political overtones with the reprinting of political tracts, statements about the arrests and trials of Soviet citizens, accounts of state persecution of informal groups for religious activity, and critiques of Soviet policies and practice. The impact of samizdat came to a head in the 1965 show trial of two satirists, Yuli Daniel and Andrei Sinyavsky, who were charged with "subverting Soviet *vlast* (power)" through "slanderous fabrications that defamed the Soviet State and social system."[3] Despite an outcry of protest from Western writers and political figures, the Soviet media labeled the two well-known writers as "renegades guilty of high treason" and duly sentenced them to five and seven years, respectively, in labor camps. This harsh recourse to Stalinist methods of repression proved to be a critical inflection point in Soviet history, prompting Soviet citizens to demand that the USSR live up to its own laws. A human rights movement began to take shape and would continue to challenge the repressive Soviet state until personal freedom was finally tolerated under Gorbachev's policies of glasnost and perestroika in the second half of the 1980s.

Before the trial began, supporters of Sinyavsky and Daniel gathered in Pushkin Square on December 5, 1965, for a "glasnost meeting," calling for fair and open trials. Roughly fifty participants and two hundred sympathetic observers gathered across from the offices of *Izvestia* on Pushkin Square, unfurling signs reading, "Respect for the Soviet Constitution" and "We Demand an Open Trial for Sinyavsky and Daniel." Among the organizers were such future dissident leaders as Alexander Esenin-Volpin, Yuri Galanskov, and Vladimir Bukovsky. Leading Soviet scientists and cultural figures, including Andrei Sakharov, Dmitri Shostakovich, and Maya Plisetskaya, signed open letters of protest. But most important, a key figure in the dissident movement, Alexander Ginzburg, compiled a thorough account of the trial and the responses of Soviet citizens to it, which became known as the *White Book*. It circulated in samizdat form and was eventually smuggled out to the West, where it was handed over to the Paris office of Radio Liberty.[4] Realizing the worldwide resonance that the *White Book* would have, the RL office passed it on to the *New York Times* for initial publication.[5] Francis Ronalds, the RL director, reasoned that the Soviet Union would have a more difficult time discrediting the *White Book* if it first appeared in the mainstream Western press.

Ginzburg's *White Book* presented a unique opportunity for Radio Liberty to report on the status of human rights from *inside the country*. Instead of relying on secondhand reports or Western news agencies, RL could now quote directly what Russians were saying about the trial and, in effect, about their government and Soviet life. Not only did the *White Book* make for compelling programming, but it also allowed RL to accomplish its mission of serving as an independent domestic radio station. RL devoted considerable airtime to the *White Book* and amplified the effect of the work, ensuring that it would be known throughout the country. Most important, it provided a historical context for the trial and the emerging dissident movement.

Among the many programs devoted to the *White Book*, one roundtable discussion stands out as an excellent example of how RL approached the emergence of samizdat and the tone it adopted toward internal change in the USSR. The program featured the who's who of the first Russian emigration: Gaito Gazdanov (1903–71), a prominent émigré writer; Vladimir Weidlé (1895–1979), a distinguished art historian and the author of a popular history: *Russia: Absent and Present* (New York,

1952); Georgi Adamovich (1892–1972), a critic and poet; and Nikita Struve (1931–2016), a professor of Russian literature at the Sorbonne. As I listened to these four eminent writers, I was immediately struck by their empathetic and dispassionate tone.[6] After all, the Sinyavsky and Daniel trial and the *White Book* exposed the cruelty and mendacity of the Soviet system and offered a convenient cudgel with which to beat the Soviet regime and mock Soviet jurisprudence. Yet the four RL broadcasters, all fervent anti-Communists, spoke in a calm, thoughtful, and deliberative manner, fully in keeping with the finer traditions of Western discourse.

Gazdanov began with a short description of the *White Book*, reminding listeners of the trial and the demonstrations. "Soviet society," he noted, "is now standing up to the authorities, publicly questioning their actions, and openly demanding that they adhere to their own laws and constitution. The demonstrators are demanding that the Soviet government simply follow its own laws; they aren't seeking a revolution or trying to subvert the political order . . . and it is significant that many prominent scientists and cultural figures are willing to openly sign letters on behalf of the arrested demonstrators." Gazdanov concluded that "public opinion in the USSR, a social phenomenon the Soviet regime has tried to quell from its earliest days in power, is now becoming a reality."

Picking up on Gazdanov's points, Weidlé noted that the *White Book* elicited feelings both of joy and sadness. "Joy," he reiterated, "because under the most difficult conditions, Russians are taking a bold and fearless stance, asserting their personal dignity as independently thinking individuals. Their demands are consonant with Western liberal values of open trials and the rule of law, and, at the same time, their bravery and high-mindedness harken back to the finer traditions of nineteenth-century Russian intelligentsia." For Weidlé, the *White Book* and the supporters of Sinyavsky and Daniel proved that despite Bolshevik rule, "true Russian patriotism is still alive." But the sad part, Weidlé conceded, "is that the trial and conviction illustrate yet again the totally arbitrary nature of Soviet justice and its reliance on repression. As in the trial of Joseph Brodsky a year earlier in Leningrad, the Soviet court called on public witnesses for the prosecution (*obshchestvennye obvin-iteli*), who, purportedly on behalf of 'the people,' accused the defendants of crimes against the state." In the case of Sinyavsky and Daniel, the prosecution called on Arkady Vasiliev and Zoya Kedrina, two members of the Union of Soviet Writers, who proceeded to accuse the satirists of "cultural heresy" and "disrespect for Russian classics" by citing words uttered by different characters in their works. "So primitive are these accusations," Weidlé lamented, "that I despair of Soviet writers (and the general public) even understanding basic literary conceits. If one were to adopt the approach advanced by Vasiliev and Kedrina, then every Russian writer could be found guilty of some crime against the state."

Like Weidlé, Adamovich had mixed feelings about the state of affairs in the Soviet Union. "On the positive ledger," he pointed out, "the Pushkin Square demonstration and the appearance of the *White Book* in samizdat indicate an evolution toward a more open and freer society in the Soviet Union. And it's my fervent hope that this evolution continues and eventually leads to a more open government and a freer society. But the very fact that Mikhail Sholokhov, a Nobel laureate, lashed out against Sinyavsky and Daniel, advocating even harsher sentences, shows just how entrenched Soviet practice has become. . . . But change will come, and Russia will inevitably evolve toward freedom."

Struve took a different tack. The trial of Sinyavsky and Daniel was sooner "a spiritual and intellectual event than a political one," he noted,

> because independent political action is still not possible in the Soviet Union. But Russia is already showing signs of an entirely new and incredibly important development—a spiritual rebirth. That rebirth has its dangers and will claim its victims, among them Sinyavsky and Daniel, but the appearance of the *White Book* offers hope to Russians. . . . Soviet trials dealing with anything political have always been unfair, but the manifestation of public opinion is a significant new factor, indicating the emergence of two Russias: one official, and the other informal. And what is most significant is that the informal Russia—the core of a civil society—thinks critically, judges fairly, and knows the difference between truth and lies.[7]

Despite the severe sentences handed down to Sinyavsky and Daniel and the hounding and arrest of the organizers of the demonstration, the outer walls of the Soviet fortress were showing visible cracks as Soviet citizens began to demand greater freedom in their personal life. And Radio Liberty was ready to take full advantage. After banning Mikhail Bulgakov's novel *Master and Margarita*, written between 1928 and 1940, Soviet censorship relented and allowed its publication in 1967, but in an expurgated form. A full version of the popular novel made the rounds in samizdat in Moscow, and Radio Liberty promptly broadcast the excised excerpts of the text. Much the same fate awaited John Reed's famous book, *Ten Days That Shook the World*, his firsthand account of the October coup d'état. Although accorded the highest Soviet honors and buried in the Kremlin Wall necropolis, Reed had virtually disappeared in the Soviet Union, primarily because he frequently cited Trotsky and other early Bolsheviks and noted the conspicuous absence of Stalin during the revolution. By 1967 Reed's book reappeared in Soviet bookstores, but in an expurgated version. This gave Radio Liberty the necessary hook to reassess Reed's version of the 1917 revolution and to remind its listeners of enduring Soviet censorship.

In 1967, in homage to Andrei Sinyavsky, RL broadcast his famous essay that had circulated in samizdat for years—*On Socialist Realism*. With wit and derring-do, Sinyavsky mocked the dreary, conflict-free strictures imposed by the Soviet state on literature and arts. He likened socialist realism to formulaic medieval Russian literature and called for greater freedom in artistic endeavors, noting the fantastical quality of Nikolai Gogol and the profound intellectual skepticism of the Russian novels of the nineteenth century. But the political sensation of the year was the defection of Svetlana Alliluyeva, Stalin's youngest child and only daughter. After seeking protection in the U.S. Embassy in New Delhi, she was whisked away to Switzerland and later to the United States. One of the few possessions she managed to bring out of the Soviet Union was her memoir, *Twenty Letters to a Friend*. Although a naive work that tried to pin most of Stalin's crimes on Lavrenti Beria, it was a major insider's account of Kremlin life and politics. Alliluyeva came to the Radio Liberty studio in New York, and in her own voice brought her story to Soviet listeners.

In 1968—proclaimed the International Year for Human Rights by the United Nations—the Soviet human rights movement came of age.[8] Although Sinyavsky, Daniel, Ginzburg, and other dissidents were in Siberian labor camps, the human rights movement continued to gain momentum and attract new adherents. The proceedings of the Ginzburg trial were recorded by other dissidents and appeared in a new samizdat publication, the *Chronicle of Current Events*, edited by the poet Natalia Gorbanevskaya. Through the efforts of many dissidents, the *Chronicle of Current Events* appeared for fifteen years, covering 424 political trials, in which 753 people were convicted of "anti-Soviet agitation." Between April and December 1968, Gorbanevskaya produced the first five issues of the *Chronicle*, cataloguing in detail the repressive measures the Soviet authorities had taken against citizens who had spoken out in support of Sinyavsky and Daniel. Many prominent members of society, university students, and even Communist Party members who had dared to voice their support for "Soviet legality" found themselves harassed, marginalized, and in some cases arrested.

In July the world discovered the name of Andrei Sakharov when the *New York Times* published his essay "Reflections on Progress, Peaceful Coexistence, and Intellectual Freedom." Advocating a reasonable approach to disarmament and the promotion of freedom of thought, this essay had circulated earlier in samizdat form and found its way to Radio Liberty, where it was broadcast to the USSR. Sakharov's foray into the world of samizdat cost him his career in military research but brought him into contact with a different slice of Soviet society, populated by fiercely independent thinkers, active critics of the Soviet government, and morally upright individuals. In time, together with his wife, Elena Bonner, Sakharov joined the dissident movement. In 1970, together with Valery Chalidze and Andrei Tverdokhlebov, he was a founding member of the Committee on Human Rights in the USSR, which collected signatures for petitions and worked closely with international human rights groups. Capitalizing on his fame as a world-renowned scientist, Sakharov became the voice of the repressed.

He would stand outside closed courtrooms to hear the latest information about court rulings against dissidents, write appeals on behalf of hundreds of political prisoners, meet with foreign correspondents to relay news about new arrests, pen essays about the need for greater democratization, and, when he felt it was necessary, go on hunger strikes until the Soviet authorities would relent and allow medical treatment for a gravely ill political prisoner or finally issue an exit visa to a Jewish refusenik. For the dissident community, Andrei Sakharov, a thoroughly secular person, acquired the aura of sainthood, and his voice and writings became a daily staple of Radio Liberty broadcasts.

The major event of 1968 was a public demonstration by a small group of dissidents in front of St. Basil's Cathedral in Red Square, protesting the Soviet occupation of Czechoslovakia. Natalia Gorbanevskaya, Pavel Litvinov, and Larissa Bogoraz were among several protesters who unfurled banners proclaiming "Long Live a Free and Independent Czechoslovakia," "Shame to the Occupiers," and "For Your Freedom and Ours." In a two-page letter to the editors of Western newspapers, Gorbanevskaya described the event: "Almost immediately a whistle blew and plainclothes KGB men rushed at us from all corners of the square. They ran up shouting—'They're all Jews!' 'Beat the anti-Sovietists!' We sat quietly and didn't resist. They tore the banners from our hands. They beat Fainberg in the face until he bled, and knocked his teeth out. They hit Litvinov. They shouted at us: 'Disperse you scum!' But we remained sitting."[9] Most of the demonstrators received sentences of three to five years in labor camps, but Gorbanevskaya, a mother of two small children, was released. As the principal writer of the *Chronicle of Current Events*, she was able to complete several more issues and record the aftermath of the demonstration. In 1969, however, she was rearrested and charged under Article 190/1 of the RSFSR Criminal Code for "dissemination of knowingly false fabrications defaming the Soviet State." She was found mentally incompetent to stand trial and was sent to a psychiatric prison hospital. A remarkably strong person, Gorbanevskaya managed to survive Soviet psychiatric torture and, with the active support of Western leaders, emigrated to the West in 1975, settling in Paris. Judged completely mentally healthy by French doctors, Gorbanevskaya continued her work in promoting human rights and became a frequent contributor to Radio Liberty programming. Her broadcasts about dissidents and the persecution of free-thinking Russians, as well as about culture and poetry, carried an authenticity that earned her respect both in Russia and the West. For many she became a symbol of freedom, and Joan Baez even wrote a song dedicated to her, entitled "Natalia," noting that "it is because of people like Natalia Gorbanevskaya that you and I are still alive and walking around on the face of the earth with dignity."[10]

As early as 1968 Radio Liberty realized that samizdat was a major phenomenon that held great promise of political and social change. To take advantage of this new source of information, RL began to collect and document samizdat. In his memoir, Peter Reddaway, a leading Western scholar, recounted how the first tranche reached Radio Liberty: "Professor Karel van het Reve worked as a correspondent for the newspaper *Het Parool* in Moscow in 1967–68 and became close to Andrei Amalrik, Pavel Litvinov, Larissa Bogoraz, and others. He was the first person to get the dissident physicist Andrei Sakharov's long essay of 1968 on progress, peaceful coexistence, and intellectual freedom out to the West. . . . When Karel finished his year in Moscow he managed to bring out a rich collection of one hundred or so samizdat documents. At my request, he sent these to Radio Liberty."[11] Very quickly the number of documents grew, and RL established an archive (Arkhiv Samizdata), under the direction of Peter Dornan and Mario Corti. The archive staff verified the documents as best as they could to ensure that they were not forgeries supplied by Soviet agents. By 1971 the Arkhiv contained over three thousand documents, and RL made the strategic decision to make those documents available both to the broadcasters and, by subscription, to academic and research institutions throughout the world. With the active support of leading scholars, RL became the major institution in the world for the study of unofficial political materials produced in the USSR. By 1992, when the Arkhiv Samizdata was closed, it contained over 6,500 documents, an indispensable source for analyzing and understanding the last decades of Soviet rule.

The samizdat materials quickly became a treasure trove for the broadcast services. Since most were written in Russian, including those from the Baltic States, Ukraine, and other republics, the Russian Service started to include them in its programs. As the samizdat archive grew, the Russian Service launched several new programs, starting with *Pis'ma i dokumenty* (Letters and documents) and later *Dokumenty nashego vremeni* (Current documents), *Obzor samizdata* (Survey of samizdat), *Dokumenty i luidi* (Documents and people), and *Prava cheloveka* (Human rights). In introducing these programs, RL announcers would explain the political or historical context of a particular document but would refrain from any commentary, assuring their listeners that RL had not edited the material. On occasion, the announcers reminded listeners that the views expressed in the samizdat document did not reflect the views of Radio Liberty. The aim of these programs was to allow Soviet listeners to hear what their compatriots were discussing and to engage in an intra-Russian debate about the future of their country. In some cases, Russians would learn about Sakharov, Solzhenitsyn, Ginzburg, Bukovsky, and many other thinkers through RL programming, and they would copy what they heard and disseminate it among their friends. That form of samizdat came to be known as *radio-izdat* and later, when recording devices were more readily available in the USSR, as *magnit-izdat*. Over the years, RL's decision to serve strictly as a *means* of communicating samizdat materials contributed to the emergence of a more critically thinking society in the USSR. In the words of Yuri Galanskov, a dissident who died in the gulag at the age of thirty-three, Radio Liberty "publicized lawlessness and acts of crude coercion by Soviet official personnel. In this way, they were stimulating our national development."[12]

Radio Liberty adopted a two-pronged approach to samizdat and human rights. The first focused on the samizdat documents and the stories by and about individual dissidents. These broadcasts formed a transmission chain: taking materials produced in the USSR and then, via Munich, broadcasting them back to the country. The second approach, principally in the program *Prava cheloveka* (Human rights), examined the bigger picture: what the Helsinki Accords meant, how they were distorted in the USSR, how the West understood human rights, what the state of human rights in other communist counties was, and what the reactions of the United States and European countries to Soviet repressive measures were. The presenter of the program would often invite Western experts to provide a broader context for the internal developments in the Soviet Union. In addition, a separate popular program, *S drugogo berega* (From the other shore)—a reference to Alexander Herzen, a nineteenth-century dissident—supplemented human rights programming (a major part of the broadcast schedule) with extensive readings and discussion of fiction and nonfiction banned in the Soviet Union.

Radio Liberty: Human Rights Broadcasts

To gain a deeper understanding of Radio Liberty human rights programming I listened to hundreds of hours of broadcasts from the 1970s and 1980s. The key was to listen (rather than to read Russian transcripts or English-language summaries) because through the immediacy of the human voice I was transported into a demonic world where the mere exchange of ideas, assertion of personal beliefs, or discussions of philosophy and history were deemed high crimes against the state. The radio voice helped me, just as it had millions of Soviet listeners, to feel the full import of Soviet injustices, not just to understand them intellectually. That critical nexus of facts and emotions made radio broadcasting a powerful weapon in the arsenal of American democracy.

The vast majority of people in the USSR who were harassed or arrested for reading and distributing samizdat were ordinary citizens with no overt political ambitions or plans to bring down the Soviet regime. As they reiterated in countless court depositions and letters from the gulag, their sole aim was to live and think as free people. But the Soviet system, as Tatiana Khodorovich, a prominent human rights activist, noted, could not countenance "free spirits" and waged a relentless war against its own citizens who did not conform to Soviet ideology. In program after program, one would learn about the squalid conditions in the prisons and labor camps, the systematic denial of medical treatment, the desperate hunger strikes, and the special punishment cells where the more outspoken prisoners would be kept for weeks and sometimes even months. In the cruelest irony of all, the "crimes" for which these political prisoners were punished—principally, sharing samizdat materials—would be ruled completely legal under Gorbachev's policy of glasnost in the late 1980s.

One of the major human rights issues for Radio Liberty was the growth of Soviet anti-Semitism in the 1960s and the plight of Jews who wished to emigrate to Israel. RL had a long tradition of focusing on persecuted minorities in the USSR, whether they were Chechens and Ingush deported during World War II or religious believers exiled to Siberia for their personal beliefs. For this reason, Soviet refuseniks— Jews not allowed to emigrate—became an increasingly prominent topic in many RL human rights programs. In 1970 a major incident galvanized the Jewish rights movement. On June 15 sixteen refuseniks— two of them non-Jewish—tried to buy all the seats on a small Soviet plane, ostensibly to attend a wedding in another city. In actual fact they planned to hijack the plane and fly to Sweden where they would seek political asylum. The organizer of Operation Wedding, as it came to be known, Edward Kuznetsov, readily acknowledged that the probability of success was nil and that all the participants knew they would end up in the gulag, but they wanted the arrests to take place at the airport, creating a media spectacle that highlighted human rights violations in the USSR.[13] The scenario worked as planned, and all the participants were apprehended at the airport in Leningrad. At the trial, they were accused of high treason, and Mark Dymshits and Edward Kuznetsov received death sentences while the others, including Kuznetsov's wife, Sylva Zalmanson, were sentenced to long prison terms.

Kuznetsov's expectations were fully realized. There was an immediate outcry in the world with denunciations of the Soviet Union by Western leaders and grassroot protests in Israel, the United States, and Europe. So powerful was the tidal wave of condemnation that the Soviet authorities relented and commuted the death sentences for Dymshits and Kuznetsov to fifteen years in the gulag and reduced the sentences of the other participants. In time, the plotters were exchanged for Soviet spies languishing in Western prisons, and by 1979 Kuznetsov was able to join his wife in Israel. The last to be released were the two non-Jewish participants—Aleksei Murzhenko and Yuri Fedorov—an irony that Kuznetsov described as "the worst example of Soviet discrimination."

In 1983 Edward Kuznetsov joined Radio Liberty as the head of the news desk. Witty, engaging, and full of good cheer, he proved to be an excellent editor, an engaging raconteur, and a fount of information about dissidents, the gulag, and underground associations in the USSR. For American specialists who knew the Soviet Union primarily through books or controlled travel in the country, Kuznetsov's stories shed light on the brutal side of Soviet life.

While still a student at Moscow State University in the late 1950s, Kuznetsov coedited a samizdat literary journal, *Sintaksis*, and compiled an anthology of poetry.[14] He was arrested in 1961 for distributing samizdat and participating in poetry readings on Mayakovsky Square and sentenced to seven years in the gulag. After his release, Kuznetsov felt that he was a marked man and that sooner or later the KGB would arrest him again. He desperately sought to leave the USSR, but when he and his compatriots were denied the basic freedom to emigrate, they organized the Leningrad hijacking, and that led to his rearrest. Despite the suffering that he had endured awaiting his execution, followed by years in the gulag, Kuznetsov was proud of the affair because it profoundly changed Soviet policy regarding Jewish emigration. During the 1960s, only four thousand Soviet citizens were allowed to emigrate; the vast majority of those who applied to leave were denied that right. In the ten years after the Leningrad trial, 347,100 Soviet citizens were allowed to emigrate, of whom 245,951 were Soviet Jews. Kuznetsov, Dymshits, Sylva Zalmanson, and the other "plotters" had changed Soviet and Jewish history in a profound way.[15]

In the 1980s Kuznetsov was a frequent contributor to the RL human rights programs. Drawing on his firsthand knowledge of the Soviet gulag system, he would report on the latest arrests of dissidents, their trials, and the fate that awaited them in the gulag. Often, he would return to the 1970 hijacking plot to explain to Soviet listeners what the participants had in mind, how they had planned the hijacking that wouldn't hurt the pilots, and the reasons for this daring act.[16] But in every program, Kuznetsov reminded his listeners that two brave and selfless participants—Aleksei Murzhenko and Yuri Fedorov—were still in the gulag and that he was committed to helping to free them. In one of the more popular programs, *Documents and People* (June 3, 1984), Kuznetsov read Andrei Sakharov's eloquent appeal to the Soviet authorities to free Murzhenko and Fedorov and ended his report by saying that he and all the other "plotters" would never forget their two righteous friends. Through their unstinting efforts, Murzhenko was released on June 15, 1984, but quickly rearrested for a parole violation. Finally, in 1987, he was allowed to emigrate to Israel and eventually settled in the United States. Yuri Fedorov was released in June 1985 but was not allowed to emigrate until 1988, when he left for the United States. Along with Kuznetsov, Fedorov organized the Gratitude Fund, a nonprofit organization intended to assist the forgotten heroes and veterans of the struggle for freedom and human rights in the former USSR.

Radio Liberty's human rights programming cast a wide net, with the intention of bringing to light many different stories about individual dissidents. Typical of the documentary-style broadcasts was a two-part series devoted to the Ukrainian activist Zinovi Antoniuk (*Documents and People*, August 11 and 12, 1980). Prepared by Egor Davydov, a former political prisoner in the 1970s, the programs drew on letters, court documents, and personal reminiscences to tell a horrifying tale of how an ordinary Kyiv engineer got swept up in the massive arrests of 1972 and became a living symbol of human dignity and spiritual strength. Sentenced to seven years in hard-labor camps, followed by three years of exile in Siberia, Antoniuk was thrust into the Soviet penal system with its prisons, camps, and hospitals. Stripped of their dignity, he and other political prisoners were subjected to ridicule and sadistic torture by the guards. The very nature of their crime—free thinking—elicited a special hatred from the camp authorities. The rights of prisoners, such as family visits, were formally accorded by Soviet law and were routinely denied. The only way to resist, Antoniuk stated, was by waging hunger strikes. Often political prisoners would band together and go on a mass hunger strike, which would further enrage the prison guards. Antoniuk's principled stance and his willingness to support fellow political prisoners led to his frequent confinement in punishment cells (*shizo*), which undermined his health. That Antoniuk survived his harsh imprisonment and was able to return to Ukraine to a play an important role in its independence movement is a testament to his own indominable spirit and belief in the righteousness of his cause. By broadcasting Antoniuk's story while he was still in exile, Radio Liberty not only gave him and fellow prisoners moral support but also helped ordinary Russians understand the essence of Soviet repression. The growing realization that the Soviet system was built on arbitrary repression led many to question the legitimacy of the USSR, paving the way for Gorbachev's policies of glasnost and perestroika.

Along with programs about ordinary Soviet citizens like Antoniuk, Radio Liberty devoted considerable airtime to prominent dissidents, including such notable figures as Sergey Kovalev, Natan Sharansky, and Yuri Orlov. The Russian Service reported regularly on their samizdat publications, arrests, trials, and conditions in prison and the gulag. Whenever possible, RL would broadcast firsthand reports of life in the camps and court transcripts of the trials. One of the more compelling broadcasts was devoted to Anatoly Marchenko, a prominent writer and human rights campaigner who became involved in dissident circles as early as 1958. Arrested for attempting to cross the Soviet border in 1961, he was sentenced to six years in labor camps. Upon his release, he wrote *My Testimony*, the first publication to describe the post-Stalin gulag system. In the introduction, Marchenko wrote, "When I was locked up in Vladimir Prison, I was often seized by despair. Hunger, illness, and above all helplessness, the sheer impossibility of struggling against evil, provoked me to the point where I was ready to hurl myself upon my jailers with the sole purpose of being killed. . . . One thing alone prevented me, one thing gave me the strength to live through that nightmare: the hope that I would eventually come out and tell the whole world what I had seen and experienced."[17] With *My Testimony* making the rounds in samizdat form, Marchenko was rearrested in 1968. He was again sentenced to hard labor and, with the exception of several short breaks, was incarcerated until his untimely death in 1986 in the Chistopol Prison. In the words of Natan Sharansky, Marchenko became "the number one Soviet prisoner of conscience . . . one of the perpetual prisoners."[18]

Over the years, RL produced many broadcasts about Marchenko and read extensive excerpts from his books and articles. On June 27, 1982, in the program *Documents and People*, RL was able to share with its listeners Marchenko's eloquent final statement at his sixth trial for anti-Soviet activity (September 1981). The court transcript had been surreptitiously copied, reproduced in samizdat, and then sent to Radio Liberty in Munich. Speaking in his own defense, Marchenko laid out his case. He claimed he had no personal animus toward the Soviet regime; no one in his family had perished in Stalin's Great Terror of the 1930s. He came from a simple working-class family and earned his living by manual labor. His rejection of the Soviet system was simple: Soviet ideology and practice denied citizens the ability to use their minds, to question, to explore new concepts and ideas. "The Soviet authorities are so afraid of their own people," Marchenko noted, "that despite their total control of all media, they ban unofficial publications as though they were weapons capable of destroying the State. The Soviet authorities resort to violence—'*b'iut ne po ideiam, a po cherepam*' [they don't fight against ideas but simply beat you over the head]." Since the Soviet government was waging a virtual war against its own people, Marchenko declared himself a prisoner of war. After his indictment of the Soviet system, the court sentenced him to ten years of hard labor in the Perm 37 camp, to be followed by five years of exile. Marchenko died five years later, at the age of forty-eight. In 1988, he was honored posthumously by the European Parliament as the first recipient (along with Nelson Mandela) of the Sakharov Prize for Freedom of Thought.

While most Radio Liberty feature programs went on air once a week, *Documents and People*, primarily edited by Rachel "Alya" Fedoseyeva, was a daily show that told the stories of Soviet citizens who had been arrested for activities that any Westerner would have considered to be normal, if not even commendable. From today's perspective, it's hard to understand why the Soviet Union would arrest Joseph Brodsky for writing poetry and send him into internal exile or why it would imprison Natan Sharansky in the Perm 37 gulag camp for committing the simple act of applying to emigrate to Israel. But in the 1970s and 1980s such actions were judged criminal. In Yuri Andropov's ominous words, the ideas propagated by the dissidents could not have arisen naturally within the Soviet Union; they had "to be implanted by our adversaries in the West to weaken socialist society."[19] Hence, in the perverted logic of the Soviet leadership, the dissidents and their domestic supporters were active "foreign agents," threatening the stability of the Soviet Union. For the aging Politburo members, the dissidents represented the infamous fifth column that had to be crushed on the battleground of ideology. If one were to stretch this war metaphor further, one could consider Alya Fedoseyeva's office, where so many human rights programs were prepared, as a "field hospital" that had to cope with news from the battlefield: incoming reports of someone's arrest for distributing samizdat, a new mass hunger strike in a labor camp, or the death of yet another political prisoner. As casualty reports poured in, RL staffers would search the samizdat archive, find materials that would provide context for the story, and then rush to the studio to air the latest news, offering hope and support to the dissidents and their families. On occasion, RL would celebrate the sudden recovery of a "wounded dissident"—his or her release from prison or the granting of an exit visa to emigrate—but generally the news was grim in those days. The best way RL could help the "wounded dissidents" was to practice glasnost—to let the world know who was being attacked and why. That public information often saved the lives because Soviet authorities, fearful of bad publicity, would usually provide better treatment to the better known "foreign agents." In some cases, when the international outcry would reach a high pitch, the Soviet authorities would even release the prisoners and exile them to the West or trade them for Soviet spies in Western prisons. Such was the fate of Solzhenitsyn, Sharansky, Kuznetsov, Ginzburg, Sinyavsky, and many other prominent dissidents who found themselves suddenly in the West. Every day Radio Liberty saved lives and gave hope to millions. In the process, it created a radio of historical record that will serve as an indispensable guide to the gruesome history of Soviet rule.

Along with documentary programs, the Russian Service addressed such broad philosophical concepts as natural rights, freedom of the press, and the free movement of people and information across borders. At the core of those programs was the Helsinki Final Act, or Helsinki Accords (1975), of the Commission on Security and Cooperation in Europe (CSCE), which stressed the primacy of liberal democratic values.[20] That the USSR had been the prime initiator of the CSCE process and had signed the Final Act gave Radio Liberty carte blanche to explore many aspects of human rights and, most important, to report on Soviet violations of those rights.

Although the Soviet authorities saw the CSCE process as legitimizing their postwar borders, the Final Act proved to be a remarkably effective tool in exposing Soviet hypocrisy and propagating the fundamental notions of human rights to millions of people behind the Iron Curtain. It was also a useful tool with which to publicly shame Soviet authorities for violating the principles they had pledged to uphold.[21] Specifically, under pressure from Western negotiators, the Soviet authorities acquiesced to Basket III, which required all signatory governments to "facilitate freer movement and contacts between people and the freer and wider dissemination of information of all kinds."[22] Basket III also contained specific provisions concerning family reunification; marriage between citizens of different states; access to oral, printed, filmed, and broadcast information; the right of citizens to emigrate; and the legitimacy of unfettered international broadcasting. As Michael Morgan notes, so radical were the Soviet concessions that when the "East Europeans read what their Soviet colleagues had negotiated on their behalf, they could not disguise their astonishment. The German Democratic Republic's Siegfried Bock fumed that the Soviets could not appreciate that their freer movement of information posed an intolerable threat to East Germany."[23] Since Brezhnev trumpeted the Helsinki process as a major Soviet foreign policy achievement, the Final Act was given wide distribution in Soviet society. That gave the dissidents a public platform to justify their activities, including the publication of samizdat, freedom of religion, and the right to emigrate. The Final Act also became an internationally accepted gauge for monitoring and assessing Soviet behavior toward its own citizens, spawning in its wake indigenous groups throughout the East bloc, including Charter 77 in Czechoslovakia, Committee for Social Self-Defense (KOR) in Poland, and the Moscow Helsinki Group.

Although many U.S. politicians initially took a dim view of the CSCE process, assuming it to be one more Soviet propaganda maneuver, in time they came to see it as a useful tool for exposing human rights violations in the Soviet Union. Shortly after the Helsinki summit, a congressional delegation, headed by Representative Millicent Fenwick (R-NJ), visited the Soviet Union and met with several dissidents. After learning about the true state of affairs in the Soviet Union, Fenwick sponsored legislation to create the Helsinki Commission on Security and Cooperation in Europe (CSCE), with the mandate to investigate and report on Soviet and East European compliance with the Final Act.[24] Initially, the Ford administration tried to block this legislation, but with criticism of détente being voiced by more and more Republicans, Ford relented, and the Helsinki Commission came into existence. Working in tandem with Radio Liberty and other nongovernmental organizations, the commission's members traveled to the East bloc and collected information about the state of human rights. As Michael Morgan noted, "By giving dissidents in Eastern Europe [and the USSR] a megaphone for their views and shining a spotlight on their plight, [the CSCE] strengthened the nascent Helsinki network."[25] Indeed, so successful was the CSCE in exposing the true nature of the Communist regimes that by 1980, Reagan, who had initially opposed the CSCE process, came to see it as an effective weapon for fighting the Cold War.[26]

For Radio Liberty the significance of the Final Act, and especially Basket III, cannot be overestimated. Much like samizdat provided RL with source material about individuals and movements from inside the USSR, the Helsinki process allowed the radios to raise broader questions about internal Soviet affairs. No matter how much Soviet officials insisted that state sovereignty superseded international agreements, the very existence of Basket III reminded the world—and through international broadcasts, the Soviet public—that the Soviet Union was a cruel and hypocritical regime, fearful of its own citizens.

Aspects of the Final Act were reflected in many RL programs, including the hourly newscasts and current-affairs shows, but the principal program that tackled this subject was simply entitled *Prava cheloveka* (Human rights). It focused on interviews with Russian and foreign experts on human rights, updates on the work of the Moscow Helsinki Group that was set up to monitor Soviet adherence to the Final Act, and extensive reports on the follow-up international conferences of the CSCE in Belgrade, Madrid, and Vienna. A sampling of *Prava cheloveka* episodes from the late 1970s and early 1980s shows extensive coverage of Andrei Sakharov's writings on freedom and world affairs, in-depth discussions of the work of Freedom House and Amnesty International, and the state of human rights in Poland and other East European countries. The editor of the program, Victor Fedoseyev, would often turn to outside experts such as Dina Kaminskaya and Lyudmila Alexeyeva to analyze the latest Soviet laws in light of the Final Act. On occasion he would invite guests to the studio to discuss major issues in the worldwide human rights movement. One notable program dealt with the Baha'i community in Iran and the discrimination it was facing from the authorities. Another focused on Stalin's deportation of the Crimean Tatars—mostly women, children, and the elderly—to Central Asia, where a staggeringly large number (46 percent) perished. Although the Tatars were formally rehabilitated in 1967, they were still denied the right to return to their native homeland in the 1980s. Intended primarily for the politically engaged listener, Fedoseyev's broadcasts may have lacked the verve of documentaries but filled an important gap in the Soviet listener's understanding of the political import of human rights.

Radio Liberty's human rights programming is so extensive that it covers practically every aspect of dissident activity in the Soviet Union. One could cite several hundred broadcasts meriting close attention. In many ways, reporting on human rights embodied RL's mission, and in the 1970s and 1980s virtually every program dealt in one way or another with the broader notion of individual freedom and human rights. These programs certainly lived up to the old adage that "the proper role of journalism is to comfort the afflicted and afflict the comfortable."[27] For years to come, historians will be able to mine these broadcasts and the samizdat archives to gain a deeper understanding of Russian political culture, Soviet history, and the emergence of Russian civil society.

VOA: Human Rights Broadcasts

Programming about human rights illustrates several key differences between Radio Liberty and the VOA. As a legally private corporation operating at arm's length from U.S. foreign policy, RL was "built on the basis of one principle: a radio of the Russian emigration to the people behind the Iron Curtain."[28] That mission allowed it to choose how and what to broadcast and to devote hour after hour to interviews with dissidents and critics of the Soviet regime. In contrast, as a federal agency, VOA was inextricably tied to the vicissitudes of U.S.-Soviet relations and often hemmed in by what the State Department or the White House considered the proper role of a government broadcaster. This was especially problematic during the heyday of détente. In his in-depth examination of VOA programming, Alexey Retivov, a longtime VOA senior editor, recounted a telling incident from 1971 when he was briefing recently hired journalists about the Russian Service. He mentioned in passing that the emerging human rights opposition movement in the USSR was a major development and "our best hope for a peaceful end to Communist rule."[29] The director of the USSR Division came up to him afterward and said that while he privately agreed with him, the State Department would not approve of that assessment. The focus of U.S. policy was to seek common ground with the Soviet Union, not to draw attention to violations of human rights or encourage Soviet citizens to challenge Soviet rule.

As détente became the principal driver of U.S. policy in the 1970s, the Soviet Union temporarily ceased jamming VOA Russian broadcasts, and the senior management responded by trying to curb programming that could be offensive to Soviet authorities. As Retivov noted, until the early 1970s the Russian Service had considerable freedom in reporting about Soviet dissidents, but in 1973, the director of the USSR Division took a different line, declaring at a staff meeting that "Soviet dissidents were just a handful of activists, and that very few people in the Soviet Union were interested in them. For that reason, it was best to broadcast as little as possible about them."[30]

This cautious approach toward domestic opposition in the USSR was on full display when Alexandr Solzhenitsyn, the most prominent critic of the USSR, was exiled to the West and his indictment of the Soviet regime—*The Gulag Archipelago*—became a world sensation. While RFE/RL, the *New York Times*, BBC, and other Western media were interviewing the author, presenting lengthy excerpts from *The Gulag Archipelago* and reporting extensively on dissidents, Jewish refuseniks, and émigré critics of the USSR, VOA found itself struggling to define its proper role. As Nicholas Cull aptly noted, "USIA director James Keogh faced the choice of playing the role of ideological howitzer and beaming Solzhenitsyn and his writings back to the USSR or supporting détente and leaving the dissident broadcasts to Radio Liberty."[31] While Keogh and other senior diplomats were deliberating, the VOA Russian Service continued to cover internal developments in the Soviet Union as it had before, broadcasting 387 items about *The Gulag Archipelago* just between December 29, 1973, and early March 1974. This programming incensed the Soviet authorities who issued démarches, stating that the Russian Service was not projecting the "correct spirit of détente." As a result, Keogh and the VOA management opted for supine diplomacy. "What we do not do, as the official radio voice of the United States," Keogh wrote to Congressman Robert L. Sikes (D-FL), "is indulge in polemics aimed at changing the internal structure of the Soviet Union. To read from the book [*The Gulag Archipelago*] would be outside the normal style of Voice of America programming and would tend to reinforce Soviet charges that the United States is utilizing these events as a political weapon and is intervening in the domestic affairs of the USSR."[32] What Keogh clearly did not know was that for decades the Russian Service had broadcast excerpts from controversial books banned in the Soviet Union and reported on dissidents and human rights issues. But with détente in full force, the State Department weighed in with a heavy hand and not only forbade the reading of excerpts from *The Gulag Archipelago* on air but also cancelled a prearranged interview with Solzhenitsyn himself.[33] It further prohibited any "in-house origination of materials" that could be construed as hostile or harshly critical of the Soviet Union.[34] The "spirit of détente" even led VOA management to discourage reporting about Andrei Sakharov and Alexandr Solzhenitsyn, not to mention lesser-known dissident figures. Retivov recalled that his attempts to report on human rights issues were met with stiff resistance, and when he submitted a lengthy piece about Solzhenitsyn he was told, "We thought you would reform but you haven't, so we're taking away your programs." Stunned by this turn of events, Retivov felt he had no option but to resign. He rejoined the VOA as a freelance contributor only in the mid-1980s when he finally had the journalistic freedom to prepare relevant and creative programs.

For State Department officials, détente meant that VOA correspondents couldn't interview anyone who might be unduly critical of the Communist system. By taking such unprecedented measures, they were imposing a form of censorship in the name of U.S. policy that violated the VOA charter. This unleashed an inevitable backlash from broadcasters, members of Congress, and the greater journalistic community. In time, VOA management felt compelled to backtrack, allowing the Russian Service to continue reporting about dissidents *so long as* the reports relied solely on news stories published in mainstream U.S. media. "On paper" this appeared to be a measure limiting sound journalism, but in actual practice, it left the door wide open to reporting on human rights abuses. The creative staff of the Russian Service took full advantage of this opportunity and translated virtually every article by U.S. and Western correspondents about dissidents in the USSR. According to an official report by the propaganda division of the Central Committee of the Communist Party, VOA reported on "the publication in Italy of *Into the Whirlwind* by Yevgenia Ginzburg; the trial of a young poet from Moscow, V. Tolstov; the *White Book* about Sinyavsky and Daniel; and the prohibition of exhibits by Marc Chagall. VOA programming also covered the 'unconstitutional behavior of the Soviet government' in its treatment of the religious and legal rights of Jews and other believers in the USSR."[35] The Russian Service reported on Alexandr Solzhenitsyn's new life in Vermont by citing the American press and on the plight of refuseniks by relying on the latest reports of the U.S. Helsinki Commission. Good journalism prevailed, but Keogh's policies hurt the credibility of VOA and soured the relationship between Solzhenitsyn and Russian Service for many years.

Proof of the continuing efficacy of VOA broadcasts, despite restrictions from senior USIA management, came in the form of a high-level visit by a Soviet delegation to VOA in July 1976.[36] Headed by N. Oganov, chief of the Government Committee on Television and Radio and M. Lomko, editor-in-chief of *Moscow News*, the delegation came to complain to the VOA director, Kenneth Giddens, that the Russian Service reports on dissidents were "counter to both the spirit of the Helsinki Agreement and the development of relations between the U.S. and the USSR."[37] Insisting that VOA devote more of its programming to "improving bilateral relations," Oganov grew testy and accused the Russian Service of being "guilty of the worst kind of propaganda, broadcasting about a small group of renegades—the dissidents—despised by the whole Soviet people."[38] He further accused VOA of "insulting" the Soviet people by dwelling too much on "negative news" that divided Americans and Soviets. "The Soviet people would like to hear support for better relations from the mouths of Americans," Oganov noted, "and not just from the President, Secretary of State, senators, artists, and so forth, but from VOA as well."[39]

According to the minutes of the meeting, Giddens stood his ground against this frontal attack, patiently explained the American approach to journalism, and expressed his fundamental support for the Russian-language broadcasts. But, unfortunately, he noted that "VOA does not broadcast about internal conditions of any country unless the facts are thoroughly checked and considered international news."[40] That concession gave the Soviet officials the excuse they needed to lambaste the reporting of U.S. foreign correspondents and to insist that the VOA Russian Service staff had no idea of the true state of affairs in the Soviet Union. The diplomatic meeting ended with the usual pleasantries, but for years Soviet authorities sent démarches and vilified the VOA in the Soviet press as an impediment to the improvement of relations between the two countries. Lost in this diplomatic to-and-fro was the overriding moral imperative for the VOA Russian Service to report on one of the biggest stories of the 1970s and 1980s—the systematic Soviet crackdown on human rights and the resulting incarceration of artists, writers, and human rights advocates. But the policy of détente and the naive belief, shared by many American academics and diplomats, that the Soviet Union and the West could not only live in harmony but even build bridges of understanding and cooperation, placed VOA Russian Service in a difficult position.

Caught between the proverbial rock and a hard place, VOA was criticized by Soviet officials for being too blatantly anti-Communist, by the State Department for upsetting the détente agenda, and by the human rights community for being too timid in its coverage of Soviet dissidents. In March 1977, Ludmila Obolensky Flam, a senior editor in the Russian Service, traveled to the USSR not in the capacity of a journalist but as a member of a State Department diplomatic program that sought better understanding between the United States and the Soviet Union. Although the U.S. Embassy tried to steer her toward more politically innocuous gatherings, she managed to meet with Yuri Orlov and other members of the Moscow Helsinki Group. As she related in her official trip report, Orlov and his fellow dissidents believed that the only way to stop Soviet "terrorism against individuals" was by publicizing the work of human rights activists through international broadcasting.[41] They criticized VOA for not broadcasting a full record of human rights violations, as noted by the Khronika Press in New York. Orlov further pointed out that VOA rarely discussed samizdat or émigré literature and ignored more critical U.S. publications. His criticism was echoed by Lyudmilla Alexeyeva: "As a longtime listener in the USSR to VOA Russian (from the 1950s to 1977), I can testify that there have been considerable swings in the station's tone, depending on the evolution of Soviet-American relations. In the détente era, the tone of the newscasts and political commentaries was saccharine, hardly differing from that of the Soviet broadcasts.... VOA's tone of loyalty to the Soviet authorities was upsetting to listeners hungry for truthful information and alternatives to Soviet official sources."[42]

Knowing the dissident community well, I believe the criticism leveled by Alexeyeva, Orlov, and other human rights advocates was not so much an indictment of the Russian Service as it was a plea for VOA to focus more attention on human rights and to publicize the heroic work of dissidents. Although the Russian Service sought opportunities to interview prominent Russian émigrés such as Mikhail Baryshnikov and the sculptor Ernst Neizvestny, it frequently came under pressure from the State Department to tone down the broadcasts. By 1980 it was clear to everyone in the Russian Service that the issue of dissidents and human rights deserved a more prominent place in the daily schedule.

Under the Reagan administration, the VOA Russian Service was given the journalistic freedom to pursue programming that the broadcasters felt was of significance to its listeners. As subsequent chapters will show, the Russian Service was able to originate in-house stories and interview virtually all major Soviet émigré writers and dissidents, broadcast extended excerpts from books banned in the USSR, and read and discuss samizdat materials. Most of the human rights issues were imbedded in programs dealing with literature, the arts, history, current events, or religion. The Russian Service even invited its erstwhile critic Lyudmilla Alexeyeva to produce a weekly forty-five-minute program on human rights. By formally ending détente as official U.S. policy toward the Soviet Union, the Reagan administration gave the VOA Russian broadcasters license to be investigative journalists and to shed the onerous burden of diplomacy. Although VOA did not deal as extensively with dissidents and human rights as RL, it could now pursue topics critical of the Soviet Union. Occasionally we would receive a cable from the U.S. Embassy in Moscow complaining that we had overstepped our remit, but we operated with a firewall that allowed us to ignore those reports. As a result, in the 1980s, VOA produced many outstanding programs that dealt with individual freedom and human rights, especially in the area of culture, that retain relevance to this day.

4

Culture and the Arts

During the Reagan administration, the relationship of the VOA Russian Service to other federal agencies, principally U.S. Information Agency and the State Department, can be illustrated through a personal story. As the director of the Russian Service of VOA (and later as USSR Division director), I would attend a weekly policy meeting in the USIA Soviet and East European Affairs office. Chaired by a senior foreign service officer, this meeting brought together senior-level directors of different USIA programs dealing with the Soviet Union, ranging from academic and student exchanges and cultural initiatives to investigations of Soviet disinformation campaigns. The chair would brief us on the latest cables from the U.S. Embassy in Moscow, share key points from NSC directives, discuss upcoming high-level meetings with Soviet or East European officials, and inform us about new initiatives undertaken by the USIA director, Charles Z. Wick. Attending these meetings was my only formal link to the U.S. policy-making community, most likely a carryover from earlier years when Russian-language programming was held under tight policy control. In the Reagan years, VOA enjoyed a privileged position within the broader foreign policy apparatus, and this meant the freedom not to attend policy meetings at the State Department or to coordinate our programming with policy officers. We could set our own agenda, selecting topics once considered provocative. Gone as well were the days when Soviet officials would meet with senior U.S. officials to complain about the attention VOA was paying to dissidents. But there still existed an old guard at USIA who believed fervently in détente, shunned vocal anti-Communists, and was wary of VOA's more critical stance toward the Soviet Union, concerned that it might exacerbate U.S.-Soviet relations. Some senior public affairs officers even privately cautioned me not to let those "crazy émigrés" run the show, but I knew I had the backing of VOA management to ignore this unsolicited advice and pursue important journalistic stories.

Although USIA policy meetings played no substantive role in shaping Russian broadcasts, I found them to be helpful in learning more about the Reagan administration policies toward the Soviet Union, building a strong professional network, and exchanging views with different experts on the Soviet Union. One of the more remarkable people I met was an elderly Russian émigré, Juri Jelagin (Yuri Yelagin), who was the editor of the USIA publication *Dialogue*. Part of the worldwide USIA publications division, *Dialogue* was a high-brow journal consisting exclusively of Russian translations of recent American articles on literary criticism, history, poetry, and philosophy that was distributed by the U.S. Embassy in Moscow as part of an overall U.S.-USSR agreement on publication exchanges.[1] Jelagin would commission translations of articles in the *New York Review of Books*, the *New Republic*, or the *New York Times Book Review* and then edit them, providing the necessary background information for Soviet readers. A deeply cultured man, Jelagin was born in Russia in 1910 and educated at the famous Moscow Conservatory of Music. An accomplished violinist, he performed in leading Soviet theaters and concert halls, despite being arrested as a teenager in the 1920s for belonging to the wrong social class. His grandfather had been a successful Russian entrepreneur, and the entire Jelagin family was part of Russian nobility. In the Soviet period they were referred to as "former people," who were frequently harassed, occasionally arrested, and sometimes even sent to the gulag.[2] During the war, Jelagin ended up in German-occupied territory, miraculously survived the war, escaped repatriation to the USSR, and emigrated to the United States in 1947. He pursued a dual career in the United States as a musician and writer. For almost twenty years he was the concertmaster of the Houston Symphony Orchestra under Leopold Stokowski. At the same time, he was active as a writer and critic, publishing numerous articles in the Russian émigré press, as well as two well-received books: *Ukroshchenie iskusstv* (Taming of the arts, 1952), a personal account of Soviet theater and music in the 1930s, and *Tyomny genii: Vsevolod Meyerhold* (Dark genius: The life of

Vsevolod Meyerhold, 1955), the first in-depth biography of one of the leading modernist theater directors of the twentieth century and a victim of Stalin's terror.

Jelagin and I became friends, and after the USIA policy meetings we would continue our discussions of the Soviet Union and the challenges facing VOA and other U.S. government programs. Full of enthusiasm and goodwill, Jelagin took me under his wing and became my mentor as I navigated the treacherous waters of émigré politics and tried to shape a new approach to VOA Russian broadcasts. As he listened to my plans for more programming about dissidents, human rights, religion, and refuseniks, he would nod along, adding "yes, yes, that's all very important, but to reach Russians you absolutely have to focus on the arts, culture, music, literature. And you must get the artists themselves on air, speaking in their own voice. . . . Let me start by introducing you to two important Russian cultural figures in emigration: Mstislav [Slava] Rostropovich and Galina Vishnevskaya." As a lifelong classical-music fan, I had attended many concerts with Rostropovich playing the cello or conducting the National Symphony Orchestra (NSO). I knew Vishnevskaya through her many recordings. Over the years, I followed their careers—artistic and political—and greatly admired the principled stance they took in support of freedom in the USSR.

Setting up the meeting proved to be a challenge. Rostropovich and Vishnevskaya had taken a dislike to the VOA Russian Service, primarily because they perceived some programs as unduly critical of their musicianship. Shortly before I joined the VOA, the Russian Service had broadcast a translation of a *Washington Post* review of Rostropovich's NSO concert that was picked up by the Soviet media and trumpeted as proof that he was past his prime as a musician and was just cynically cashing in by making anti-Soviet pronouncements. Gossip and backbiting in émigré circles further alienated Rostropovich and Vishnevskaya. To overcome their resistance, Jelagin decided that he would convince them that my coming to VOA represented a new chapter and that they should give VOA another chance.

True to his word, Jelagin set up a meeting for me with Slava at the Kennedy Center for the Performing Arts after one of his National Symphony Orchestra concerts. With trepidation, I knocked on the door of his private dressing room, not knowing how I would be greeted. To my amazement, Slava flung open the door, gave me a bear hug, and told me that any friend of Jelagin's was his friend for life. His warmth, charisma, and good cheer overwhelmed me. Rather than talk about VOA and our policies, however, he wanted to know more about me. He was keenly interested in my family background, how I had learned Russian, and what my experience as a Fulbright scholar in the Soviet Union had been. He knew my paternal grandfather, the Right Reverend Michael Pomazansky, a noted Orthodox theologian, and was pleased to learn that my maternal grandfather, Sergey Markoff, had been a Russian pilot in World War I and later served in the White Army during the civil war. For Rostropovich, an avowed anti-Communist and proud Russian, I had the right pedigree. By the end of our chat, Rostropovich offered to give me a series of exclusive interviews for VOA and promised to help bring other notable cultural figures to the VOA studios.

Within a week I was back in his dressing room at the Kennedy Center with a VOA engineer to conduct the first interview, but before starting, Rostropovich handed me several photocopies of articles about him in Soviet encyclopedias. "Look," he said, as I recall,

> in the 1955 edition, when I was not even thirty years old, I merited a lengthy write-up that listed my numerous awards, such as the 1951 Stalin Prize and the 1955 Russian Republic award. It also mentioned my father, the famous cellist Leopold Rostropovich, and my many concerts in the USSR and Europe. In the 1975 edition, however, when I was already having run-ins with the KGB, primarily for helping Solzhenitsyn and standing up for human rights, the entry was cut by two-thirds and mentioned only the bare facts of when and where I was born and that I was a musician.

"In the latest, 1980 edition," he noted angrily, "I have been virtually crossed out of Soviet musical history. All my awards and achievements were excised and the entry simply read, 'In 1978, Rostropovich and his wife, G. P. Vishnevskaya, were deprived of Soviet citizenship for undermining the prestige of the USSR.'"³ This may seem petty to an outsider, Rostropvich told me, "but it is a great insult and injustice, especially after all that we, Soviet artists, had done for our country and how we had raised the prestige of the USSR in the world. The editing of my biography," he concluded, "showed that in the Soviet Union bureaucrats determine who you are and what you've done; you yourself are but a pawn in their hands."

We started the recorded interview not by delving immediately into the latest developments in U.S.-Soviet relations or discussing the plight of dissidents and artists but by talking about modern music. Noting the recent Kennedy Center celebration of the Polish composer Krzysztof Penderecki, I asked Rostropovich how musicians, to say nothing of listeners, can begin to understand and appreciate radically modern music. Acknowledging Penderecki's growing popularity in the Soviet Union, despite antipathy toward him within the Ministry of Culture, Rostropovich responded that listeners, if they are open-minded and ready to embrace something new, can come to love modern music. "My great pride in Washington," he exulted, "is that if we advertise a Shostakovich program, the Kennedy Center is immediately sold out. It was completely different when I got here seven years ago. That means that people in Washington are beginning to really appreciate more modern music."⁴ But understanding new music, Rostropovich averred, was a challenge even for professional musicians. "I can't say that at first I myself understood Penderecki's cello concerto," he confessed.

> First, I took separate parts that aroused in me a certain emotional excitement. Then, only much later, did I connect these pieces. If a person hears the music only once, he might be simply confused. But if he manages to listen to it a second time, if he has the patience and desire, he will begin to perceive those islets of understanding which he will then remember. And Penderecki is full of innovation. When, for example, in his *Requiem*, right before the "Lacrimosa," when the choir and orchestra do a glissando upward and then the music disappears into the heavens in a pianissimo . . . I can say without exaggeration that I myself seem to fly.

At that moment of artistic exuberance, when he was trying to put into words the transformative power of music, Rostropovich suddenly sat back and in a tone of deep regret reminded our listeners that the freedom Penderecki could express, even in Communist Poland, was missing in the Soviet Union. "I consider that the Soviet musical establishment is making a great mistake because the people in power dictate what kind of music can be composed and limit music to a very base level."

Rostropovich's heartfelt description of Penderecki's music prompted me to ask if he saw a direct connection between music and religious experience. A deeply religious person, Rostropovich spoke eloquently about music and the divine in Bach and other composers and finally came back to Penderecki, whose *Requiem* was grounded in ancient Polish hymns and dedicated to Lech Walesa, Cardinal Stefan Wyszynski, and the Solidarity movement. Poland, Rostropovich told VOA listeners, was the true catalyst for change in the Communist world because it had freedom of art and religion, and those essential freedoms laid the groundwork for independent movements such as Solidarity. "Of course, life is very difficult in Poland now," Rostropovich went on to say, but "heroic figures such as Walesa, Wyszynski, and Penderecki do appear. I don't think Penderecki is a political activist any more than I am. We simply stand for truth. And the freedom to be who we are is what Walesa and the Solidarity movement are fighting for." We ended our first session with an extended excerpt from "Lacrimosa," part of Penderecki's *Requiem* that had its world premiere in Washington DC under the baton of Slava Rostropovich.

In the second half of the interview, we turned to Russian culture. Noting Yuri Lyubimov's success in directing plays and operas in the West, I asked Rostropovich to comment on the recent firing of Lyubimov from his celebrated Taganka Theatre and his forced exile in the West. "I know Lyubimov well," Slava responded, "and recently met with him in Paris. He did not want to leave his homeland, and I advised him to return to Moscow, telling him that it's still our country. . . . But the Soviet authorities exiled one of the finest representatives of Soviet art. And not for the first time. Where is the Soviet Union's best film director—Tarkovsky? In Italy. The best Russian writers? In Paris, Vermont, Washington. The best Russian dancers? In New York. The best Russian musicians—everywhere in the West." Rostropovich's emotional response prompted me to probe further, asking why even apolitical art elicited such vehement reactions from the Soviet state. Because, Slava said, all great artists want to fully realize themselves, to search for new expressions of their art, and in the Soviet Union they can do only what the culture bureaucrats allow them. "You can explore this form of art, but not that form, the bureaucrats will tell our artists," Rostropovich lamented. And the result is that "Makarova, Nureyev, Baryshnikov, Ashkenazy glorify Russian culture in the West, but not in Russia. . . . The authorities have expelled the very best of Russian culture."

Because my interview with Rostropovich was the first in a projected series of VOA "radio conversations" with major Russian émigrés, I had the interview transcribed and translated into English and sent a copy to the VOA director with a short cover note describing the contents. Unbeknown to me, Tomlinson sent the interview and my memo to various professional radio hands in the United States as an example of the more dynamic and sophisticated programming that VOA was embarking on. Tomlinson later told me that he had received many positive responses and shared with me a particularly poignant letter from Barry Farber, the radio talk show host and political gadfly. Farber began his letter by noting that one of his colleagues had read the transcript first and exclaimed, "Is VOA trying to grab the world with THIS?" "He made a comment disparaging enough," Farber noted,

> so that when I began to read it [the Rostropovich transcript] I feared the worst . . . but it was excellent! My friend's comment helped me understand the value of it all the more. I'd assumed everybody grew up with the same awareness I did of the difference between grabbing a maximum share of the local audience and satisfying the need the Voice of America has to fill among populations denied all basic freedoms. My friend lacked all sensitivity to that point. To him, it's all showbiz. And Rostropovich's musings ain't showbiz. This is an exquisite piece. Rostropovich begins by giving the Soviet Union its due as a superior steward over younger talent. This builds credibility. . . .

Then, in surgically precise strokes, he dismantles the Soviet dictatorship in a way sure to convince every artist, intellectual, bureaucrat, and even common worker inside the Soviet empire. And he does it with nice payloads of heart, wit, and soul.[5]

Several months after my initial interview with Rostropovich, I received a call from Galina Vishnevskaya, who told me that her memoir was about to appear in both English and Russian, but prior to publication, she wanted to offer the VOA Russian Service an exclusive interview, followed by extended readings from her book.[6] I realized instantly that this was the radio coup of the year! Not BBC, Deutsche Welle, or Radio Liberty, but VOA would be the go-to station for one of the biggest Russian cultural stories of the year. Not only had Vishnevskaya, a much beloved artist and a decorated "hero of the USSR," been stripped of Soviet citizenship, but also her name and very existence were expunged from Russian history. Photos of her triumphant performances at the Bolshoi Opera were doctored so that her face and name simply vanished; her recordings were no longer sold; and her name could not be uttered on Soviet radio or television. She became a nonperson for speaking her mind honestly and for helping Solzhenitsyn and his family to survive when they were under assault by the KGB.

I remember her coming to the VOA, manuscript in hand, greeting our staff, and then heading to one of our humble studios for several hours of recording. A serious person, not given to empty chitchat, Galina wanted to read *her story* to *her people* and to be connected to *her beloved homeland*, if only through the medium of shortwave broadcasting. And Galina had an extraordinary story to tell. Born in 1926, she grew up in extreme poverty, hardly knew her parents, survived the siege of Leningrad during World War II, and managed by dint of sheer willpower to learn music and to audition for operatic roles. She began her career shortly after the war with the Leningrad District Operetta Theatre, but her big break came in the early 1950s when she successfully auditioned for the Bolshoi Theatre in Moscow. She went on to sing virtually all the main roles in the standard operatic repertoire at the Bolshoi Theatre, in addition to the leading opera houses in Europe and the United States. In time, major composers noted her unique gifts. Dmitri Shostakovich composed a song cycle for Galina in 1961, entitled "Satires," while Benjamin Britten composed the soprano part for her in his monumental *War Requiem*.

Early in our conversation, I asked her what aspect of her life was the most difficult to write about. I expected she would say her early childhood when she lived in dire poverty or the blockade of Leningrad, when she survived by working in a brigade collecting corpses on the street, but to my surprise she said it was about the great people she had known, among them Dmitri Shostakovich and Alexandr Solzhenitsyn. "You carry an enormous responsibility before history when you write about them," she told me. "You have to be careful in your conclusions and even in how you reacted to what you saw with your own eyes and heard with your own ears."[7] She then raised the example of Solomon Volkov's controversial book *Testimony*, which purported to be the memoirs of Shostakovich. Although acknowledging that many of the stories in Volkov's book, specifically those describing Shostakovich's anti-Soviet views, were well known among Russian musicians, Vishnevskaya was dismissive of the book as a whole. "Shostakovich was a tragic figure of our time. Soviet musicologists are trying to cover up his thorny and difficult life, but in the West, those who have escaped from the Soviet prison, the so-called witnesses, are looking for cheap sensation, a way to make money. I would say it's unethical and dishonest to toy with such great people as Shostakovich who are the pride of our culture."

Galina's passionate response about Shostakovich prompted me to ask about Solzhenitsyn. "Unwittingly, we played a big role in his life," she told me. "If he had not come to live with us for four years, his fate would have been different. . . . Slava met him in the fall of 1969 at a concert in Ryazan and invited him to come and live with us because he simply had no place to go. We had a second house on our dacha property, and I was happy to offer him shelter." Knowing that our listeners were hearing only vile descriptions of Solzhenitsyn in Soviet media, I pressed Vishnevskaya to share her sense of his personality. She responded:

He has but one goal in his life: to do what he set out to do. He's the type of person who wouldn't just sit around and chat or socialize. I know a lot of people are miffed at him . . . that he's anti-social . . . but he simply values his time. . . . He set himself the task of writing the history of the Russian revolution, and he values every minute. . . . And that's the way he was with us for four years. . . . If we invited him to have dinner with us, he would come, in order not to offend us . . . but it was obvious he was anxious to leave because his desk was waiting for him.

From Shostakovich and Solzhenitsyn we segued to Galina's personal life. In a certain way, her life story could be seen as an exemplar of Soviet success. Here was a girl born into a destitute family, at the lowest rung of the social ladder. She was given opportunities to realize her ambitions, and her hard work and innate genius were recognized by the Soviet state. Later, she went on to conquer the artistic world in the USSR and in the West. But Galina's book is not a story of theatrical events and glamorous trips. At its core, it is an insider's look at the Soviet system itself: its exploitation of artists, its control over what one says and what one does, its arbitrary rewards and punishments, its fundamental denial of artistic freedom. "We were serfs," Galina told me in an acerbic tone. "If we did what we were told, we were rewarded. If not, we would be punished." Not a meek person, Galina periodically rebelled, and that resulted in cancelled concerts and trips. Finally, the Soviet authorities, fed up with her honesty, simply cancelled her existence. "It was awful, simply awful, that so many years of my life were spent in Russia," Vishnevskaya fumed, "and I was dependent on those bastards every minute of my life. . . . By 1976 my name was crossed out of all the books about the Bolshoi Theatre. . . . A jubilee album had come out—*Two Hundred Years of the Bolshoi Theatre*—and my name was not there, as if I had never been there, as if I had never worked there, had never been born in Russia, and had never done anything there for those twenty-three years at the Bolshoi Theatre."

Toward the end of the interview, Galina shared with me an amazing story illustrating just how absurd Soviet practice had become: "The

Soviet Union continues to sell my recordings abroad, although we don't get any money for this. The film *Katerina Izmailova*, the Soviet title of Shostakovich's opera *Lady Macbeth of Mtsensk*, is not shown in Russia, but the video is sold in the West. Slava and I started watching it, and I see '*Katerina Izmailova*, Lenfilm, 1966.' The cast—'Katerina Izmailova'... and then a blank, no name. What idiocy! They sell the film in the West, and any normal person watching it would want to know, who is the artist? But my name can't be mentioned."

On that note, Galina began to read extensive excerpts from her memoirs. It was her opportunity to strike back and achieve some form of justice. Her readings, full of passion and fury, scaled operatic heights of indignation—"Mother Russia, avenge your ravaged, tortured children"—only to melt into the most ethereal pianissimos, as when she addresses her beloved grandmother: "God rest your soul, Darya Alexandrovna Ivanova, your good, kind Russian soul. Why did you have to die like that? Tormented by hunger and cold, covered with scabs and lice, with none of your children or grandchildren at your side. Strangers' hands closed your eyes. May the earth nestle you like down." We accompanied these readings with excerpts from her many operatic recordings and the entire "radio package" was one of our proudest achievements. We submitted it to the all-VOA competition for the best cultural programming of 1984 and were thrilled when it received first prize, knowing full well that this was just one more triumph for the indomitable Galina Vishnevskaya.

The participation of Rostropovich and Vishnevskaya in the Russian broadcasts signaled a new era for the Russian Service when it could openly broadcast interviews and works by Russian émigrés who were hostile to the Soviet Union. Prior to the early 1980s, senior editors in the Russian Service—principally Natalie Clarkson, Ludmila Obolensky Flam, Barbara Cummins, and Tatiana Retivov—worked hard to include reports about Russian émigrés who were harsh critics of the Soviet Union but had to contend with occasional rebukes from American management. Through their efforts, the Russian Service regularly reviewed new publications of literature by émigré presses, including Ardis Press in Michigan, and interviewed such well-known artists as Mikhail Baryshnikov, Mikhail Chemiakin, Ernst Neizvestny, and Alexander Galich. "One of my favorite VOA stories," Tatiana Retivov reminisced, "was about the unofficial artist Aleksandr Kalugin, who had been placed in a mental institution [in the USSR]. An American art collector brought back some of Kalugin's journals that he kept while in the mental institute, and so VOA did a special program dedicated to Kalugin and his artwork. We read excerpts from his diaries, and shortly afterwards he was released."[8]

The Russian Service also presented works by Joseph Brodsky, Sasha Sokolov, Vladimir Maximov, and Vladimir Voinovich, who did shy away from expressing their views of the Soviet Union. Though popular with listeners, this cultural programming was often dismissed as "bad radio" by senior American managers, who had come to VOA from American commercial radio, where an artificially upbeat tone, snappy reports, and catchy musical bridges were the rage. I recall siting through many evaluation sessions where VOA radio experts would assess the quality of the Russian broadcasts, even though they didn't know a word of Russian. All they cared about was the "sound." Was the broadcast clock observed? Were the segues smoothly done? Was there a variety of voices? Was the tone lively? I would acknowledge the need to improve the technical quality of our broadcasts but would strenuously push back against any attempt to excise readings from books or to do away with lengthy interviews. From a strategic point of view, the most valuable programming VOA could offer its listeners was truthful information about their country and its role in the world and a sense that independent Russian culture was thriving in the United States. Fortunately, in the 1980s we were free to ignore previous policy injunctions about sound and style, dispense with centrally produced English-language texts, and create our own programming. Taking full advantage of our new journalistic freedom, we doubled down on programming about writers and cultural figures who were either banned outright in the Soviet Union or unknown even to better-educated Russian listeners. Central to that effort was the introduction of a new program simply entitled *Literary Readings*.

Among the first books we selected was Juri Jelagin's *Taming of the Arts*. In this personal story, Jelagin drew on his experience as a musician at the Moscow Art Theatre and the Vakhtangov Theater to paint a compelling picture of theatrical life in the 1930s. His principal goal was not to review the artistic accomplishments of Soviet theater but rather to provide an insider's look at life during Stalin's rule. Jelagin recounted how artists served the Soviet state, occasionally even performing at late-night Communist Party bacchanals, and how they were treated as dispensable serfs who would be arrested (and sometimes shot) when new artistic norms were dictated from above. What made Jelagin's memoir such gripping radio programming was his ability to draw on personal family stories to paint a larger picture of the life of the creative class in the Soviet Union.

A good example of Jelagin's technique was an extended excerpt about how his mother received permission to reside in Moscow. As background, Jelagin recounted how his father, the son of a well-to-do factory owner in tsarist Russia, was arrested in the late 1920s for "the crime of being a member of the wrong social class" and sent to the gulag. In keeping with a longstanding Russian tradition of aiding political prisoners, dating back to the Decembrist Revolt in 1825, Jelagin's mother voluntarily followed her husband to Siberia, settling near the camp so she could visit him periodically and try to sustain him physically and emotionally. Despite her best efforts, Jelagin's father died after several years, and his mother returned to Moscow. During her absence, the Soviet authorities had introduced an internal passport system that determined who could live in major cities, principally Moscow. As the wife of "former person," Jelagin's mother had no right to live in her native city but was required to reside in a small town or village at least 100 kilometers away from the capital. Within days of her arrival in Moscow, local police informed her she had to depart or she too would be arrested and sent to the gulag.

Knowing that internal exile in the brutal conditions of Soviet life would be certain death for his mother, Jelagin took all the steps he could to save her. At this point, the listener begins to enter the theatrical world of the 1930s. As Jelagin notes, theaters were one of the few privileged sectors of Soviet life that brought together the party bosses, the urban workers, the "former people," and an emerging

Soviet upper class. Theaters represented a much-needed escape from a dismal Soviet existence that was becoming ever harsher and more dangerous. For the new ruling elite, theaters were their domain to flaunt their newly acquired status, parade as conquerors before the masses, enjoy the good life, and seek out their mistresses and lovers. For the growing urban class, theaters were an oasis, a place for old-fashioned entertainment and a needed respite from the din of agitprop and Communist indoctrination. For the "former people" this was their sanctuary, a place to hide from the authorities, to earn at least subsistence wages, and to preserve the right to continue living in the major cities where they had been born. As Jelagin points out, virtually all of the major actors, theater directors, musicians, and even stagehands were from the nobility or the tsarist bourgeoisie. His stand partner in the Vakhtangov Theater orchestra was Count Sheremetyev, a scion of the richest family in tsarist Russia. A prominent member of the chorus was one of Tsar Nicholas's reputed lovers, and the theater usher was an old aristocrat. They were tolerated by the authorities because they were the only people who knew how to create the magic of theatrical life that so much of Soviet society craved. For this reason, Jelagin felt that despite his wrong pedigree he could use his theater status to save his mother.

The Vakhtangov Theater enjoyed the patronage of Vyacheslav Molotov and several senior officials of the OGPU (the earlier incarnation of the KGB) and that *krysha* (protection) emboldened the theater administrator to call the head of the Moscow passport office to arrange a meeting for Jelagin. Thrilled by the opportunity to plead his case, Jelagin met with the director only to learn that the theater administrator's *blat* (bureaucratic pull) could get him a polite meeting but not a residence card for his mother. In desperation, Jelagin went to the top political bosses at the Vakhtangov. They assured him that they could contact a very important official at the OGPU, but Jelagin first had to write a memo stating that his principal duty was to serve the Soviet state at the highest professional level. For that, he needed "the peace and quiet that only his elderly mother could provide." When Jelagin averred that this was not necessarily true, he was told bluntly that without a valid reason showing fealty to the state, nothing could be done. Jelagin complied and several days later set off to the headquarters of the OGPU, where he received the all-important papers. As Jelagin noted, such was the reality of the "first egalitarian, socialist society." Even though by Soviet law his mother had no right to reside in Moscow, the OGPU overruled the passport office as a favor to the Vakhtangov Theater. This was a clear indication of the political status that a major Soviet theater enjoyed—a status, however, that could vanish overnight.

As I listened to Alexey Kovalev's masterful reading of the *Taming of the Arts* some thirty-five years after the initial broadcast, I was struck by the eloquent narration that captured the feel of Soviet life for the "little people," those eking out an existence in the darkening days of Stalin's rule.[9] So long as Jelagin and his fellow artists were needed by the authorities, they were periodically given small tokens of appreciation, privileges denied to most citizens. But they knew that they lived on the edge of a precipice and that at any moment those privileges could be yanked away. As members of wrong social class, they could be condemned to the gulag or simply shot. As Stalin's terror intensified through the 1930s, even highly prized and venerated artists came under verbal attack that often led to their eventual arrest. In one of the searing chapters of the *Taming of the Arts*, Jelagin relates the fate of a person he knew well: Vsevolod Meyerhold, the world-famous Russian theater director and cofounder of the Moscow Art Theater. As his modernist productions fell into disfavor, Meyerhold was accused of being a "formalist" (a code word for a Western-oriented, decadent artist), and his all-important bureaucratic ties started to disappear. His theater was closed, and he could survive only by staging occasional productions in other theaters. In June 1939 Jelagin attended a major conference of theater directors, where Meyerhold inveighed against ideological campaigns waged by the theater authorities. According to Jelagin's notes, Meyerhold stated, "If what you have been doing with the Soviet theater recently is what you call antiformalism, if you consider what is now taking place on the stages of the best theaters in Moscow as an achievement, then I would prefer to be considered a formalist. . . . In attacking formalism, you have destroyed art."[10]

Shortly after that speech, Meyerhold was arrested; his wife, the famous actress Zinaida Reich, was stabbed to death. Meyerhold himself underwent excruciating torture and was shot in February 1940. His fate served as a coda to the book, with Jelagin reminding readers that the Soviet authorities tried over and over again to *tame* the Russian arts, to bring them under their full control, to master them as one would a circus animal, but they could never succeed. No matter how oppressive the Soviet regime became, Russian art would always rebel and assert its full freedom. The only option left for the authorities was to exterminate its most creative proponents.

Extended literary readings, especially about the 1930s, seemed old-fashioned, if not irrelevant, to many VOA radio specialists. These programs bore no direct relationship to the VOA mission of explaining U.S. policies and American life. But during the Cold War, the Russian Service could pursue the kind of programming we felt our listeners would want to hear. In our strategy meetings we mapped out a new approach to our cultural programming, building on the success of Vishnevskaya's memoir and Jelagin's *Taming of the Arts*. Our intention was to provide a deeper examination of Soviet history and life—denied to our listeners by Soviet censorship—and, at the same time, highlight the creative freedom of Western life and the enduring ties between Russian émigrés and their homeland. We realized that the most effective way to create lively radio programs was by having Russian writers read their own texts and comment on them. With many well-known Russian writers living in the West, we had a unique opportunity to connect artists with their audience, overcoming the barriers imposed by Soviet authorities.

One of the highlights of VOA cultural programming was a series of readings by Vasily Aksyonov from his novel *Skazhi izium* (*Say Cheese!*, 1984). A popular writer of youth prose, Aksyonov came of age in the "thaw years," that freer period of Soviet life after Stalin's death when wholesale terror had subsided and the Soviet Union was beginning fitfully to open up to the West. The son of Yevgenia Ginzburg, the author of the harrowing memoirs of the Soviet Gulag, *Krutoi Marshrut* (Into the whirlwind), Aksyonov knew the horrors of Soviet life firsthand. But rather than dwell on Stalinist terror, he embraced Western fashions, a libertine lifestyle, jazz, and popular culture. He came to be a free spirit in totalitarian Russia, and his works, full of slang and youthful irreverence, became a symbol of the first Soviet counterculture movement, commonly known as *stilyagi* (those with style). In the 1960s and 1970s, he was a popular writer whose works had an ironic edge, a flair for the forbidden, and an easy, almost conversational style that appealed to virtually all classes of Russian readers. By the 1970s, with Brezhnev's conservative stagnation steadily strangling the arts, Aksyonov began to experience repeated run-ins with the authorities. After his involvement with an independent literary almanac, *Metropol*, as well as the publication in the West of his two celebrated novels, *Ozhog* (*The Burn*) and *Ostrov Krym* (*The Island of Crimea*), he was forced to emigrate. Shortly afterward, Aksyonov was stripped of his Soviet citizenship. He settled in the hip Adams Morgan section of Washington DC, taught Russian literature at George Mason University in Northern Virginia, and continued to write, now as a free man.

Like Galina Vishnevskaya, Aksyonov came to the VOA, text in hand, ready to communicate with his many readers in the Soviet Union. The novel he chose, *Say Cheese!*, was in many ways autobiographical, recreating the genesis and eventual fate of *Metropol*. In the novel, however, Aksyonov replaced literature with photography, the only art form that technically was not controlled by an official, government-sanctioned union. This ostensible freedom from bureaucratic constraints allowed the hero, Maxim Ogorodnikov, and his fellow photographers to collect and exhibit photos of true Soviet reality. Such outrageous behavior led to inevitable confrontations with the KGB, and the novel chronicled the escapades of the photographers as they tried to present their art in public. Aksyonov depicted the Soviet society as a battleground where the forces of state power were pitted against personal freedom. This was a serious indictment of the Soviet system, but the message was delivered with irony, humor, and a touch of the absurd.

In conducting research for this book, I listened with pleasure to the broadcasts of Aksyonov's novel. Alexey Retivov, a VOA broadcaster, and Aksyonov intermixed excerpts from the novel with lively discussions about the characters and the political implications of the story.[11]

Aksyonov's reading of his own text lent the program a sense of intimacy, as though we were guests in his home where we listened to his views on literature, enjoyed his witty asides, chuckled along with him as he read the humorous parts of his novel, and basked in the warmth of Russian bonhomie. With Aksyonov there was no hectoring, no imposition of ideology, no moralizing. Rather, his gravelly voice embraced his listeners, and he expressed even the most serious ideas with a light touch.

In time, Russian literature and culture became a central part of the Russian broadcasts as we presented the works of major (and many minor) Russian émigré writers, among them Alexandr Solzhenitsyn, Ivan Elagin, Nikolai Morshen, Vladimir Voinovich, and Georgiy Vladimov. At the height of the Cold War, we felt it was our principal duty to provide our listeners with uncensored Russian culture that was otherwise inaccessible to them. This did not mean, however, that we ignored VOA's mission of reflecting American life in all of its diversity. The Russian Service had the luxury of broadcasting twenty-four hours a day, seven days a week, and that provided ample airtime to satisfy many different tastes. Each hour began with a live ten-minute newscast, produced centrally by the VOA news desk, followed by current-affairs or feature shows. In the 1980s we had four current-affairs programs and forty-six weekly feature shows, ranging in subject matter from science and technology, medicine, and agriculture to the role of women in contemporary society, hobbies, and sports. Along with our literary readings, we had eight weekly programs that dealt exclusively with cultural topics: *Books and People*, *Pop Concert*, *Jazz* (with Willis Conover), *Country Music*, *Cinema*, *Broadway*, *Art in America*, and *Theater*. Our music programs, hosted primarily by American broadcasters who had mastered the Russian language, were popular with young people in the USSR, and our broadcasters would receive considerable fan mail. When I traveled throughout Russia in the 1990s, Russians would tell me that they came to know and love such American icons as Frank Sinatra, Johnny Cash, or Simon and Garfunkel through the VOA music shows. Generally, music programs were not heavily jammed and provided a continuing cultural bridge between the United States and the Soviet Union despite the vicissitudes of Cold War politics. For many of our staffers, music programming was "the fun stuff" that made VOA a great place to work.

VOA programming about theater and the arts, in contrast, tried to appeal to educated, urban listeners who were interested in the latest trends in the Western art world, especially about artists and movements censored by official Soviet media. Anchored by a husband-and-wife team, Alexey Kovalev and Zhanna Vladimirskaya, who had been professional actors in the Soviet Union, our weekly *Theater* program set a high professional standard. A good example of their work was an hour-long program devoted to Samuel Beckett and the prominent American theater director Alan Schneider, who staged many of Beckett's plays in the United States. Rather than just describe the plays and quote from various reviews, Kovalev and Vladimirskaya translated several scenes from three Beckett plays—*Happy Days*, *Waiting for Godot*, and *Endgame*—and then acted them out in professionally produced mini "radio plays." They interspersed the scenes with discussions about Beckett's plays in the USSR, Schneider's conception of the works, and the general reception of Beckett in the United States. Shorn of any political coloring, this program was intended for the cognoscenti who would be interested in learning more about a complex artist virtually unknown in the USSR. This was a timeless piece, a serious but highly entertaining program that explored new trends in Western theater. It didn't score political points, denigrate the Soviet Union, or promote the West. Rather, VOA presented radio theater that searched for artistic truth and questioned the meaning of life, making the broadcast as relevant today as it was when it was first produced and aired in 1986.

Not all episodes of the *Theater* program were aimed exclusively at elite audiences. Most combined general news and gossip about the theatrical world, updates on the latest American hits, reports about important festivals in the United States (such as the Spoleto Festival in Charleston, South Carolina), and, most important, reviews of visiting Soviet theatrical groups in the United States. When the Leningrad Kirov Ballet came to the Wolf Trap theater near Washington in June 1986, VOA devoted considerable resources to covering the event. After a lengthy absence, Soviet artistic troupes were again beginning to perform in the

United States after Gorbachev announced his policy of glasnost. But instead of taking politics as the hook for the story, the Russian Service approached the Kirov performance as it would any theatrical event in the United States. Its correspondent, highly knowledgeable about ballet, attended the performances, explained the popularity of the Wolf Trap theater, gave a professional assessment of the latest achievements of the company, went backstage to speak with the artists, and conveyed to Soviet listeners the warmth and enthusiasm of the American audience. By avoiding politics, the VOA broadcast showed how normal U.S. and Russian interactions could be and how warmly welcomed the Kirov Ballet was in the United States. Given the heavy political content of our current-affairs programming, we generally stayed clear of politics in most of our Americana stories, convinced that straight reporting about culture was the most effective way to communicate American values.

As a classical music fan, I would occasionally urge the cultural editors to devote more airtime to opera and symphonic music, especially since Russians were passionate about these musical genres. But mostly I got pushback from the editors who noted that shortwave broadcasting would significantly distort the fidelity of the sound and that our listeners already had access to musical concerts on Soviet radio and television. They acknowledged that programming about Rostropovich and Vishnevskaya, accompanied by musical excerpts, would be effective but were adamant that we would receive few, if any, accolades for broadcasting a two-hour concert from the Kennedy Center. I accepted their arguments but was nonetheless pleased when VOA would occasionally devote a program to a classical musician or musical event.

One of the more memorable programs during my time at VOA was a two-part broadcast about the outstanding Russian American pianist Vladimir Horowitz (1903–89), replete with extended excerpts from his piano repertoire. In 1986 Horowitz announced that after an absence of sixty-one years, he wished to return to his native country to play concerts as part of the Reagan administration's recently relaunched cultural-exchange program with the Soviet Union. Although Gorbachev's policy of glasnost had already been articulated, Soviet media outlets were still unsure how to treat an émigré artist and, to play it safe, virtually ignored Horowitz's visit and concerts. In sharp contrast, Western media, notably CBS, transmitted the entire Moscow concert to American and European audiences, thereby providing VOA with considerable material for its own broadcasts. As was the custom in the Soviet Union, the best seats in the Grand Hall of the Moscow Conservatory were reserved for high party officials, and only a few were sold to the public. Fearful of the political repercussions of attending an émigré concert, many Soviet dignitaries simply didn't show up, leaving the best seats empty. Meanwhile, the musical and artistic cognoscenti of Moscow stormed the balcony with some even climbing onto the roof so they could hear the music through the skylights that provided natural light to the theater. The Horowitz concert had all the elements of drama and made a perfect subject for VOA.

The first part of the program presented a biographical sketch of the artist, with occasional piano selections. In a straightforward manner, the presenter of the program described Horowitz's early life in Kyiv, his years at the Kyiv Conservatory, and his spectacular success in Moscow and Leningrad. As his fame spread across the musical world, he received an invitation in 1925 to play concerts in Berlin. Horowitz applied for a Soviet exit visa and was granted one for only six months, but he knew he would not return to the USSR. After success in Germany and France, he came to the United States and was immediately greeted by an old friend, the Russian-American composer Sergei Rachmaninov. Within forty-eight hours of his arrival in New York, Horowitz and Rachmaninov were in the Steinway music store in midtown Manhattan, trying out instruments and playing duets. With initial help from Rachmaninov, Horowitz's career took off, and quickly he became one of the preeminent pianists in the United States.

The program about Horowitz drew on a long tradition at VOA of presenting American success stories with Russian roots. Horowitz considered himself fully American. He taught many of the finest American pianists, represented America abroad, and was proud of his adopted country. But his ties to Russia went deep. His piano technique was nurtured by the famous Russian Piano School; his initial success was in playing Russian music; and many of his close friends were of Russian heritage. By presenting Horowitz's life, the VOA not only was able to showcase music in America but also gave Soviet listeners a better understanding of the vibrancy and achievements of the Russian emigration. Far from withering away, as Soviet propagandists declared, many Russian émigrés were highly successful in the United States and became an integral part of the American cultural fabric.

Looking back at the 1980s, some thirty years after the fall of the Soviet Union, one can appreciate how well the Russian Service handled cultural programming. True to its charter, VOA focused primarily on American arts and tried to communicate a sense of American cultural values. But the Russian Service was also able to focus on Russia-related stories and connect directly to our audience. Where possible, we tried to give Russian artists an opportunity to speak directly to their compatriots, and not only through their works. I recall how the famous violinist Victoria Mullova came to the VOA studios for an interview shortly after defecting to the West. After explaining why she had defected, she turned to us with a personal request. Distraught that she could not reach her mother, she asked if she could simply address her over the VOA airwaves. We readily acquiesced, and she assured her mother that she was safe. In those dark days of the Cold War, we felt the VOA Russian Service had a special mission of helping Russians to connect with their homeland, if only by means of shortwave broadcasts.

In reviewing VOA cultural programming, I was heartened to come across an interview with Vladimir Voinovich, one of Russia's greatest satirists, speaking about what it was like to be a creative writer in Brezhnev's Soviet Union. With sadness, he related how the propaganda machine of the USSR was slowly but inexorably crushing the very spirit of free art, how Soviet bureaucrats were trying to control writers through a system of "carrots and sticks"—enticing those who followed the party line with material goods and foreign trips and sending the obstreperous and willful to the gulag. And yet what Russians truly wanted, Voinovich said with an air of resignation, was to live like normal people, to express their views freely, to read foreign publications, to be themselves. Yuri Lyubimov, the most prominent theater director of his generation, echoed those very sentiments in another VOA interview, describing to his many fans what it was like to be in full control of the staging of plays, how normal and exciting it was to work at Washington DC's Arena Stage Theater. Neither Voinovich nor Lyubimov was calling for the overthrow of the Soviet regime; they were simply appealing for more humane conditions. As Voinovich said, just let Russians be free, and they will create a successful and dynamic country.

Radio Liberty Cultural Programming

Programming about culture and the arts was the lifeblood of Radio Liberty. For Russian broadcasters, whether of the first, second, or third wave of emigration, true Russian culture could thrive only when it was free of official Soviet ideology, when artists could fully express themselves in a multicultural environment. As a surrogate station, Radio Liberty saw its mission as embodying that independent spirit and communicating artistic freedom back to the home country. From its first broadcasts, RL presented Russian culture in a broad context, ranging from tsarist, émigré, and underground Soviet culture to Western art, popular music, and cinema. Its programs ran the gamut from reviews of art exhibits, classical music concerts, book fairs, and the latest literary works to comic skits, satirical songs, pop music, jazz, and spoofs of Soviet films and popular plays. In Ivan Tolstoy's words, "The history of RL Russian broadcasts is in fact a history of Russian culture of the second half of the 20th century."[12] Russian culture and the Radio Liberty broadcasts are so thoroughly interwoven that their relationship merits a separate full-length study. My examination here merely touches on several salient examples that can provide but a glimpse of the richness of the programming.

In sharp contrast to the commonly held assumption that early RL programming was ponderous, highly politicized, and aggressively anti-Communist, many broadcasts in the 1950s actually strived to be humorous and entertaining. We find, for example, witty satires of Khrushchev's policies, including his infamous Virgin Lands campaign, an ambitious effort to boost the Soviet Union's agricultural production to alleviate endemic food shortages. In the spirit of late-night U.S. television comedy, the Russian staff—principally Leonid Pylaev and Galina

Zotova—riffed on important Soviet pronouncements, composed little ditties about the latest economic successes, and mocked the party's grandiose promises. Pylaev also authored a long-running radio play about boozing Russian officers stationed in Soviet-occupied Germany that was punctuated by old war songs and slapstick routines. Far from being the angry rants of traitorous émigrés, as Soviet propaganda would portray RL broadcasts, these programs were Russian versions of French *variété*, music-hall spectacles intended for popular appeal. These corny skits, rather quaint by today's standards, showcased the spirit and talent of the staff: how well they sang Russian songs, how creative they were in writing and acting out comic scenes, and how much fun they were having on air.

Most of the popular music programming drew on rich traditions of Russian cabarets in New York and Paris, but RL also included Western music. A very talented singer, Galina Zotova translated and performed popular American songs. Her renditions of Simon and Garfunkel's "The Sound of Silence" and "Scarborough Fair" were musical gems. For years, Boris Orshansky hosted a jazz program; Igor Berukshtis acquainted his listeners with American pop tunes; and the RL Paris office made sure to feature French chanson, including songs by Brigitte Bardot. In the 1960s, in step with the worldwide craze, RL played all the records of the Beatles.

The star of early RL cultural programming was Vladimir Dukelsky (1903–69). Born into a noble Russian family, Dukelsky graduated from the Kyiv Conservatory and began his musical career as a composer of classical music. His family fled Russia during the revolution and made its way to the United States. In 1922 George Gershwin befriended Dukelsky and suggested he Americanize his name to Vernon Duke. As Duke, he composed many popular American songs, including "Taking a Chance on Love," "I Can't Get Started," and "April in Paris." As a regular contributor to Radio Liberty broadcasts, Dukelsky produced many musical programs that featured not only his compositions but also the works of other Russian émigré musicians.

Radio Liberty tried to present a broad range of music and even devoted an entire program to the popular rock-opera *Hair*. After playing several better-known songs, it aired an incisive review of the *Hair* phenomenon by Georgi Adamovich, an eminent émigré poet and frequent contributor to RL's more high-brow programs. Despite his use of a high literary style, Adamovich conveyed how much he enjoyed talking about *Hair* and its place in youth culture. He communicated the spirit of *Hair*, its rebellious nature, rejection of staid traditions, and revelry in free expression, including its celebration of nudity on stage. In communicating that liberating freedom, Adamovich reminded RL's listeners that it was not only the youth who loved the work but also their parents who stood in long lines to attend performances. To be free, Adamovich was saying, was to be daring and to challenge conventions. That subtle political message—the delight of art and culture untrammeled by ideological strictures—infused early RL programming and balanced the heavy political fare with a much-needed lighter touch.

Along with programming about Western and Russian émigré culture, RL focused on the emergence of the underground arts in the USSR—"*podpol'shchina*" as one Russian commentator ironically referred to them. With the beginning of the cultural thaw in the 1950s, Soviet citizens began to look for ways to freely express their ideas, emotions, and desires. In one of the more insightful RL broadcasts, Vladimir Frumkin, a noted musicologist, described the growing popularity of youth songs. Drawing on his experience as a conservatory student in Leningrad working "voluntarily" on construction projects in the summer, Frumkin related how Soviet youth would gather in the evenings to relax and sing songs that they had composed themselves. What was remarkable, Frumkin noted, was the conspicuous absence of the pompous, patriotic songs promoted by the state and played endlessly on Soviet radio. Frumkin knew that official songs were mandated by the Komsomol (Communist Youth League), schools, and other official organizations and that students were required to sing them. But he was pleasantly surprised to learn that they were not at all popular. When given the slightest chance, young people in the USSR wanted to express themselves through humorous, sentimental, and sometimes even absurd songs. As Frumkin was quick to point out, these songs were not political and did not challenge the legitimacy of the state or party, but as personal compositions devoid of Communist ideology they embodied an underlying sense of protest, a desire to break free of Soviet clichés. That stirring of personal freedom was seen as dangerous by the Soviet authorities.

The freer amateur art form noted by Frumkin evolved over time into a genre commonly known as *avtorskaya pesnya* (bard songs)—music not officially sanctioned by the state—that ranged from witty Aesopian satires to outright anti-Soviet protests. Given the connection between free expression and political subtext, it is no surprise that the best-known and most influential representatives of this genre—Bulat Okudzhava (1924–97), Vladimir Vysotsky (1938–80), and Alexander Galich (1918–77)—were mainstays of RL broadcasting. Okudzhava, the acknowledged elder of the triad, was a poet, writer, musician, novelist, and singer-songwriter of Georgian-Armenian ancestry. His songs avoided overtly political themes, but their directness, freshness, and independence challenged Soviet orthodoxy, and that made him "politically suspect." Vysotsky was a poet, songwriter, and actor who had an immense influence on Russian arts and has continued to be popular well into the twenty-first century. A successful playwright and poet, Galich began composing popular songs that over time evolved into biting commentaries on Soviet life. By the early 1970s he was considered a dissident figure and forced to emigrate. He settled in Paris and became a regular contributor to Radio Liberty. If one types the names of these three bards in the Radio Liberty/Open Society archives (www .osaarchivum.org), one finds 79 entries for Vysotsky, 148 for Okudzhava, and over 500 for Galich. And these entries account only for programs in which they sang their songs, commented on them, or spoke directly to their millions of fans in the USSR. This astoundingly rich collection underscores the central role Radio Liberty played in supporting and propagating Russian culture that was popular with Soviet citizens but restricted by the authorities.

One of the more popular music programs, entitled *Oni poiut* (They are singing), featured many songs by the three bards. As the emcee, Galina Zotova would introduce the songs, often commenting on their merits, and then play them on air. These were relatively short programs—up to ten minutes—and provided a needed break from heavier political fare. On occasion, the bards would be part of larger programs that would examine their art within a wider context of cultural developments in the USSR. Among the more memorable broadcasts was Okudzhava's miniconcert and open discussion with RL journalists (May 27, 1990). He spoke about the long-term significance of RL programming and why he was a regular listener. He also answered questions from the staff and, of course, sang some of his better-known songs. This program was aired in the waning months of Soviet rule and the back-and-forth between Okudzhava and the staff showed how fear of Soviet authorities had all but disappeared. Several years later, Okudzhava came to the fortieth anniversary of Radio Liberty, celebrated in Moscow, and reminisced about his years as a dedicated RL listener, commented on the critical role RL played in conveying artistic freedom to the people of the Soviet Union, and even sang a song composed in honor of Radio Liberty.

A cult figure in Russia, Vladimir Vysotsky gained worldwide fame as a balladeer whose songs of love, war, the gulag, and everyday life carried an honesty and directness that was in sharp contrast to the clichés of Soviet art. His early "criminal songs" (*blatnye pesni*) were not only witty satires of Soviet life but also poetic expressions of the eternal questions of life. Despite their bitter tone, full of street jargon, these songs embodied a Russian spirit that transcended political barriers and found resonance among different classes in the Soviet Union, as well as with different waves of Russian emigration. In one of the many RL tributes to Vysotsky, Rostislav Polchaninov, a member of the first emigration, spoke about the "common language" he shared with Vysotsky and how both the first and second emigrations viewed him "as one of our own." Andrei Sinyavsky referred to him as "our national poet," noting that his poetry captured "the national we" (*on pisal ne ot ia, a ot my*).[13] Though he was not formally banned, the Soviet authorities treated him as a dangerous artist who challenged the dominance of the state and had the audacity to gain national popularity while spurning the Soviet Ministry of Culture. His close relationship with RL no doubt raised further concerns. The Soviet authorities' inability to completely quash Vysotsky was an early indication that the free spirit he embodied was whittling away the state's control over personal artistic expression. The Soviet culture bureaucracy was waging a losing battle against the free arts and, by the 1980s, was so brittle that it crumbled less than a decade after Vysotsky's death.

As prominent as Okudzhava and Vysotsky were in RL programming, they could not rival Alexander Galich's place of honor. Soon after arriving in France, Galich began to host a weekly program, *On Air with Galich*, in which he spoke directly to RL listeners in an intimate way, as though he were chatting with friends at home. He would come to the Paris studio with just his guitar, introduce his songs, often relating how and why he had composed them, and then would sing them on air. Galich deftly captured the absurdities of Soviet life but at the same time gave his listeners a sense of hope through his love of country, a yearning for normalcy, and a fervent belief in a better future for Russia. He avoided cheap sentimentality, even though he spoke openly of nostalgia, love for his neighborhood, the sounds and smells of his youth—sentiments that have always resonated with Russians. His well-known song, "Kogda ia vernus'" (When I return), expressed poignantly that particular interweaving of youthful love and abandon with cold, underlying political reality. This same "Galich mix" was fully expressed in one of his New Year's Eve broadcasts (December 31, 1975). Galich invited his friends from the other language services of RFE/RL to a "party on air," with vodka, hors d'oeuvres, laughter, jokes, witty stories, and, of course, plenty of songs in Russian, Georgian, Armenian, Czech, and Polish. Everyone was singing, telling stories, having fun, and sharing that experience with RL's listeners. No one spoke explicitly about politics; this was a celebratory evening. And yet, despite all the merriment, everyone understood that this kind of personal freedom, with its political jokes and sly innuendoes, could not be displayed in a public forum in the Soviet Union.

In the 1970s RL introduced a regular program, *Culture and Politics*, that examined Soviet practices and contrasted them with cultural life in the West. Frequently edited by Vladimir Matusevich, a talented broadcaster, *Culture and Politics* had a broad remit, ranging from reviews of literary works, reports on academic conferences, and radio essays by émigré writers to analyses of the latest cultural developments in the Soviet Union. Serious in tone, these broadcasts were intended to appeal to educated, urban listeners keenly aware of worldwide cultural developments. Though critical of Soviet practices, *Culture and Politics* adopted a high-brow tone, preferring to examine subjects ignored by mainstream Soviet media, whether essays about Czeslaw Milosz, Vladimir Nabokov, and Vaclav Havel or reports about cultural trends in the Soviet republics.

Occasionally, *Culture and Politics* would tackle a major artistic movement or a new approach to research in the arts. One memorable program in this vein (June 3, 1981) was a review of an academic conference on émigré writers, held in Los Angeles. Maurice Friedberg, a leading American scholar of Russian literature, began with an examination of what constituted émigré literature, reminding his Russian listeners that Thomas Mann, Bertolt Brecht, Alfred Döblin, and Theodor Adorno, among many others, were émigré writers living in Los Angeles after fleeing Nazi Germany. He noted that many of Poland's leading writers—including Adam Mickiewicz, Juliusz Słowacki, and Henryk Sienkiewicz—had lived abroad and were in effect émigré writers. Having set a broad context, Friedberg and Anatoly Gladilin, the RL editor of the program, began to discuss the specifics of Russian émigré writing, focusing primarily on the question of language. Could writers preserve a *living language* if they were residing in a foreign linguistic environment, or would their language become stilted, artificial, and academic? Would they become "American" or "German" writers who happened to write in the Russian language? In short, would they "write with an accent"? With artistic flair, Friedberg compared the émigré writer to a blind man who may have lost his sight—his natural, daily connection to his native readers—but made up for this disability by developing a heightened sense of touch and smell that resulted in a more nuanced, symbolic language. Friedberg contended that the works of older émigré writers—Nabokov, Bunin, Zaitsev—as well as those of more recent émigrés—Solzhenitsyn, Voinovich, Aksyonov—would in time return to Russia and find their rightful place among the classics. Gladilin added that Soviet readers were already viewing Ivan Bunin as a thoroughly Russian writer with a rich stylistic palette even though he had written many of his best works in emigration. From today's perspective, when we know how the Soviet Union collapsed and how émigré writers were welcomed back in post-Communist Russia, it is remarkable how prescient Gladilin and Friedberg were and what an astounding program they presented to Russian listeners.

A more common format of *Culture and Politics* was a profile of a Russian writer or an in-depth examination of a specific literary work. These two approaches came together in a remarkable program dedicated to the seventieth birthday of Victor Nekrasov (1911–87), which aired on June 19, 1981. An actor and journalist, Nekrasov fought in the battle of Stalingrad and later drew on his experience to produce a heralded novel—*V okopakh Stalingrada* (*Front-Line Stalingrad*)—which was awarded the USSR Prize for Literature in 1947. The novel propelled Nekrasov's career, but rather than becoming a Soviet icon, he caught the freer artistic spirit of the 1950s and began to adopt a more critical stance toward the Soviet Union. His next two works dealt with personal dramas, reflective of the turn away from rigid ideological narratives. In 1959 he was the first major Soviet writer to call for a monument to be built at Babii Yar, the ravine outside Kyiv where the Nazis had massacred over thirty thousand Jews (September 29–30, 1941). Still an official writer, Nekrasov was allowed to travel to Europe and the United States, and he subsequently wrote a travelogue—*Both Sides of the Ocean* (1964)—that presented a nonideological picture of the West that avoided Soviet clichés about the ills of the capitalist world. Nekrasov's expression of personal freedom incurred the wrath of the party bureaucracy, and Khrushchev even personally denounced him. By the mid-1960s, Nekrasov began to sign letters in support of the inchoate human rights movement, and that led to repeated interrogations by the KGB. Finally, he was expelled from the Communist Party in 1973 and forced to emigrate in 1974. He joined the editorial board of the émigré journal *Kontinent* in Paris and became a regular contributor to Radio Liberty.

RL's tribute to Nekrasov as a model of moral righteousness included his own description of what it was like to be harassed by the KBG, shunned by official writers who earlier had shown him solicitude and respect, and then expelled from a country that he had served heroically and defended with his life. What is significant in Nekrasov's story is that he was not a revolutionary who sought to overthrow the Soviet system or even an ardent dissident. He was simply a Russian patriot who wanted to live honestly and to express his views openly. In the RL program, he recounted his war experiences in a way that would appeal to virtually every Russian. He spoke about the dangers, hardships, exhilaration of liberating Poland and Czechoslovakia and the warm reception the Red Army initially enjoyed. Nekrasov recalled how ordinary people invited Soviet soldiers into their homes, gave them what little food they had, cheered them as they moved forward against the Germans. Nekrasov noted that common Soviet soldiers saw Poles and Czechs as brothers, but the Soviet high command "came not to liberate Eastern Europe, but to conquer it." And that for Nekrasov was a war crime. It not only destroyed fraternal ties, but it led to Soviet military control and the suppression of freedom.

As one scans the thousands of programs that deal with culture and the arts, one quickly realizes that Radio Liberty performed a truly heroic act of preserving, nurturing, and transmitting Russian and Western culture when it was under siege by the Soviet authorities. It would be hard to name a single major (or even minor) independent Russian writer of the second half of the twentieth century whose works were not reflected in RL broadcasts. Programs such as *Pisatel' u mikrofona* (Writer on air), examined modern Russian literature by presenting insightful book reviews and inviting writers to the RL studios to read from their works. Future biographers of Aksyonov, Voinovich, Solzhenitsyn, Sinyavsky, Dovlatov, Vladimov, and many other writers will find unique primary sources at Radio Liberty that would be indispensable for their research. The same would hold true for musicologists tracing the emergence of popular music in the USSR or historians exploring the interrelationship of Soviet rule and the arts in general.

In sum, Radio Liberty was so much more than just a radio broadcaster. It was a home for Russian artists, musicians, and writers where they could create their work and then connect directly with their compatriots. And RL not only gave them ready access to the airwaves but also paid them for their work. Those payments and honoraria were modest, but they allowed Russian émigré artists to maintain a decent standard of living and to continue to produce their art. Someday Russian historians will look back at the second half of the twentieth century and stand in awe of how American taxpayers, through open congressional appropriations to RFE/RL and VOA, supported the very best of Russian culture and allowed it to blossom at a time when the Kremlin was all too ready to snuff it out.

1. Board for International Broadcasting (BIB) board of directors. *Seated (left to right):* Arch L. Madsen, Steve Forbes (chair), Ben Wattenberg, James A. Michener. *Standing (left to right):* Gene Pell, Kenneth Tomlinson, Michael Novak, Lane Kirkland, Clair Burgener, Edward Ney. Courtesy of Radio Free Europe/Radio Liberty.

2. (*opposite top*) Steve Forbes, chair of the BIB, and Mark Pomar aboard the *Capitalist Tool*. Courtesy of Radio Free Europe/Radio Liberty.

3. (*opposite bottom*) Mark Pomar (*left*) and Gene Pell, president of RFE/RL (*right*). Courtesy of Radio Free Europe/Radio Liberty.

4. (*above*) BIB directors with Vaclav Klaus, minister of finance, Czechoslovakia (1989–92), president of the Czech Republic (2003–13). *Left to right:* Kenneth Tomlinson, Michael Novak, Steve Forbes, Klaus. *Facing away:* Barry Zorthian (*left*), Cheryl Halpern (*right*). Courtesy of Radio Free Europe/Radio Liberty.

5. (*above*) BIB directors meeting with officials in Budapest. *Left to right:* Jane Lester (secretary of the board), Laszlo Ribansky (director of the RFE Hungarian Service), Mark Pomar, Ross Johnson (director of RFE), Kenneth Tomlinson, Gene Pell, Ben Wattenberg, Steve Forbes. Courtesy of Radio Free Europe/Radio Liberty.

6. (*opposite top*) Mstislav "Slava" Rostropovich, Russian human rights advocate and director of the National Symphony Orchestra, addressing the BIB directors. *Standing:* Mark Pomar and Rostropovich. *Seated (left to right):* Steve Forbes, Daniel Mica. Courtesy of Radio Free Europe/Radio Liberty.

7. (*opposite bottom*) Ludmila Obolensky Flam, senior Russian correspondent, in the VOA studio. Courtesy of author.

8. (*opposite top*) Mark Pomar with Lech Walesa, Solidarity leader and president of Poland (1990–95). Courtesy of author.

9. (*opposite bottom*) *Left:* Vladimir Matusevich, director of the RL Russian Service. *Right:* Mark Pomar. Courtesy of author.

10. (*above*) Mstislav "Slava" Rostropovich, Russian human rights advocate and director of the National Symphony Orchestra, Washington DC, addressing the BIB. Courtesy of Radio Free Europe/Radio Liberty.

11. (*above*) Natan Sharansky, prominent human rights activist in the Soviet Union and an Israeli politician, addressing the Board for International Broadcasting. Courtesy of Radio Free Europe/Radio Liberty.

12. (*opposite top*) ID #1—RFE/RL employee ID for Mark Pomar (September 1982). Courtesy of author.

13. (*opposite bottom*) ID #2—Conference ID for Mark Pomar, U.S.-Soviet Information Talks, held in Moscow, September 26–28, 1988. Courtesy of author.

14. (*top*) *Seated*: Zhanna Vladimirskaya, VOA Russian writer and editor (*left*), Ludmila Foster, VOA Russian editor (*right*). *Standing*: Valery Golovskoy, VOA Russian staff. Courtesy of author.

15. (*bottom*) *Front row*: Boris Brodenov, James Schigorin, Elena "Helen" Bates/Yakobson (*seated*), Victor Franzusoff. *Rear row*: Katherine Elene, Vladimir Postman, Tatiana Hecker. Courtesy of Harry S. Truman Library.

16. (*opposite*) Marina Oeltjen, chief producer of Russian Service, VOA. Courtesy of author.

17. *Left:* Gerd von Doemming, chief, USSR Division, VOA. *Right:* Alan Heil, deputy director, VOA. Courtesy of author.

5

History

On my first day at Radio Liberty in the summer of 1982, I was assigned to be the content editor of the principal program about Russian history, aptly titled *Russia: Yesterday, Today, and Tomorrow* (RYTT). The program had been mired in controversy. The more conservative broadcasters praised it for addressing important issues in Russian history that had been distorted or ignored by Soviet propaganda, primarily the conservative traditions of the Slavophiles and late nineteenth- and early twentieth-century figures, such as the philosopher Vladimir Soloviev and the prime minister of Russia Petr Stolypin. The incoming director of Radio Liberty, George Bailey, believed that Russian national ideas and conservative traditions deserved to be treated seriously in the Russian broadcasts and encouraged more freelance contributions from religious dissidents and nationalist writers. George Urban, the incoming director of Radio Free Europe, noted that conservative broadcasts could wean RL listeners away from communism and socialism by appealing to traditional values and especially to Orthodoxy.[1] Russian nationalism was deeply imbedded in Russian émigré communities, principally in Paris and New York, and the emigrants saw themselves as the true embodiment of Russian culture. Many recent Soviet émigrés, however, saw *RYTT* as a nationalistic screed that glorified Russian political figures who had exemplified age-old Russian xenophobia or the darker impulses of authoritarian rule. As a result, the director of the Russian Service decided that a fresh, critical examination of the history broadcasts was needed. My task was to find a way of presenting Russian politics and philosophy *within a Russian cultural tradition* while at the same time ensuring that the programs adhered to the norms and practices of Western discourse.

One year earlier, the RL history program had come under sharp criticism in a report prepared by James Critchlow, a senior member of the Board for International Broadcasting staff in Washington. Responding to critical remarks voiced by several recent Soviet émigrés, Critchlow traveled to Munich, surreptitiously listened to several history broadcasts, and subsequently issued a scathing thirty-page report. He began by noting that "the Soviet Union is a society where no spontaneous public discussion of current issues is allowed. This curb has led to widespread use of historical parallels as 'code' for public expression of political ideas."[2] Critchlow then presented a long list of "historical codes" that he claimed were policy violations, including antidemocratic, anti-Western, anti-Polish, and anti-Catholic references in the programs. Although he was critical of the nationalist approach of RYTT, one program in particular roused his ire: a profile of Konstantin Pobedonostsev (1827–1907), a noted Russian jurist, statesman, and adviser to three tsars. That program, Critchlow claimed, included "expressions of Russian nationalistic and xenophobic views [and] encouraged attitudes of aggression towards other people." Specifically, it conveyed a pessimistic view of democracy in Russia and portrayed the Russian Orthodox Church as the foundation of Russian culture and the only true faith.[3] So damning was Critchlow's report that I decided that before assuming responsibility for RYTT, I should examine the list of policy violations and listen to the infamous broadcast to understand how a figure like Pobedonostsev could stir up so much vituperation.[4]

That thirty-minute broadcast of RYTT, which aired on May 21, 1980, dealt with four major figures: Stalin, Solzhenitsyn, Sakharov, and Pobedonostsev. An unlikely quartet, these starkly different historical figures were linked together by their contrasting notions of progress in Russian society. The first segment described Stalin's meeting with academicians in 1938, in which he expressed his preference for practical knowledge over purely academic work and stressed that the overriding aim of Soviet policy was industrialization. Citing the transcript of the meeting, which had been published in *Pravda*, the RL writer noted that Stalin had been dismissive of traditional Russian rural life and the Euro-centric academic institutions, favoring materialism at the expense of traditional Russian values.

In sharp contrast, the second segment began with a long excerpt from Solzhenitsyn's *Letter to the Soviet Leaders*, which catalogued the ecological ruin of the Russian countryside. In Solzhenitsyn's conception, the new Soviet industrial state had destroyed old Russia, caused untold damage to rural Russia, and left the Russian people destitute. The third piece then contrasted Solzhenitsyn's effusive evocation of a mythic Russian past with Sakharov's measured response. Taking a middle ground between Stalin and Solzhenitsyn, Sakharov maintained that Russia needed to be part of the modern world and that required industry and innovation, but without wanton destruction of the environment. The last segment on Pobedonostsev examined a conservative thinker who rejected many Western values and extolled an Orthodox Russia. While noting that Pobedonostsev was skeptical of Western democracy, abhorred a free press, and believed that Orthodoxy was the basis of Russian culture, Boris Paramonov, a freelance contributor to Radio Liberty, presented him as a major Russian thinker. Paramonov's intention was to show that by learning about conservative thinkers such as Pobedonostsev, who were shown only in a negative light in the Soviet Union, Russians would gain a deeper understanding of their historical traditions.

My first question after listening to the program was, Did this short profile merit Critchlow's damning criticism? Did it contribute, in Gene Sosin's words, to "anti-Semitic sentiments creeping into the broadcasts"?[5] My sense was that by examining the program on Pobedonostsev out of context and then listing short excerpts that purportedly violated RL policy, Critchlow did a disservice to RFE/RL. In the 1980s, critics of RFE/RL would often cite Critchlow's report as evidence of Russian antidemocratic programming without ever listening to the actual broadcasts or understanding how the programs were developed.[6] In one egregious example, William Korey, director of policy research at B'nai B'rith, stated Pobedonostev was responsible for promoting anti-Semitism "and yet RFE/RL chose to praise him as a great conservative thinker."[7] Certainly Pobedonostsev had anti-Semitic views and was a monarchist, which was acknowledged in the program, but so were Dostoevsky and many prominent Russian literary and political figures in the nineteenth century. The key was not to ignore them but rather to set them in a proper critical context. Mindful of RL's policy guidelines, Paramonov studiously avoided Pobedonostsev's anti-Semitic writings or his explicit criticism of democracy and parliamentary rule. He also made clear at the outset that Pobedonostsev was a controversial figure who was reviled by Russian and Western liberals. And, significantly, the profile of Pobedonostsev was part of a long series of programs that featured conservative, liberal, and moderate Russian political figures.

Although Critchlow's criticism was highly selective, he raised a fundamentally important question: Was a conservative reading of Russian culture, history, and philosophy appropriate for a radio station receiving U.S. government funding? Did this funding obligate RL broadcasts to cover only those events in Russian history that echoed, if only faintly, American values of democracy, freedom of the press, and individual rights? Or did the mission of the surrogate radios allow for Russians to speak to other Russians within their own cultural world and adhering to their traditional values, even if those values went against the grain of American liberal beliefs? Critchlow believed that RL should focus primarily on those aspects of Russian political culture that echoed Western liberal traditions, but the incoming RFE/RL management, in line with the Reagan administration, favored nationalism, religion, and conservative philosophy as the most effective ways to counter the Soviet Union. This set up a turbulent period for the radios as they tried to reflect a broad range of political views, from liberal to conservative, knowing full well that this exposed them to selective criticism. *Russia: Yesterday, Today, and Tomorrow* offers a telling case study.

I decided the best way to approach my task was to understand the mindset of the conservative broadcasters and especially the main editor of the history program, Gleb Rahr. Born in 1922 to Russian parents, Rahr grew up in the Baltic States and was an urbane, multilingual, first-emigration journalist and political activist.[8] Fervently Orthodox and highly patriotic, Rahr had been a longtime member of an anti-Communist émigré organization, the National Alliance of Russian Solidarists (Natsional'no Trudovoi Soyuz Rossiiskikh Solidaristov, or NTS). Founded in 1930 in Belgrade, the NTS rejected both communism and liberal capitalism, preferring a centrally controlled government headed by a powerful leader and supported by a council of wise men. Their ideology was corporatism, which advocated the organization of society by corporate groups, such as agriculture, labor, military, science, or guild associations, on the basis of their common interests and contribution to the state. The NTS believed that if each group performed its functions harmoniously—like a human body (corpus)—under the guidance of an absolute leader, then society would prosper and the state would become powerful. This approach led them to reject parliamentary democracy and advance the notion of a temporary dictatorship in post-Communist Russia that would bring about the nation's moral and spiritual regeneration.[9] Such a political structure echoed Italian fascism, as well as Portuguese and Austrian corporatism. After the fall of communism, NTS established itself in Russia, and its philosophy found many adherents in Putin's Russia.

Well versed in Russian and European history, Rahr enjoyed the give-and-take of debate but was so firmly set in his views that no argument of mine could shake his faith in core conservative Russian values. When confronted with the issue of Russian aggression in Eastern Europe, for example, he would acknowledge it but would find a convoluted way of explaining why Russians had to invade Poland or the Baltic States to set up buffer states. Rahr, a deeply cultured man, would not consciously seek to offend Poles, Ukrainians, or other nationalities in the Soviet Union, but many of his heroes, among them Konstantin Pobedonostsev, Konstantin Leontiev, Ivan Ilyin, and Feodor Dostoevsky, were Russian nationalists who were highly critical of the West. When I would counter that many of Pobedonostsev's views were odious to Western liberals and that he would be presented "warts and all" in the West, Rahr would contend that Soviet publications presented *only* the negative side of Pobedonostsev, and hence RL's mission was to balance that view by presenting his other writings. This line of reasoning was often voiced by other conservative RL broadcasters. For example, they would argue that if Solzhenitsyn was labeled a fascist in the Soviet press and Russians did not have access to his writings, then RL's task would be to broadcast extended excerpts from his publications so that

Russians could make up their own mind. According to their logic, if Pobedonostsev was presented as thoroughly evil force in Russian history, then RL's duty was to fill out the picture with extensive excerpts from his writings so listeners could judge for themselves. If Soviet listeners were subjected only to the achievements of industrialization, then RL should talk about the pernicious effects of that industrialization on the environment. The mission of Rahr's history programs was to challenge the Soviet historical narrative and, by doing so, undercut the dominance of Communist ideology. Rahr did not fully appreciate that his approach left him open to charges of distorting history or that Western concepts of fairness and balance had their own power of persuasion. In the end, he would make the cuts demanded by American management but viewed them as the high price he had to pay for the opportunity to convey true Russian culture to his enslaved compatriots.

In the highly politicized world of the Russian diaspora, Rahr's program came under harsh criticism from the more liberally minded dissidents and émigrés. In her *Helsinki Watch Report*, Lyudmilla Alexeyeva took Rahr to task for "drumming into listeners the conceptions of the contemporary Russian nationalist movement as elaborated by Solzhenitsyn and his followers."[10] "Nearly every script about Tsarist Russia," Alexeyeva continued, "painted a picture of a wise government, a flourishing economy, and an ideal state of society.... When discussing relations between the authorities and society in Russia, [Rahr's] authors were unconditionally on the side of autocracy."[11] Alexeyeva's criticism of the history programs was picked up by journalists, diplomats, congressional staff, and academics, which resulted in a skewed picture of Radio Liberty programming. From today's perspective, with Soviet communism on the ash heap of history and Putin's Russia resurrecting its past in a *distinctly conservative, nationalist vein*, it is well worth examining RYTT broadcasts in a dispassionate way, noting their weaknesses along with their strengths and assessing what lasting impact they may have had on today's deliberations about Russian history.

From 1980 to 1984, Rahr produced over two hundred half-hour programs that covered many different periods of Russian history. These were not scholarly works but thoughtful examinations of seminal events and historical personages. The programs usually had three topics loosely connected thematically. Often, they would note anniversaries of important historical events and use the commemoration to draw on recent articles and publications for extended commentary. The topics ranged from the 600th anniversary of the battle at Kulikovo, when the Russian forces under Dmitri Donskoi defeated the Mongols for the first time, to the 350th anniversary of the founding of the University of Tartu (in today's Estonia), which played a significant role in the development of Russian higher education. More recent anniversaries included the February 1917 revolution, the killing of the tsarist family, and the Molotov-Ribbentrop Pact.

The programs of RYTT primarily examined subjects in Russian history that were ignored or distorted in Soviet scholarship. The Reverend Alexander Schmemann, for example, produced a series of talks on Russian intellectual history, focusing on the Slavophiles and early twentieth-century thinkers such as Nicholas Berdyaev and Petr Struve. Boris Paramonov developed a series of portraits of major conservative and moderate political figures that included the broadcast about Pobedonostsev. Other topics dealt with reform movements in late tsarist Russia, the legacy of Lenin and Stalin, and the policies and practices of the Soviet Union. Often the programs would conclude with a book review of a recent Western publication. Typical was an insightful review of Marc Raeff's *Understanding Imperial Russia*, which provided listeners with a dispassionate and erudite analysis of the complexities of their historical past. Equally, reviews of Russian authors, notably Roy Medvedev and Alexander Nekrich, offered fresh perspectives on the Soviet Union.

Like many patriotic, Orthodox nationalist thinkers, the contributors to RYTT rejected the Soviet version of Russian history, but they were also wary of the secular and analytical schools that dominated Western universities and intellectual circles. They readily hewed to Nikolai Karamzin's view of tsarist rule as the embodiment of the Russian nation and stressed the central role of Orthodoxy in Russian statehood. They were convinced that Western historians were too dismissive of the accomplishments of tsarist rule, especially its role in forming the

Russian state and its potential for reform. In their view, Western historians minimized the role of the Russian Orthodox Church and readily acknowledged the Soviet Union as a legitimate successor state and a representative of Russian culture. The Russian conservatives had deep respect for the older generation of Western historians, including Robert Conquest and Isaiah Berlin, and appreciated the works of contemporary historians who analyzed archival materials. But they could not countenance the revisionist historians who rejected the term *totalitarianism* and tended to cast the Stalinist period in a more benign light. Curiously, the one major historian who caused Russian conservatives the greatest heartburn was himself a conservative and a staunch anti-Communist: Richard Pipes.

A prolific author of over twenty books on Russian history, a distinguished Harvard professor, and a member of the National Security Council under Reagan, Pipes cast a long shadow over Russian studies and the radio broadcasts of RL and VOA. Many conservative Russians, including Rahr and Solzhenitsyn, agreed wholeheartedly with Pipes on two fundamental points: the Soviet Union was an expansionist, totalitarian state that posed an existential threat to the world, and the October Revolution was in fact a coup d'état foisted on the population by a small group of extremists. What the conservative thinkers could not abide was Pipes's central thesis—expressed most eloquently and acerbically in his book *Russia under the Old Regime*—that the origins of Soviet rule could be traced to tsarist policy and practice, even to early manifestations of totalitarian rule in fifteenth-century Muscovy Russia. Conservative Russians bristled at Pipes's disdain for Russian political and religious culture and traditional way of life, but what truly galled them was the last chapter of *Russia under the Old Regime*, entitled "Towards the Police State." Here Pipes stressed the sheer ineptitude and venality of the tsarist bureaucracy, mocked tsarist rituals, reminded his readers that Russia had created the first domestic political police force, and argued that Russia differed fundamentally from all states in Europe because it had a poorly developed concept of private property. According to Pipes, the relationship between state and subject in tsarist Russia differed little from that in the Soviet Union. "Since 1845," he wrote, "Russian Criminal Codes have each contained a political 'omnibus' clause worded with such imprecision that under its terms the organs of state security have been able to incarcerate citizens guilty of crimes no more specific than intent to 'weaken,' 'undermine,' or 'arouse doubts' or 'disrespect' for existing authority. A juxtaposition of such clauses from three consecutive Criminal Codes—1845, 1927, and 1960—gives an instructive demonstration of the continuity of the police mentality in Russia irrespective of the nature of the regime."[12] To add sting to his analysis, Pipes concluded that the Russian Criminal Code of 1845 inspired similar legislation in Fascist Italy and Nazi Germany and "became to totalitarianism what the Magna Carta was to liberty." Pipes acknowledged that the Great Reforms of the 1860s represented a major corrective and opened a path to a more just society, but blamed the radical intelligentsia, terrorists, and the conservative backlash in the 1870s for sabotaging true reform. In Pipes's conception, after the assassination of Alexander II, his successor, Alexander III, instituted the legal structure of a "full police state."[13] But tsarist Russia was too incompetent to fully realize the police state that it had set in motion. In Pipes's view, Lenin and Stalin simply took the basic tsarist police structure and through terror imposed it on the whole country.

Many Russians of varying political persuasion found Pipes's thesis not only highly questionable but also personally demeaning. To draw a direct line from Muscovy Russia to late tsarist rule and then to Lenin and Stalin was to put into question their core beliefs and their very identity as Russians. How could a tsarist government they respected, a tsar whom the Russian Orthodox Church canonized, and a religious culture they revered be equated with a vicious, murderous regime that killed tens of millions of its own citizens? No one was more vocal in denouncing Pipes's thesis than Alexandr Solzhenitsyn. Writing in *Foreign Affairs*, he stated:

Richard Pipes's book, *Russia under the Old Regime*, may stand as typical of a long series of such pronouncements that distort the image of Russia. Pipes shows a complete disregard for the spiritual life of the Russian people and its view of the world—Christianity.

He examines entire centuries of Russian history without reference to Russian Orthodoxy. . . . Instead of being shown a living being of a nation, we witness the dissection of a corpse. Pipes devotes one chapter to the Church, which he sees only as a civil institution and treats it in the spirit of Soviet atheistic propaganda. . . . The author willfully ignores those events, persons or aspects of Russian life which would not prove conducive to his thesis, which is that the entire history of Russia has had but a single purpose—the creation of a police state. . . . The book allows only one possible conclusion to be drawn: that the Russian nation is anti-human in its essence, that it has been good for nothing throughout its thousand years of history, and that as far as any future is concerned it is obviously a hopeless case.[14]

Solzhenitsyn was so outraged by Pipes's interpretation of Russian history that he even turned down an invitation to meet with President Reagan, a politician he deeply admired, because Pipes, at the time a member of the NSC staff, would be present.[15] Pipes returned the favor by asserting that Solzhenitsyn was unschooled in history and accused him of being an anti-Semitic Russian nationalist who sought to blame communism on Jewish revolutionaries rather than on Russian political culture.

Soon after the publication of Solzhenitsyn's essay, Rahr addressed Pipes's interpretation of Russian history in two programs. The first, broadcast on July 2, 1980, began with a report on the trial and execution of Marshall Tukhachevsky and the purges of the upper ranks of the Soviet military. Based on Robert Conquest's book *The Great Terror: Stalin's Purges of the Thirties*, this segment painted a graphic picture of Stalinist rule. It was then followed by a report by Boris Shragin, a well-known émigré writer, about a raging debate in émigré circles between those who believed that the Soviet Union was a logical extension of tsarist rule and those who saw it as an aberration, an irreparable rift in Russian history. Shragin reminded his listeners that this topic had been first broached in a samizdat work, *Metonoia*, that included a Russian translation of the last chapter of *Russia under the Old Regime*, "Towards the Police State." This issue provoked heated debate in the Russian dissident community, with several liberals agreeing with many of Pipes's assertions and the nationalists rejecting the thesis in toto. That debate gained international scope with the publication of Solzhenitsyn's critique in *Foreign Affairs*, which prompted additional attacks on Pipes by Russian émigrés, principally Vladislav Krasnov, a teacher of Russian at the Defense Language Institute in Monterey, California. In the RL broadcast, Shragin carefully laid out the arguments on both sides, noting that Krasnov merely amplified Solzhenitsyn's emotional response while Pipes reiterated that political cultures evolve over time but are always tied to their past and that new regimes are not simply created ex nihilo. At the conclusion of the piece, Rahr told his listeners that this discussion would be continued in a week and then switched to the last segment of the program, a profile of a liberal Russian reformer, Vasili Krivoshein, who had worked in the latter years of tsarist rule. With a touch of irony, Rahr suggested that perhaps a more thorough understanding of the agricultural reforms introduced by Stolypin and Krivoshein could help to settle the debate between Pipes and Solzhenitsyn.

One week later, on July 9, 1980, Rahr returned to the question of whether Soviet policies and actions were imbedded in Russian political culture or were the product of Communist ideology. He began the program with a short segment on Soviet history, focusing on the fiftieth anniversary of the 16th Party Congress that cemented Stalin's control over the Communist Party and laid the groundwork for the collectivization of the peasantry. Then Rahr segued to Shragin's report on the key debate, this time emphasizing Krasnov's rebuttal of Pipes's views. An attentive listener to the program could not help but sense that Shragin, while trying to be an honest broker, was beginning to side with Pipes. As he summarized Pipes's main arguments, his tone became assertive in stressing Russia's aggressive foreign policy, and he even stated, quoting Pipes, that Soviet ambitions to reach the Indian Ocean had been first developed by tsarist generals in the nineteenth century. On the completion of the report, Rahr broke with his usual calm tone and chided Shragin, asserting that tsarist policies in the Balkans were driven exclusively by humanitarian concerns for fellow

Orthodox Christians and that Russian expansion into Central Asia was dictated by the rules of the Great Game, the rivalry between the British and Russian empires in the nineteenth century. Despite the passions that Pipes's thesis evoked, RL presented both sides of the argument.

In conducting research for this book, I listened to many of Rahr's broadcasts and came to appreciate how challenging it was to develop history programs for Russian listeners in the USSR. Many older Russian émigrés saw communism as an alien ideology and hence did not believe that Soviet reform movements could bring about positive political change. Equally, they felt that Pipes's vision of a power-hungry totalitarian empire was not only wrong but also self-defeating. To read Pipes's works on air, as Pipes himself had urged VOA and RL to do, would be tantamount to telling Russians that major reforms were doomed at the outset. Why struggle to defeat communism if a successor regime would most likely behave in the same way? Reports on the gulag, the Great Terror, or collectivization made for depressing radio programming and reminded listeners yet again of their tragic history. Unlike the history programs of RFE that could offer their listeners hope (as well as solace) by casting Poland or the Baltic States as victims of Russian and Soviet aggression, the Russian Service had to contend with a Soviet political culture that was despotic, imperialist, and often cruel to its own people. Appealing to democratic values might be an effective way to reach a small disenchanted urban elite but probably meant little for the vast majority of the Russian population. Democracy, after all, was a thin reed in Russian historical discourse and practice, and there were few if any historical examples of democratic rule one could point to in Russia's past. Moreover, while Poland, Hungary, and the Czech Republic saw themselves as fully European, Russia had always had an ambiguous relationship with Europe. Its high culture and academic institutions were thoroughly European; its politics and religion stood in opposition to the West. For centuries the Russian Orthodox Church inveighed against the heretical West and presented itself as bearer of true Christianity. To further complicate matters, the Soviet Union was an empire, and even the most fervent anti-Communists at RL were proud of that empire and dreamed of it becoming a Russian one.

Faced with such a unique set of challenges, Rahr and his contributors cast *RYTT* as a *message of hope*, a program intended to show Russians that they were a dynamic nation with a glorious past and the potential to be a leader in the world. Rahr often mentioned to me that his ideal listener was a Russian military officer, deeply loyal, proud of Russia's achievements, maybe even religious, but thoroughly disgusted with Communist rule that was destroying his country. To reach that listener, *RYTT* focused on the reform movements in the second half of the nineteenth century and early twentieth century and the vibrancy of Russian intellectual traditions, including the role of Orthodoxy in shaping Russian identity. Virtually every broadcast under Rahr's editorship dealt with at least one of these themes. Rahr tried to show his listeners that the most hopeful periods in Russian history brought together a strong state with individual freedom, economic opportunities, and social reforms. His hero was Petr Stolypin (1862–1911), and he devoted many programs to him and to his followers. Even programs that did not explicitly mention Stolypin relied on his ideas as the standard against which to measure other political movements in Russia.

One of the last major statesmen of Imperial Russia, Stolypin served as prime minister from 1906 to 1911, when he was assassinated by a revolutionary, Dmitry Bogrov. Faced with mounting domestic terrorism, a fractured duma, and an ineffectual tsar, Stolypin sought to unite Russia and save the monarchy by resorting to martial law and, at the same time, introducing far-reaching agrarian and economic reforms that would stem peasant and urban unrest. Stolypin's vision of Russia's future projected a powerful state led by a strong leader who supported a market-oriented economy, the protection of private property, effective local government, and basic human rights. Stolypin was not a democrat in the Western sense of the word, but he clearly wanted to make Russia a more European country that guaranteed full civil equality for all the peoples of the Russia Empire, including Jews and national minorities. For many Russians, especially conservatives, his death marked the end of any hope for a reformed tsarist government.

On July 30, 1980, Rahr devoted the better part of *RYTT* to Stolypin. After a short segment about the disaster of Soviet collectivization,

Boris Paramonov presented a detailed profile that described Stolypin's land reform, the break-up of communal ownership (*obshchina*), and the granting of private property to the peasants. Stolypin believed that constitutions, laws, and press freedoms, trumpeted by the liberals, meant little if the majority of Russians lived in abysmal conditions and toiled as though they were still serfs. Having lived in the western provinces of the Russian Empire—today's Lithuania—he saw firsthand how private property and a market economy nurtured a more prosperous and engaged citizenry. Significantly, Paramonov reminded his listeners that Stolypin's land reforms were opposed by the Far Right that wanted to preserve Russia's communal roots, by the Far Left that rejected all forms of private ownership, and even by the liberal Kadet Party that was in favor of expropriating the land of the wealthy aristocracy. To illustrate how radical Stolypin's program was, Rahr invited Arkady Stolypin, Petr Stolypin's only surviving son, then in his eighties and living in France, to read from a correspondence between his father and Leo Tolstoy about the land reforms. A family friend, Tolstoy sent several letters to Stolypin, castigating him for trying to destroy Russia's age-old customs of common land ownership and driving Russia toward European norms. In his response to Tolstoy, Stolypin respectfully disagreed, arguing that only private property widely distributed and protected by law could save Russia from revolution and ruin. This exchange of ideas, forcefully and eloquently presented, was among the more effective RL history programs, giving listeners an insider's look into the critical question facing Russia in the early twentieth century: Would it remain an outlier pursuing its own unique political path, or would it adopt the norms of a Western market economy?

A critical Western listener could take issue with some of the points made in this program, in particular, the fanciful assertion that by 1906 Russia was a constitutional monarchy. There was also gratuitous criticism of the Kadet Party and the radical intelligentsia, but the program as a whole illustrated the fundamental mission of RL: to provide listeners with factual information about their past that would help them conceive a better future for themselves. The broadcast presented a serious examination of how land reform could function in Russia and made a strong case for the importance of the rule of law.

Stolypin's focus on an entrepreneurial market-based economy had a profound impact on post-Communist Russia, far exceeding the expectations of Rahr and his cohort of writers. In the early 1990s Boris Fyodorov, a prominent member of the state duma and later minister of finance, became a devotee of Stolypin, collecting his works and popularizing his ideas. In 1995 Boris Nemtsov, then governor of Nizhny Novgorod, urged Russians to adopt Stolypin's reforms: "Petr Stolypin's reforms produced astounding results. . . . Between 1906 and 1915, thanks to the efforts of Stolypin's farmers, the productivity of crops nationwide grew by 14 percent, in Siberia by 25 percent. In 1912, Russia's grain exports exceeded by 30 percent those of Argentina, the United States, and Canada combined."[16] Not to be outdone, Putin, in his first state-of-the-union address on June 8, 2000, referred to only one historical figure, Petr Stolypin, noting how he "combined patriotic responsibility for the future of the country with basic civil freedoms."[17] Throughout his tenure as president and prime minister, Putin made numerous references to Stolypin as a model politician and encouraged the creation of the Stolypin Foundation in Moscow. In 2011, on the one hundredth anniversary of Stolypin's assassination, Putin praised Stolypin for his "unbending will" in striving to ensure economic growth in a difficult period in Russia's history. He then expressed the need for a statue of Stolypin at the entrance to the Russian Government Building (the "White House"). As word spread in the 1990s and early 2000s about Stolypin's vision for Russia, he became a popular figure not only among the emerging urban elite but also in the country as a whole. By 2008, in a nationwide poll to identify the most significant Russian historical figures, Petr Stolypin came in second, a result that would have pleased the conservative writers at RL.[18]

In 1984 the editorship of *RYTT* was transferred to a recent Soviet émigré and a professionally trained historian, Vladimir Tolz. Although relying on many of the same freelance contributors, Tolz reconceptualized the broadcasts. He continued with profiles of major nineteenth-century Russian political figures and noted major anniversaries, but he shed overt political messaging, invited major Russian writers to participate in discussions on air, and reached out to Western experts. Early in his tenure, Tolz covered a major Slavic studies conference in Washington DC and interviewed several prominent historians, including Richard Pipes. With a light touch and in fluent Russian, Pipes explained on air how he approached the study of Russian history and why émigré attacks on him distorted his scholarship. Tolz also sought out American professors who spoke native Russian, including Boris Gasparov (Berkeley) and Herman Ermolaev (Princeton), who were able to give Russian listeners a deeper understanding of how Western scholars analyzed Russia and the Soviet Union. But most striking was the absence of an editorial position. As a general rule, Tolz's broadcasts presented different points of view about Russia's past and future. Liberals and conservatives of various hues were welcomed on air so long as they presented fact-based, thoughtful analyses. In any given month, one could hear Nikita Struve speak about Orthodoxy and the Slavophile movement and Mikhail Vozlensky, a former high-ranking Soviet official, discuss corruption and intraparty politics in the Soviet Union. Prominent dissidents and writers, among them Vladimir Voinovich, Vasily Aksyonov, and Vladimir Bukovsky, were frequent guests. So too were such American scholars as Murray Feshbach and Robert Daniels. Tolz's intention was to offer Russian listeners a variety of different approaches to Russia's past and future. As the policy of glasnost grew bolder in the late 1980s, Soviet scholars began to participate in RYTT, and that made the broadcasts even more relevant for the audience.

Significantly, Tolz's broadcasts shifted away from some of Rahr's favorite subjects, including Stolypin and lesser known Orthodox thinkers. Gone were the conservative émigré conceptions of Russia that had been imbedded in many of Rahr's programs. Instead, RYTT turned to the urban educated elite that Rahr had generally avoided. Tolz selected subjects that would resonate with younger, better educated listeners. When, for example, he marked major anniversaries, such as the eight hundredth anniversary of *The Tale of Igor's Campaign*, an epic poem in Old East Slavic, he presented a linguistic analysis of the work and then placed it in the context of current Soviet scholarship. Typical of his approach was Herman Ermolaev's two-part analysis of how Iuri Trifonov's works were able to circumvent Soviet censorship and deal subtly with Stalin's reign of terror. In Tolz's hands, *RYTT* became a dispassionate, comprehensive, and judicious program that offered listeners a serious, often sophisticated examination of their culture from both a Russian and Western perspective. These broadcasts stand as one of the finest chapters in RL history.

It would be easy to conclude that *RYTT* under Gleb Rahr's editorship was a throwback to an earlier, more aggressive period in RL history, while Tolz's programming showed a maturing, more professional radio sound. Many RFE/RL executives and outside evaluators would have concurred in this judgment. But during the Cold War both approaches coexisted. There was the passionate, politically engaged, culturally exclusive, and emotionally "Russian" sound ("our country," "our people") and the journalistically balanced, measured, dispassionate Western voice. Rahr's programming appealed to his core listeners and tried to buoy their spirits, sometimes pandering to their biases as well. His aim was to give his audience hope that Russia could emerge from under the rubble of communism and resurrect its culture and religion, asserting its rightful place among the great nations of the world. When I would challenge Rahr, noting that his approach could alienate many listeners, he countered that those listeners could easily find programs to their liking on BBC or VOA, but only RL could reach the vast majority of conservative, Orthodox, patriotic Russians. And, he asserted, communism would be defeated only if that ignored majority were to rise up against the regime. Today's Russia clearly shows how prescient he was. If one were to conduct an internet search in Russian of Pobedonostsev in 2021, one would easily find videos and articles, some citing the very texts that Critchlow had found objectionable in the early 1980s. There is even a popular podcast by a young Russian who cites Pobedonostsev's diatribe about democracy and urges his compatriots to adopt Pobedonostsev's approach to politics. Putin himself has expressed admiration for many of the nineteenth-century figures that Rahr had presented in his programming, notably Stolypin, the émigré philosopher Ivan Ilyin, and the reactionary philosopher Konstantin Leontiev.

In hindsight, it is clear that Rahr identified an important audience in the Soviet Union that believed that communism was an alien ideology and responded positively to a new nationalist spirit.

If Rahr's programs were part of a long tradition of politically engaged broadcasts, Tolz's programs hewed closer to the purist line of balanced, unemotional, and scholarly broadcasts. A broad sampling of RL broadcasts from the 1950s to the 1990s would reveal many programs that were apolitical, dispassionate, and judicious in their assessments of Russian politics. From its earliest days, RL invited important Western scholars to participate in its broadcasts and reached out to both liberal and conservative thinkers. The noncontroversial nature of these broadcasts may have kept them out of the public eye, but that does not diminish their major contribution to RL programming. At its best, Radio Liberty tried to be "all things to all listeners" within the framework of fact-based programming. In hundreds of hours of listening to RL Russian broadcasts, I never came across any conspiracy theories or outright distortions of history, though on occasion I would spot questionable political judgments. But given that RL was on the front lines of the war of ideas and faced a menacing foe that attacked it every day in the media, the broadcasters showed remarkable restraint and adhered to high journalistic standards.

6

Solzhenitsyn

Shortly after joining VOA, I received an unexpected phone call from Natalia Dmitrievna Solzhenitsyn. I had met her in 1979 when I was asked to be an interpreter at a press conference in Montpelier, Vermont, at which Representative James Jeffords introduced a prominent Russian dissident, Alexander "Alik" Ginzburg. A poet, journalist, human rights activist, and close friend of the Solzhenitsyn family, Ginzburg was among the early dissidents in the Soviet Union. He was responsible for the first samizdat literary magazine, *Phoenix*, and, in 1965, for the documentation of the trial of Yuli Daniel and Andrei Sinyavsky, published as the *White Book*. Ginzburg was sentenced several times by the Soviet authorities and spent years in the gulag, but each time after his release he would resume his human rights work. In 1972, together with Alexandr Solzhenitsyn, he formed the Fund to Aid Political Prisoners, which distributed the royalties from the publication of *The Gulag Archipelago* to the families of political and religious prisoners across the Soviet Union. In 1978 he was rearrested and this time sentenced to eight years of hard labor. Through Solzhenitsyn's intercession, the U.S. government was able to exchange Ginzburg for two Soviet spies and literally overnight he landed in Vermont. The press conference went well, and we spent the rest of the day discussing the political situation in the Soviet Union. I met with Alik Ginzburg many times afterward but didn't see Natalia Dmitrievna and considered our meeting to be a one-time business matter.

When Natalia Dmitrievna called me in early 1984, she recalled our meeting in Vermont but said she was calling for a different reason. Alexandr Isayevich, as she referred to him in public, had noted significant improvements in the broadcasts of the VOA Russian Service and wanted to offer us an exclusive interview and extensive readings from his latest work, *August 1914*. Here was a harsh critic of VOA who only a few years earlier had lambasted the Russian broadcasts in *Foreign Affairs*, calling them frivolous and inconsequential. Now he was offering us, not other international broadcasters, a radio exclusive. Natalia Dmitrievna explained that I needed to travel to their home in Vermont with a radio engineer and spend at least three days with Alexandr Isayevich as he read chapters from his novel to me. I could also do an extensive interview with him on literary and cultural topics.

Only when I hung up the phone did it dawn on me that I had just committed the VOA to broadcast an author who had been virtually banned in the Ford and Carter years. And this was a world-famous writer who could not be edited and had a reputation of being demanding and dismissive of government bureaucrats. I called the VOA front office and explained to the secretary that I had to see Kenneth Tomlinson, the director, and his senior deputy, Ambassador Melvin Levitsky, right away. After being ushered into Tomlinson's office, I recounted the phone call and explained that Solzhenitsyn was the most famous Russian writer alive and whatever he said or did was front-page news throughout the world. Our Russian audience had doubtless heard a great deal about him but in all likelihood had never heard his voice or extended excerpts from his writings. By broadcasting his voice, we would make literary and political history and show our major rivals, principally BBC and Radio Liberty, that VOA had come of age. Tomlinson and Levitsky readily agreed and told me that our parent agency, USIA, and the White House would be supportive. However, they cautioned that there could be protests from advocates of détente in the State Department and on Capitol Hill and promised to maintain a firewall to protect us from undue criticism.

In May 1984 I traveled to Cavendish, a small village in the bucolic hills of southern Vermont. After checking in at the only hostelry in town, I drove to the Solzhenitsyn compound, some ten miles away, until I came to a massive steel gate and a tall fence ringed with barbed wire. In an effort to guard his privacy, Solzhenitsyn had built a veritable fortress. After I entered the prescribed code in the call box, the gate opened, and I proceeded along another dirt road to a modern, chalet-style house with large windows, open decks, and stunning views of verdant Vermont.

Alexandr Isayevich came out to greet me and immediately took me to his library, a separate building where he worked. Prerevolutionary editions of Russian books were strewn about, as were photocopies of early twentieth-century Russian newspapers. In an old Russian tradition, Solzhenitsyn took out a bottle of vodka and suggested that we each have a shot to break the ice and then get down to business. Rather than talking about our project, he began by peppering me with questions— Where did I grow up? Who were my parents? How did I learn Russian? He was curious to know who I was and tried to figure out if I would be able to understand his literary works. The fact that my paternal grandfather was a noted Orthodox theologian and my maternal grandfather had been a pilot in the Russian air force in World War I assured Alexandr Isayevich of my bona fides. Initially Solzhenitsyn showed little warmth, but having decided that I qualified to be an intelligent interlocutor, he began to relax and invited me to join him for an old-fashioned Russian family dinner. We went to the main house, where I greeted Natalia Dmitrievna and met her mother and their three boys, then teenagers. After one of the boys said a prayer, we all sat down to an informal home-cooked meal. The conversation was light; the boys talked about their school day; we chatted about Vermont, my home state, and its old tradition of town meetings, which Solzhenitsyn heartily approved. After dinner, Solzhenitsyn's son Ignat, already a promising musician, played several piano pieces as we drank tea and chatted in a warm, familial setting. I felt I had been magically transported to an idealized country estate somewhere in the heartland of Russia.

Early the next day we began our work. I started with a far-ranging interview, asking Alexandr Isayevich to explain the origins of the novel *August 1914*, part of a cycle of novels called *The Red Wheel*, and why he wanted to focus on the assassination of the Russian prime minister, Petr Stolypin. "This is a long narrative about the fate of Russia during the revolution," Solzhenitsyn began, "not of separate people or even separate classes of people, but of all of Russia as a whole, from the peasant in the remote village, from the worker in the Petrograd factory, to the tsar; from Petersburg to the far corners of Russia."[1] Solzhenitsyn explained that he had first conceived a novel about the passing of Imperial Russia as early as 1936, when he was still a student, and originally planned to write about the October Revolution. But as he read more about the events of 1917, he realized that to analyze the "October coup" (as he referred to it) required a thorough understanding of the February Revolution, and that in turn brought him to World War I. Since World War I was an unwieldy subject, Solzhenitsyn decided to focus on one major battle, the Samsonov catastrophe, which formed the heart of the first volume, *August 1914*. "I worked on this battle in great detail," Solzhenitsyn told me, "but it turned out I could not start from there either because all the historical figures, all the characters, the contemporaries of that time, carried the past within them, that last decade prior to World War I, and you cannot understand the course of events if you don't go back still further and explain how those people were formed, how public attitudes and historical interpretations were formed. So I went back to the Stolypin era."

As I listened to Solzhenitsyn's detailed explanation of the genesis of his work, I could see that the very mention of Stolypin's name brought a smile to his face. "The Stolypin era," he would utter with great enthusiasm, "what a remarkable era . . . only five or six years in all. . . . After being rocked by revolution, Russia was almost in ruins. She pulled herself together and returned to normalcy again in an incredibly short time: five years. This is the part I will be reading from the book."

The actual writing of the multivolume work began in earnest only in the 1960s. By 1970 Solzhenitsyn had finished the first volume, *August 1914*, and submitted it for publication only to have the Soviet censors reject it. After he was exiled from the USSR in 1972, he returned to the novel, spending considerable time researching early twentieth-century Russian history and revising the original version of *August 1914* by adding a lengthy prequel about Stolypin and his assassin, Dmitry Bogrov. Based on his research, Solzhenitsyn became convinced that Stolypin was the last best hope for Russia and that his death marked the end of reforms that could have transformed Russia into a stable, prosperous European state. He concluded by saying that the chapters on Stolypin were his most successful attempt at a cloak-and-dagger story that tried to reveal the mindset of terrorists.

Before commencing our recording, I asked Solzhenitsyn about his use of historical documents, mostly newspapers and memoirs that were so fundamental to describing the minutia of Russian history. "There were many publications in the early Soviet years, but by 1928 they were drying up," he responded. He continued:

> And I was able to use part of this material when I was still living in the USSR. . . . When I arrived in the West, an enormous amount of literature opened up to me: an abundance of émigré literature and even more unpublished memoirs. I appealed to the old emigration to write memoirs about the revolution and received almost five hundred works, containing over three hundred eyewitness accounts of the revolution. . . . When you read them, you have the impression that you are living at that time, talking with the participants of those events. . . . And here in the United States there are excellent libraries with the richest archives on Russian history, especially at the Hoover Institution. There I was able to get many memoirs, publications, newspapers. I now have microfilms of all the newspapers of that time in Petersburg and Moscow, for every day of the February Revolution.

The excerpts he would read, he said proudly, were written in the United States and relied heavily on sources available in U.S. libraries. That made the chapters in a sense American and, he added with a chuckle, even appropriate for VOA. At that point, Alexandr Isayevich sat down at his desk, and I across from him. And for three days, with only occasional short breaks, he read his tale in a firm, "radio voice." When he had finished, we had over twenty hours of recording from which we would fashion a long series of broadcasts.

The first part of the Stolypin chapters, roughly fifty pages of text, is a dramatic portrayal of the young anarchist, Dmitry Bogrov, who shot Stolypin point-blank on September 5, 1911, in the Kyiv opera house, where the tsar and his entourage were celebrating the fiftieth anniversary of the emancipation of the serfs. Drawing on documents, court records, and private letters, Solzhenitsyn painstakingly recreated the last fateful days in Kyiv, including the exact locations of Stolypin, the tsar, Bogrov, and the Okhranka, the tsarist secret police. His aim was to present a hyperrealistic description of the plot to kill Stolypin and to bring the reader into the vortex of the assassination plot. To do this, Solzhenitsyn drew on common literary techniques, principally stream of consciousness and internal dialogue, to delve into Bogrov's inner thoughts, worries, and aims. Like Raskolnikov in Dostoevsky's *Crime and Punishment* or Nikolai Ableukhov in Andrey Bely's *Petersburg*, Bogrov is torn between the fear of arrest and his determination to follow through with his daring criminal act. He questions his motives, devises intricate schemes to confuse the Okhranka, and fantasizes about his role in Russian history as the superman who would push Russia off the precipice and into the maelstrom of the revolution. With an actor's gift of inflection, Solzhenitsyn imbued Bogrov's inner struggles with emotion and conviction. By reading his own text, akin to a composer performing his own composition, Solzhenitsyn was able to create a personal radio drama that touched the emotions of the listeners and made them *feel* the full enormity of the terrorist act and its tragic consequences for Russia. By the time Bogrov pulls the trigger in the Kyiv opera house, we, the listeners, have been with him at every step; can sense his mood, his worries; know every hallway in the opera house; can identify every Okhranka policeman; and know the exact spot where Stolypin was shot.

After the fatal shot, Solzhenitsyn abruptly switches styles, and the second part of the Stolypin chapters is set in a different literary world. The traditional techniques of inner monologue, dramatic ellipses, and metaphorical writing are replaced by a documentary novel with its everyday language, historical personages, newspaper clippings, duma speeches, private letters, and government decrees. Gone are intrigue, dramatic tension, and naked emotion. In their place, we find a hagiographic portrait of Stolypin as the ideal statesman who could have built a powerful Russia. In these chapters, we no longer see Solzhenitsyn's artistic flair, biting irony, or any shades of gray. Instead, we are presented with a conservative, nationalist interpretation of the early twentieth century of Russian history.

In essence, the nationalists viewed Nicholas II as a weak tsar but a good man, the revolutionaries as devils who wanted to destroy Russia, the duma as an ineffectual legislative body prone to bickering and posturing, and the tsarist bureaucracy as wholly incompetent and corrupt. The conservative nationalists contended that Russia needed a strong leader who could save the monarchy, defeat the revolutionaries, strengthen the Russian Orthodox Church, and introduce economic reforms. And they found their ideal hero in Petr Stolypin. This vision gained currency among the first wave of the Russian emigration in the 1920s. It became an integral part of the political programs of émigrés and, after the fall of communism, found adherents in Russia. As noted in the earlier chapter on history programming, Stolypin became a revered figure in post-Communist Russia. For that reason, it was not surprising that shortly after assuming the Presidency in 2000, Putin visited Solzhenitsyn at his home outside of Moscow and Russian central television showcased their discussion of Stolypin and his vision for Russia. Putin even added that "Stolypin's views need to be known by all Russians."[2]

Listening to Solzhenitsyn depict the "savior of Russia" reminded me of my earlier discussions with Gleb Rahr at Radio Liberty when I would argue that an idealized portrait of Stolypin was not convincing and could be viewed as a caricature. Now I had to contend with a Nobel laureate who was creating that same idealized picture. For hours Solzhenitsyn intoned about Stolypin's accomplishments, from his land reforms and civic freedoms to his crushing of the terrorists. In Solzhenitsyn's rendering, Stolypin could do no wrong. Even his use of courts martial to allow the quick arrest and execution of suspected revolutionaries was presented as a necessary and positive step in saving Russia.

When Solzhenitsyn resorted to a more literary style, he depicted Stolypin as the apotheosis of maleness. Stolypin was strong, athletic, decisive, handsome, fearless, selfless, and duty-bound. He was the proud father of five children; he rode horses; he never flagged; he was a fabled Russian *bogatyr* (giant hero). When Fedor Rodichev, a Kadet member of the duma, accused Stolypin of harsh measures to quell terrorist activity and called the noose "Stolypin's necktie," Solzhenitsyn's style conveyed a sense of indignation. "Stolypin was not the kind of minister," Solzhenitsyn wrote, "who would respond to his defamer by seeking the appropriate recourse in law. Here he was in his full glory. To answer the reckless, unrestrained, dissolute freedom of speech of the 20th century, he had to act like a man and like a knight challenge him to a duel."[3]

Despite Solzhenitsyn's effusive praise of Stolypin, the central message of the documentary-novel was to present a vision of a future Russia. To draw on a term from Socialist Realism, Stolypin was the "positive hero," whom readers should venerate. Solzhenitsyn stressed that Stolypin rejected both the Far Right and the Far Left. Significantly, both the anti-Semitic Union of the Russian People and Left anarchists considered him an archenemy. Stolypin believed in civic rights and equality before the law and wanted to work with the duma, but he was not a Western democrat. He was an imperialist and monarchist at heart who believed that the tsar embodied the core values of "Russianess" that could keep a multiethnic empire from disintegrating. Stolypin's life was dedicated to a great Russia with Russian culture, religion, and language as the building blocks of the Russian State. To achieve this grand vision, Russia needed a strong leader at the helm who governed with a firm hand and respected the law but could breach it if the state was in danger.

In Solzhenitsyn's artistic vision, Stolypin was not just a political strongman. He embodied an aura of sainthood and martyrdom. In hagiographical literature, it is common for the author not only to provide an account of the hero's miraculous deeds and accomplishments but also to depict in excruciating detail his martyrdom. In the Christian tradition, deeply embedded in Russian culture, it is suffering that ensures heroic stature. In keeping with this tradition, whether consciously or not, Solzhenitsyn described Stolypin's defeat and humiliation in the duma. In spring of 1911 Stolypin circumvented the duma by pushing through a law allowing Russia's western provinces—today's Poland, Lithuania, and Ukraine—to form local governing councils (or *zemstvos*). Although this was a minor matter, it was not the first time Stolypin had technically broken the law to enact measures he thought were necessary for the welfare of Russia. This time, however, the duma rose up against him in anger. With sorrow and indignation, Solzhenitsyn recounted how unfair this public trial had been. Here was the positive hero toiling ceaselessly for the good of Russia, only to have the duma members, preoccupied with their petty interests, fail to appreciate his work in behalf of Russia. Drawing extensively on duma speeches, Solzhenitsyn described Stolypin's public mortification. The first attack came from Vasiliy Maklakov, a member of the liberal Kadet Party, who began by cataloging Stolypin's illegal and arbitrary actions that had turned Russia into "Stolypin's patrimony" (*votchina*). He accused him of violating the letter of the law and thereby weakening Russia's rule of law. This attack from the Left was followed by a more vicious assault from the Right. Vladimir Purishkevich, an ultranationalist, mocked Stolypin for his desire to give Jews and national minorities full civic equality, claiming that Stolypin's pet project of setting up zemstvos in the western provinces was simply a ploy to stir up Polish nationalism. As a saintly figure, Stolypin stoically endured those blows—"slaps in the face," in Solzhenitsyn's words. But Solzhenitsyn himself could not help but come to Stolypin's defense. He countered Maklakov's and Purishkevich's accusations by claiming that Stolypin was the wise leader who stood above party politics, supported the tsar, and was motivated solely by his dedication to a great Russia. He needed the support of the duma and not bickering parliamentarians interested in a game of legal technicalities. In defending Stolypin, Solzhenitsyn displayed his utter disdain for party politics and his belief that chaotic democracy, a stultifying tsarist bureaucracy, and an ineffectual Nicholas II actually destroyed Stolypin. Bogrov's bullet was simply the final blow.

Solzhenitsyn ended his hagiography with a detailed description of Stolypin's vision of a future Russia, based on notes and letters he had found in the archives. In his version, Stolypin envisioned a powerful and prosperous Russia by the 1920s that included industrialization and the development of an entrepreneurial economy. He made plans for universal education, world-class universities, a new banking system open to foreign investors, and a foreign policy dedicated to world peace. Solzhenitsyn noted that Stolypin saw the United States as Russia's true ally and was planning to invite U.S. senators, congressmen, and journalists to Russia shortly before he was killed. Stolypin even sketched out a world parliament that would adjudicate disputes between countries and create a world bank of sorts that would lend money to countries in times of dire need. In short, Solzhenitsyn painted a utopia that in his mind only Stolypin could have conceived and implemented. But the revolutionaries, short-sighted politicians, and corrupt and incompetent bureaucrats destroyed this national potential and put Russia on the path to eventual Bolshevik rule.

After this lengthy documentary-novel, Solzhenitsyn turned to the third part of the Stolypin chapters: a fast-paced narrative that traced the days and hours before the assassination from Stolypin's perspective. As preparations for the Kyiv celebration unfolded, Stolypin remained hard at work on important government matters while the tsar was preoccupied with the pomp and circumstance surrounding his visit. Though warned of a possible attempt on the life of Stolypin, the Okhranka officials continued to muddle along, interested primarily in their own comfort. No special precautions were taken and, according to Solzhenitsyn, the bureaucracy sensed that Stolypin was in disfavor and therefore saw little to be gained by taking extra protective measures. Stolypin was unguarded during the second intermission when Bogrov walked up to him. In Solzhenitsyn's flight of fantasy, Stolypin recognized Bogrov as the assassin and leapt at him, trying to disarm him. But Bogrov pulled the trigger twice, pinning Stolypin to the orchestra railing. Bleeding profusely, Stolypin looked up to the royal box where the tsar and his family were seated and muttered, "What will now happen with Russia?" Struggling, he tried to bless the tsar, but couldn't lift his right hand. "Then Stolypin raised his left hand," Solzhenitsyn writes, "and with it, in a measured way, religiously, without hurrying, blessed the Tsar with the sign of the cross and collapsed."[4] As Stolypin lay dying, Solzhenitsyn noted, the tsar did not walk up to him, but simply turned away, not realizing that those fateful bullets had killed the Romanov dynasty as well.

For several days, Stolypin struggled to stay alive, and during that time he hoped the tsar would visit him so he could offer his advice, but the tsar never came. In scenes of lament and sorrow, typical of hagiographic literature, Solzhenitsyn depicted the death of Stolypin and the end of a true Russia, destroyed by the elite segments of society, the callous tsar, the depraved courtiers, the fervent revolutionaries, the corrupt police, and the reckless pamphleteers. In Solzhenitsyn's grand vision, without Stolypin, Russia was ready to be misled by Lenin and the Bolsheviks. The scenes of death become operatic in tone and scope. Like Siegfried's funeral in Wagner's *Götterdämmerung*, Stolypin's last days and hours heralded not just the death of one person but also the destruction of an empire in the fires of an impending revolution, an artistic and fanciful vision of the tragic end of tsarist Russia.

Putting Solzhenitsyn on Air

On my return trip to Washington, I struggled to determine what to do with this unique recording. To the best of my knowledge, VOA had never broadcast twenty hours of readings by any Russian writer. Editing the readings was not an option, but simply putting them on air would disrupt the VOA schedule and call into question our journalistic judgment. The only way to proceed was to repackage the readings, providing historical context, and include them as part of our regularly scheduled arts and cultural programming. Several years earlier, the Russian Service had started a program, *Books and People*, that presented mostly short readings from new Russian publications, along with discussions about new literary works. The Stolypin chapters would thus find a home among other works of fiction, and that would obviate the need to account for the historical accuracy of the events depicted in the novel. I explained this approach to Tomlinson, and he assured me that the White House supported our decision to broadcast Solzhenitsyn.

We knew that broadcasting Solzhenitsyn's work would be controversial. We anticipated that some Soviet émigrés as well as American academics would take issue with the depiction of Stolypin as Russia's "best hope" and would be highly critical of the conservative nationalism that pervades the entire novel. To address that criticism, I held a town hall meeting with the entire USSR Division to explain how the recording was done and why these readings represented an important chapter in Russian broadcasting. What we did not expect was a full-fledged anti-Solzhenitsyn campaign. "It is no secret," Lyudmila Alexeyeva wrote in the *Helsinki Watch Report*, "that several successive heads of the Russian Service have been in regular telephone contact with Solzhenitsyn's wife. . . . Program directives were tied to such telephonic guidance. . . . In 1984, the VOA Russian Service, in an unprecedented step, gave abundant air time to Solzhenitsyn for readings from his new composition, *The Red Wheel*."[5] Her criticism focused on Solzhenitsyn's depiction of the assassination: "Inasmuch as Stolypin, according to Solzhenitsyn, was Russia's only hope for the future, his death represented the collapse of that hope and brought the inevitability of revolution. Solzhenitsyn's work suggests that this development in the conflict of interest between the Jews, represented by Bogrov, and Russia, represented by Stolypin, was responsible for the revolution and all the troubles that ensued for Russia and the world."[6] Her words lit a match, and she threw it into a barrel of oil.

The charge of anti-Semitism caused a conflagration in Washington. The foes of Solzhenitsyn picked up the charge and, without reading the novel, let alone listening to the actual broadcasts, started criticizing our decision to broadcast it. I would hold meetings with various critics to explain how we were broadcasting the readings in the vain hope that this would quell the passions, but the battle lines were firmly drawn. Many older émigrés and American programmers welcomed our journalistic coup, but some of the recent émigrés sided with the critics. The divisions in the service quickly hardened into factions. And the accusations and controversy spilled out of the VOA building, reaching not only the émigré press but also congressional offices and the U.S. media. For the most part, charges and countercharges were driven by political considerations. Congressional offices, critical of the Reagan administration, welcomed any news that put USIA and VOA in a bad light. When I met with congressional staff to discuss the actual broadcasts, I found there was little interest in understanding the issue. Anti-Semitism was a convenient club with which to fight the administration.

With public controversy swirling, the *Washington Post* decided to weigh in. In early 1985, Joanne Omang wrote:

> A new version of Alexander Solzhenitsyn's famous novel "August 1914," being broadcast by the Voice of America into the Soviet Union, has the Soviet-watching community in an uproar over charges that parts are subtly anti-Semitic. The book has not been printed in English, and the flap is largely in the form of clashing analyses. At heart, the debate continues an ancient quarrel over the implications of ethnic Russian—as distinguished from Soviet or communist—nationalism and its suspicions toward Jews and other minority groups. But it also involves longstanding feuds within the Russian emigre population over the accuracy of Solzhenitsyn's view of the world, particularly his account of the origins and nature of the communist regime. It is, in short, a very Russian dispute, convoluted and steaming with nuance and grudge invisible to non-Russians.[7]

As a professional journalist, Omang asked me for my comments and then reached out to different Russian experts in the United States. Driven by his longstanding animus toward Solzhenitsyn, Pipes predictably noted, "Solzhenitsyn does not say anything that is explicitly anti-Semitic. It's not overt in any way, but to a Russian audience it's very clear in the way he dwells on Bogrov's Jewishness that he is blaming the revolution on the Jews." Meanwhile, John Glad, from the University of Maryland, noted that "as an artist, Solzhenitsyn tries to make Bogrov comprehensible to readers as a dedicated but misguided figure who brought about a tragedy and happened, like many other revolutionaries, to be Jewish." Norman Podhoretz, editor of *Commentary*, summed up the controversy by stating, "While there is no clear sign of positive hostility toward Jews in Solzhenitsyn's books, neither is there much sympathy. I can well imagine that in his heart he holds it against the Jews that so many of the old Bolsheviks, the makers of the revolution that brought the curse of communism to Russia, were of Jewish origin but whatever there may be in his heart, there is no overt anti-Semitism in any of his translated works."

Despite the charges and countercharges, we broadcast the readings as we had planned. A close reader of the text, especially in today's more politically correct era, might find Solzhenitsyn's focus on Bogrov's Jewish heritage inappropriate and even offensive. In fairness, Solzhenitsyn's critical comments about Jewish revolutionaries were more than outweighed by his descriptions of the daily discrimination that Jews faced in tsarist Russia and their legitimate fear of pogroms. One can also sense Solzhenitsyn's utter rejection of the major anti-Semitic groups in Russia, the Union of the Russian People, the Black Hundreds, and the Union of Archangel Michael. Though they enjoyed the support of Nicholas II, these groups are unequivocally condemned as evil forces destroying Russia.

In conducting research for this book, I listened again to Solzhenitsyn's reading of the entire Stolypin cycle. As a whole, *The Red Wheel* is an unwieldy work, spanning many volumes, with a multitude of characters, no unifying plot, and seemingly endless digressions. But the Stolypin chapters in *August 1914* are an exception; this is dramatic writing with a spellbinding narrative and highly artistic language. Solzhenitsyn's depictions of Bogrov and Stolypin are firmly in the tradition of classical Russian literature. Dostoevsky and Tolstoy would have recognized Solzhenitsyn as their student. But Solzhenitsyn's unique artistry reaches its apex in his portrayal of secondary characters, principally the Kyiv police chief, Nikolai Kuliabko, and Tsar Nicholas II. Through Solzhenitsyn's reading of his own text, I felt I had come to know these characters as though I had spent hours or days with them. They are "fully rounded," to use E. M. Forster's famous characterization. We sense their pettiness, vanity, small-mindedness, fears, and even cruelty. We see them laughing, interacting with friends, eating their favorite foods, boasting about their beautiful homes, naively trusting their advisers. We sense their foibles, and we understand just how ordinary and unimportant they are as human beings. And yet, fate had placed them in critical positions, and their actions, selfish and incompetent, paved the road to Russia's ruin. Solzhenitsyn's reading transported me to the early twentieth century, and I felt that I had actually lived through that turbulent period in Russia's history. If that was my reaction, I can well imagine the overpowering effect it had on millions of Russian listeners who, thanks to VOA, could experience something denied to them by their own government—their Nobel laureate, their history, their literature. So successful were Solzhenitsyn's readings with our audience that three years later, my successor as the head of the VOA Russian Service, Natalie Clarkson, traveled to Vermont and recorded Solzhenitsyn reading more chapters from *The Red Wheel*, this time about the February 1917 revolution.

The Solzhenitsyn readings were clearly one of the major achievements at VOA in the Reagan years when the Russian Service had the freedom to practice serious journalism. But with that freedom came a responsibility to be professional and to know how to handle controversial material. The Solzhenitsyn readings tested the Russian Service in battle, and that resulted in three fundamental principles that characterized subsequent programming.

The first was the need to set any potentially controversial programming in an overall context that explained its contents, showed how it adhered to the overall mission of VOA, and preempted any potential criticism. That context would then have to be thoroughly discussed and refined with the editors, the entire staff, and, most important, the senior management of the VOA. In the case of the Solzhenitsyn programming, we had taken all these steps but were nonetheless blindsided by the attacks that focused on charges of anti-Semitism. In retrospect, I would have flagged the passages that could have raised concern and would have brought in outside experts to discuss how best to handle them. We would have proceeded with the readings as planned, but prebroadcast feedback would have made it easier to explain what we were doing and to allay the concerns of our critics.

The second point was the critical need for firewalls. The Russian Service was exceptionally fortunate that the directors of both VOA and our parent agency, USIA, understood the importance of journalistic independence and were willing to support our decision to broadcast Solzhenitsyn's work. After all, we were reversing longstanding U.S. policy that had kept Solzhenitsyn off the air in the 1970s, and we had to expect political pressure and outright criticism. Gaining the acquiescence of the White House proved to be indispensable. As I recall, I did not receive a single cable from the U.S. Embassy in Moscow questioning our Solzhenitsyn readings.

The third point, and the most important one, dealt with the need for greater diversity in programming. Rather than keeping potentially controversial writers off the air—as VOA had often done in the détente years—the Russian Service chose to make the VOA studios available to a broad range of responsible voices, from liberal to conservative. Even though I felt strongly that Lyudmila Alexeyeva's attack on our broadcast of Solzhenitsyn was unfair, I thought she was a very important figure in the human rights movement, and we invited her to become a regular contributor to VOA broadcasts. Over the years, she voiced many reports and had the freedom to express political views that were different from Solzhenitsyn's. Similarly, we invited other Russian writers who did not agree with Solzhenitsyn, notably Vasiliy Aksyonov and Vladimir Voinovich, to read from their works. In retrospect, the Solzhenitsyn readings represented a new era for the Russian Service, characterized by bold programming that went beyond the news and politically safe stories. VOA was now competing head-to-head with Radio Liberty and the BBC, directly challenging Soviet propaganda, and serving as a sophisticated means of communicating with our growing audience in the Soviet Union.

7

Religion

Daily editorial meetings at VOA and RL Russian Services focused considerable attention on the latest monitoring reports of Soviet media. To develop the most effective programming, we needed to know what our listeners were seeing on television or reading in the Soviet press, which stories were being ignored, and which ones distorted. By parsing Soviet media, we were able to prepare a relevant news and current-events lineup and select appropriate topics for our strategic programming on culture, human rights, arts, and history. Only one important programming area was rarely discussed at these meetings, and that was the subject of religion. Until Gorbachev's policies of glasnost took root, mainstream Soviet media rarely covered religious issues, did not broadcast religious services, and avoided free-flowing discussions of non-Marxist philosophy. For the most part, Soviet coverage of religion consisted of barbed commentaries or trite criticism of cults. This reticence to engage seriously with religious issues handed VOA and RL a virtual monopoly on programming that directly addressed questions of Church history, philosophy, theology, liturgical rites, faith, and belief.

From its earliest days in power, the Soviet regime waged an aggressive war against all expressions of religious life, with the twin goal of exterminating any trace of Russian Orthodoxy, seen as the bulwark of traditional Russian culture, and establishing a new Soviet state, based on atheism. During the Red Terror after the October 1917 coup, Soviet forces killed tens of thousands of priests and religious figures, but resistance to Soviet closure of churches and the confiscation of church property continued even after the civil war had come to an end. One telling example of Soviet brutality occurred on March 15, 1922, at the height of the first Soviet famine. Local townspeople in Shuia, some two hundred miles north of Moscow, stood their ground as GPU troops (the successor to the Cheka) tried to remove icons, crosses, relics, and other artifacts from the main church. So enraged were the government forces that they gunned down the resisters, arrested several dozen people, and summarily executed them. Four days later, Lenin wrote to Molotov: "It is precisely now, and only now, when in the starving regions people are eating human flesh, and hundreds if not thousands of corpses are littering the roads, that we can (and therefore must) carry out the confiscation of church valuables with the most savage and merciless energy.... We must lay our hands on a fund of several hundred million gold rubles.... Confiscation of church valuables should be conducted with merciless determination. The greater the number of clergy and bourgeoisie we succeed in executing, the better."[1]

As a prominent American historian, Douglas Smith, has noted, the Shuia incident alone "brought in over twelve tons of gold, silver, diamonds, pearls, and other precious stones. A public show trial, the first in Soviet history, was put on for the resisters in April [1923]. Over twelve hundred clergymen were found guilty and put to death. It is estimated that, all told, at least eight thousand people were executed or died defending their places of worship."[2]

In 1925 the USSR formed the League of Militant Atheists, which was responsible for closing most churches across Russia, Ukraine, and other Soviet republics, as well as for the arrest and execution of priests and church prelates. Soviet policies included antichurch campaigns, the promotion of atheism in schools, the outlawing of baptism, the censoring of theologically and religiously oriented literature, and the closing of seminaries. During WWII, in a desperate attempt to bolster Russian patriotism, Stalin relented and allowed the Orthodox Church to operate, but only under the strict control of the state. Many high-level Church officials were co-opted by the KGB (or were de facto KGB agents), and the official Church became another tool of the Kremlin. In subsequent years, there were periodic antireligion campaigns, affecting not only the Orthodox community, but also Jews, Baptists, and Muslims. The Communist Party viewed any form of religion as a dying practice that would disappear once the older generation passed away.

Far from dying away, however, religion steadily grew in popularity in the post-Stalin years. By the 1960s, religious activists formed an important segment of the Soviet human rights movement, and religious issues were the subject of many samizdat works. As we saw in our examination of human rights in chapter 3, Soviet citizens gathered in informal groups to discuss religion, grapple with non-Marxist philosophy, and explore the faith of their parents and grandparents. According to RL audience research, roughly half the Soviet population had some religious affiliation or professed a keen interest in learning more about a specific religion.[3] This assessment was further confirmed by travel reports of Western students and scholars, U.S. Embassy cables, Western media sources, and anecdotal evidence. We knew that the overwhelming majority of Russians who were interested in religion identified with Orthodoxy, both for cultural and religious reasons. The data and sundry reports, however, suggested a broader swath of religious interests. Drawing on her many years in the human rights movement in the USSR, Lyudmila Alexeyeva noted that by the 1980s there was not only "a religious revival of all traditional religions that have existed in Russia—Orthodox, Catholics, Jews, Muslims, as well as congregations of Baptists, Pentecostalists, Seventh-Day Adventists, and Jehovah's Witnesses but also religions quite new to the country, such as the Hare Krishna and the Children of God."[4]

Early in my tenure at VOA, I met regularly with the director, Kenneth Tomlinson, to discuss the overall strategic approach of the Russian broadcasts, identifying programming areas that were relevant to our listeners and embodied fundamental American values. Prominent on our agenda was the subject of religion. Tomlinson told me that the White House and the NSC were keenly interested in how VOA treated religion. I explained that the Russian Service had a long tradition of religious broadcasting, including a one-hour liturgy on Sundays, special Church services on major holidays, and weekly Sunday sermons, prepared and voiced by a noted Orthodox prelate, Archbishop John (Shakhovskoi) of San Francisco. Archbishop John's homilies were in the Orthodox style, based primarily on biblical readings of the week and assertive in proclaiming the preeminence of the Orthodox faith. Archbishop John did not seek to convert nonbelievers or use religion to score political points. Rather, he tried to make listeners feel good about their Orthodox beliefs, provide moral sustenance, and create an emotional bond between believers in the United States and those in the Soviet Union.

To balance these parochial programs, the Russian Service aired an ecumenical program that presented news about different denominations in the United States and was intended for Soviet listeners who were curious about the role of religion in modern society. Most of the programming consisted of translations of relevant articles from the U.S. press and English-language scripts prepared by the VOA Central News Division. In the mid-1970s VOA hired a recent Jewish émigré writer, Vladimir Matlin, who took over the editorship of this program. Realizing the growing interest in religion in the Soviet Union, Matlin suggested recasting the religious broadcasts by creating two separate shows: one focused on Christianity and the other on Judaism. Significantly, these broadcasts were not intended to be simply about religion but rather would be faith-based programs that sought to address the spiritual and cultural interests of the listeners. To develop these programs, VOA took an unprecedented step of hiring a well-educated young Orthodox priest as a full-time broadcaster. The Reverend Victor Potapov, whose parish was in Washington DC, had grown up in the United States, spoke Russian at home, and received his theological training at the Holy Trinity Orthodox Seminary in Jordanville, New York. So unusual was his appointment that initially the VOA management was not sure how to treat an Orthodox priest in a federal workplace. They insisted that he not dress as a cleric and asked that he try to blend in with the rest of the staff. For the first several months they did not even let him introduce himself on air as a priest, and he remained a curious anonymous voice.[5] In time, everyone felt comfortable calling the Reverend Potapov simply Father Victor. He was friendly, unassuming, and deeply respected by the entire Russian Service staff. Father Victor took over the editorship of the Christian program, which quickly grew into a full-fledged forty-five-minute weekly program—*Religion in Our Life*—focusing primarily on Orthodoxy. Meanwhile, Matlin developed an analogous Jewish program aimed at both religious and secular Jews in the USSR. The weekly programs were supplemented by special broadcasts geared to major holidays and religious events.

Tomlinson was supportive of our approach to religious programming and was especially pleased that both the Orthodox and Jewish communities were involved. He encouraged me to bolster our religious broadcasts and, where possible, to draw connections between the freedom to practice religion and the political freedoms enjoyed in the West, noting that religion was one of the most effective ways of undermining communism. Tomlinson further assured me that he would discuss our programming on religion at senior-level policy meetings at USIA and the NSC, as well as in his testimony before relevant congressional committees. Religious programming, he told me, had a clear strategic component that resonated well with the overall Reagan administration policy toward the USSR. For Reagan, religion exemplified the fundamental American value of freedom, responded to the growing needs and interests of Soviet citizens, and directly challenged the dominant position of Marxist ideology and state atheism. Russian broadcasts were the most effective way to communicate that message.

VOA: Orthodox Programming on Air

To listen to Father Victor's programs was to enter an Orthodox world.[6] Although he occasionally discussed different religious issues, Father Victor primarily focused on Russian Orthodoxy, and his intended listener was an Orthodox Christian. When Father Victor spoke about the meaning of the liturgy, the celebration of Communion, or the significance of fasting, he was speaking in an intimate and personal way to a fellow communicant who would partake in these rituals and sacraments. When he described the life of Archbishop Ioann (of Shanghai), Pavel Florensky, or Archbishop Antony (Khrapovitsky), he was not examining their political or theological significance but rather was sharing traditional hagiographic portraits of major religious figures. When he turned to miracles, sainthood, mysticism, or even the occult, his words were always anchored in Orthodox theological writing. When he spoke about the Reverend Gleb Yakunin, Alexandr Solzhenitsyn, or religious dissidents in the USSR, he was drawing close ties between the defenders of the faith in the Soviet Union and their brethren in the West. Father Victor's programs were unabashedly faith-based and celebrated the centrality of Orthodoxy in Russian life. His tone was gentle and uplifting, shorn of any hard edge or gratuitous criticism of the Soviet Union. In the darkest days of the Cold War, he was reaching out to fellow Orthodox Christians with a message of unity and hope: "You, my listeners, may be living in an atheist country, but you're not alone; we are all part of one Orthodox world. Together we will create a sense of community."

Among the major themes in Father Victor's programs was the role of Orthodoxy in the Western world. In an interview with Ernest Gordon, the Presbyterian dean of the Princeton University Chapel, for example, Father Victor explored the influence of Orthodox religious writings on Gordon's academic work and conception of faith. Likewise, he devoted several programs to the establishment of Russian theological institutions in the West, primarily the St. Sergius Institute in Paris and the St. Vladimir's Orthodox Seminary and the Holy Trinity Seminary in the United States. Drawing on the writings of prominent émigré writers, he explained how the intellectual and political freedom in the West facilitated the development of Russian religious philosophy. These programs were enhanced by examinations of noted Russian theologians and philosophers of the twentieth century, including Semen Frank, Sergei Bulgakov, Nikolai Berdyaev, Nikolai Lossky, Alexander Schmemann, and John Meyendorff. A good example was a program devoted to George Florovsky, a major philosopher and historian of Russian Orthodoxy.[7] Born in Odessa in 1903, Florovsky emigrated to Europe after the 1917 revolution; there, he received his higher education. A prolific writer on theology and philosophy, Florovsky entered the priesthood and became a professor of theology at the St. Sergius Institute in Paris. In 1949 he emigrated to the United States, where he initially served as dean of St. Vladimir's Orthodox Seminary. In 1955 he became a professor of divinity at Harvard University and later joined Princeton University as a distinguished professor. His magnum opus, *The Ways of Russian Theology*, grappled with questions of Christian scholasticism, pietism, and idealism, as well as the enduring significance of patristic writings. Father Victor explained Florovsky's conception of Orthodoxy, his initial flirtation with Eurasianism, and his views on ecumenicalism. An active participant in an Orthodox-Anglican dialogue in the 1930s, Florovsky lectured frequently in Great Britain, explaining how Orthodoxy conceived of one universal church. Although a worldly European, Florovsky was by nature a conservative in theological matters and argued for the primacy of the Byzantine Church fathers. He was a towering intellectual figure, part of the rich Russian émigré school of Orthodox theology whose works were indispensable for an understanding of Russian intellectual history. But in the Soviet Union, Florovsky and other major émigré philosophers were virtually unknown and their works unavailable. Through Father Victor's programs, Russian theologians "came home" and now, in post-Communist Russia, have reclaimed their rightful place among the major thinkers of the twentieth century.

In a similar vein, Father Victor described the work of Ivan Gardner, one of the world's leading experts on Russian church singing.[8] Born in Crimea in 1898 to a family of Scottish ancestry, Gardner studied musicology and theology before the revolution, focusing on chants in Subcarpathian Rus, now in Ukraine. After the 1917 revolution, he emigrated to Serbia and later to Germany, where he received a doctorate in musicology at the University of Munich. His research culminated in a multivolume work, *Russian Church Singing: Orthodox Worship and Hymnography*, published in New York in the 1970s. In his program, Father Victor provided an in-depth review of the book, noting how in tsarist Russia church singing in Saint Petersburg and Moscow had come under heavy Western influence, while the older, more traditional style of singing was best preserved in Russian monasteries. According to Gardner, after the 1917 revolution, the older style of church singing could be heard primarily in Russian émigré churches. By reviewing books by Gardner, Florovsky, and other theologians, Father Victor acquainted his listeners with Russian scholarship virtually inaccessible even to experts in the Soviet Union.

Father Victor's programs also tried to appeal to secular listeners, primarily by focusing on religious dissidents. On March 22, 1980, for example, he broadcast Solzhenitsyn's fiery statement condemning the arrest of the Reverend Dmitri Dudko and the Reverend Gleb Yakunin and then included a comprehensive report about the two notable religious dissidents. Born into a peasant family in 1922, Dudko served in the Red Army during WWII, entered the Moscow Theological Institute after the war, but was arrested in 1948 for writing a poem criticizing the destruction of Russia's historical monuments. He was sentenced to ten years of hard labor in the gulag. After being amnestied in 1956, he resumed his religious studies and became a dissident priest, bucking the authority of the official Church. He gained a cult following as a priest of the people. Yakunin was a major figure in the human rights movement, a member of the Moscow Helsinki Group, and an elected member of the Russian Duma from 1990 to 1995. In 1965 he wrote a letter to Patriarch Alexei I (published in samizdat), arguing that the Church had to be liberated from state control. In 1976 Yakunin established the Christian Committee for the Defense of the Rights of Believers and published hundreds of articles about the suppression of Orthodoxy and other religions in the Soviet Union. He was promptly arrested and convicted of anti-Soviet agitation. Yakunin was amnestied in 1987 by Gorbachev, but fully rehabilitated only in 1991.

After describing the latest persecution of religious figures, Father Victor turned to an interview with a remarkable Russian dissident, Anatoly Levitin-Krasnov. Born in 1915, Levitin-Krasnov became involved in Orthodox circles in the 1930s and was periodically detained by the KGB. In 1949 he was arrested and sentenced to ten years of hard labor in the gulag for calling Stalin Russia's "chief thug" in what he thought was a private conversation. After being amnestied in 1956, Levitin-Krasnov resumed his religious work, primarily as a samizdat journalist cataloging Soviet repressive measures against religious activists in the USSR. He was periodically rearrested, but he persevered in his work, once claiming in court that he would always defend religious activists if they were repressed for their views, but he would also defend atheists if the government were to persecute them. In 1974 Levitin-Krasnov was forced to emigrate and settled in Switzerland, where he continued to document religious persecution. By inviting Levitin-Krasnov to the

VOA studio to talk at length about the role of religion in the human rights movement, Father Victor communicated to his listeners the fundamental American value of religious freedom.

On occasion, Father Victor's programs brought together religion, human rights, and politics. On November 14, 1981, he devoted the entire broadcast to the new martyrs of the Russian Orthodox Church, canonized earlier that year by the conservative Russian Orthodox Church Abroad for their stalwart defense of the Orthodox faith in 1918. Religious listeners were able to hear the church service, including prayers, chants, and excerpts from a sermon about the significance of the canonization. The politically inclined listeners heard a Russian cleric extolling religious freedom in the United States that allowed the Russian Orthodox Church to thrive and prosper. Secular listeners learned about a 1976 samizdat document regarding the early victims of Soviet terror. In a somber voice, Father Victor intoned the names of those who were tortured and killed by the Bolsheviks in the most gruesome way: beheadings, amputations, and burials while alive. At the end, he stated that there were 8,010 specific victims from across all of Russia who had died defending the Church during the Red Terror of 1918 alone. Their sainthood was a testament to the enduring strength of the Russian Church in the face of Soviet terror. By combining history, theology, church rituals, and basic human rights, Father Victor educated and comforted his listeners, reminding them that they were not abandoned by their fellow American communicants.

VOA: Jewish Programs on Air

The issues of faith, tradition, and human rights were just as prominently featured in the weekly Jewish program, edited by Vladimir Matlin. In light of the growing anti-Semitism in the Soviet Union in the 1970s and the marginalization of Jews in Soviet society, Matlin saw his primary task in giving Soviet Jews a sense of pride in who they were.[9] He thought he could accomplish this most effectively by drawing on popular American books intended for general readers because they offered concise and lucid expositions of the traditions, beliefs, practices, and history of the Jewish people. Among the more memorable broadcasts were excerpts from Herman Wouk's *This Is My God* that focused on the Shabbat, High Holidays, Jewish prayer, Torah, Talmud, and Zionism. A Pulitzer-prize-winning author of *The Caine Mutiny*, Wouk sought to explain Judaism from a modern Orthodox perspective that would attract both Jewish and non-Jewish readers. Matlin supplemented Wouk's book with readings from Rabbi Milton Steinberg's *Basic Judaism* and from Dennis Prager and Rabbi Joseph Telushkin's *Nine Questions People Ask about Judaism*. In the 1970s Prager and Telushkin became involved in supporting Soviet Jewry and were inspired to write their book after meeting with Soviet Jews. They corresponded extensively with Matlin about the translation and transmission of their book and discussed how best to communicate the values of human rights to a Soviet audience. Using American works about Judaism had the additional bonus of establishing closer ties between Jews in the United States and their fellow communicants in the USSR, and that linkage proved indispensable in helping to free individual refuseniks.

Since a principal aim of the program was to provide moral sustenance to Soviet Jewry, Matlin drew on the works of recent émigrés to forge a special relationship. Rabbi Victor Rashkovsky, a regular contributor to the program, had been a film director in the USSR, but after emigrating to the United States, he enrolled in the Hebrew Union College in Cincinnati, Ohio, and became head of the Jewish Congregation of Oak Ridge, in Tennessee. Knowing the needs and interests of his listeners, Rashkovsky was able to explain the origins and meaning of Jewish holidays, as well as to provide traditional Jewish music, cantor melodies, and Israeli songs. Rashkovsky's talks were supplemented by numerous interviews Matlin conducted with such prominent Jewish leaders as Natan Sharansky, Vladimir Slepak, Ida Nudel, Yosef Mendelevich, and Yosef Begun.[10] These interviews provided a living link with refuseniks and were supplemented by statements of concern, support, and protection from U.S. presidents, senators, representatives, and public figures, in addition to ordinary American citizens.

Over the years, Matlin received thousands of letters from listeners and organizations noting the impact of his programming. Among those letters was one from the president of the Union of Councils for Soviet

Jews, Pamela Brown Cohen. In the 1980s Cohen traveled to several Soviet cities to meet with Jewish activists. Upon her return she wrote to the VOA director that "in every meeting, and nearly every discussion, reference was made to information received over the Voice of America. . . . The impact of the radio is enormous. Time after time, reference was made to broadcasts in which the Union of Councils and its positions were aired. The information provided by VOA is vital and provides individuals with a special kind of protection. It gives them a tremendous sense of hope to know that they are not forgotten, that their situations are reported in the United States and then transmitted into the Soviet Union."[11] So effective were Matlin's programs that the Jewish Federation of Central New Jersey bestowed its 1985 Human Rights award to the Russian Service. As the director, I was invited to the awards ceremony to speak to an overflowing crowd about how we developed our programming in the Russian Service and the pride we took in the Jewish broadcasts.

If one were to search through publications or government documents about VOA during the Cold War, one would be hard-pressed to find any explicit references to religious programming. The VOA Charter makes no mention of religion and contains only an oblique reference to reporting about social issues: "VOA will present a balanced and comprehensive projection of significant American thought and institutions." In his exhaustive examination of VOA programming, Alan Heil does not treat religious broadcasts, while in his history of USIA, Nicholas Cull makes only passing references to Islamic-focused programming. Yet for decades the Russian Service broadcast church services, sermons, Bible lessons, interviews with clerics, religious music, samizdat, and reviews of theological literature. Religious programs were a prominent part of the daily lineup and were rebroadcast throughout the week. We knew there was a thirst in the USSR for personal freedom, a desire to explore the world in one's own way, and a growing belief that everyone had the right to make up one's own mind about enduring values and the meaning of life. Through our religious programs, we wanted to help Russians to realize that personal freedom.

From today's perspective, with religion freely practiced in Russia and the Orthodox Church having reclaimed its traditional role of state ideologue, it may be hard to understand why the Soviet state viewed VOA religious programs as hostile and dangerous. Throughout the 1980s, even as glasnost became official policy, Soviet bureaucrats and the mainstream press continued to attack VOA religious broadcasts for "sowing doubts in the minds of Soviet citizens about socialism and leading the youth astray." Yet today, the VOA Orthodox and Jewish programs would undoubtedly be seen as noble, truthful, and high-minded. Most important, they were honest in their approach. They did not try to balance religious and secular values and search for just the right mix of diverse views. Openly and proudly, they spoke to believers, their fellow communicants, in the language of their culture and beliefs and thereby gave millions of Soviet citizens comfort, solace, and hope.

Radio Liberty: Orthodox Programs

Like VOA, Radio Liberty considered programs about religion to be central to its mission, and from its first days it broadcast a weekly liturgy and Sunday talks. However, in contrast to the more traditional sermons by Archbishop John of San Francisco aired on VOA, RL offered more intellectual fare. The Reverend Alexander Schmemann, dean of St. Vladimir's Seminary in New York, adopted an informal style and spoke to his listeners as if they were well-educated college graduates. He didn't simply assert theological principles, proclaim the preeminence of Orthodoxy over other Christian faiths, or restate the words of the Bible. Rather, he assumed his listeners might be skeptical of religion and tried to reason with them. His talks about the significance of the liturgy, for example, drew on ancient Greek and Hebrew sources to explain how the liturgy evolved into a communal affirmation of Christian service to others. Similarly, his talks about classical Russian writers provided a Christian lens through which to see Russian culture. In discussing classical Russian literature, for example, Schmemann sought to explain the concept of beauty within a Christian context, as a ray of the divine in an otherwise ugly or sinful world, thereby giving Soviet-educated listeners new tools for comprehending Dostoevsky's famous assertion that "the world will be saved only by beauty." Likewise, Schmemann's discussion of Alexander Pushkin as a "Christian poet" for whom the beauty of language or nature was a way of perceiving a higher being revealed important aspects of Pushkin's art. Schmemann's intention was to engage his listeners in new ways of looking at Russian culture and, in the process, to show the limitations of the Soviet-Marxist model.

In 1978 Radio Liberty began a weekly religious program, aptly named *Not by Bread Alone*. It included Father Alexander's talks, explications of the Gospels, sermons by other Orthodox prelates, discussions of religious samizdat, and reports about religious life outside the USSR. To underscore its ecumenical outlook, in the inaugural broadcast (July 8, 1978), the editor, Gleb Rahr, interviewed an American rabbi who was serving as a U.S. Army chaplain in Germany. The rabbi explained how the chaplaincy worked, how he ministered to the needs of Jewish soldiers and officers, and, most surprising, how members of the armed forces who were of other denominations or of no religion came to him to talk about family issues. Rahr's intention was to illustrate that the West took religion seriously and that chaplains had a positive impact on army morale. In the same vein, several weeks later, Rahr aired two programs about religious life in Hungary and Poland. In sharp contrast to the USSR, in Communist Eastern Europe one could easily buy Bibles, attend church, and form discussion groups that dealt with religion and philosophy.

In the late 1970s, as Soviet authorities mounted another anti-religion campaign, Rahr began to incorporate religious samizdat in his programs. On July 22, 1978, he devoted the entire broadcast to one of the more fearless religious dissidents, Zoya Krakhmalnikova. Born in 1929, Krakhmalnikova became a member of the Union of Soviet Writers and the Soviet Academy of Sciences, despite the fact that her father had been arrested in 1936. In 1971 she was baptized into the Russian Orthodox faith, and this resulted in her dismissal from the Union of Soviet Writers. A woman of indomitable spirit, Krakhmalnikova began publishing a samizdat journal, *Nadezhda* (Hope), that included articles on philosophy and religion. Despite her apolitical stance, she was arrested in 1982 and held in the notorious Lefortovo prison for over a year. In 1983 Krakhmalnikova was sentenced to five years of exile in a remote region of Altai. To underscore the severity of the judgment, the authorities granted her husband and daughter only one visit a month, and Krakhmalnikova herself was not allowed to attend church services. In 1986, ten months after Mikhail Gorbachev became the general secretary of the Communist Party, Krakhmalnikova's husband, Feliks Svetov, was arrested for promoting religion and exiled to Siberia. Only in July 1987, with glasnost in full force, were Krakhmalnikova and Svetov finally pardoned.

By the early 1980s Radio Liberty became an authoritative voice supporting the cause of religious freedom. As one listens to *Not by Bread Alone,* one learns not only about the fate of the better known figures such as Father Gleb Yakunin and Father Dmitri Dudko but also about such lesser-known but important dissidents such as Tatiana Shchepkova, Lev Regelson, and Alexander Ogorodnikov. *Not by Bread Alone* also included discussions about the religious upbringing of children, abstract concepts of holiness, the significance of icons and relics, the canonization of Nicholas II and his family, and extended readings about Russian saints. In a general sense, Rahr's program resembled Father Victor's religious broadcasts on VOA, as they both sought to create an Orthodox world. But in one important respect, Rahr's program was different: it carried a distinctly political message. Not only did Rahr portray Orthodoxy as the true religion of Russia, but also, drawing on his nationalist sensibilities, he tended to conflate religion with an idealized vision of tsarist Russia. A telling example was a series of readings from Ivan Shmelev's religious novel, *Bogomol'e* (The pilgrimage). Written in Paris in 1931, the novel told the story of a carpenter in Moscow who makes a pilgrimage to Sergiyev Posad, the seat of the Russian patriarch and the spiritual center of Russian Orthodoxy. Shmelev uses the common literary device of a journey to paint age-old Orthodox Russian towns and villages, with their habits, attitudes, and everyday life.

Such idealized portrayals of prerevolutionary Russia would occasionally prompt sarcastic comments by recent émigré broadcasters who felt that paeans to Orthodoxy were of little interest to Soviet listeners. Lyudmila Alexeyeva even noted in her *Helsinki Watch Report* that these readings "contained little or no information about the religion of the Russian people.... There was nothing of what one might expect in a series on Christianity ... [only] a sugarcoated, romanticized depiction of life in Old Russia."[12] In his critique of Russian broadcasts for the BIB, James Critchlow disparaged *Not by Bread Alone* as a voice of official Orthodoxy that invariably denigrated other religions of the Soviet Union.[13] Rahr would counter these criticisms by noting that many Russians in the 1980s were yearning to learn more about their culture and history and that émigré literature offered unique insights. And to some degree, he was proved right. Just several years after Rahr's broadcasts were aired, Shmelev's literary works were published in the USSR to considerable acclaim. In post-Communist Russia, *Bogomol'e* has continued to be a popular book and has even appeared as an e-book online. Shmelev himself became a venerated figure in Putin's Russia. Fifty years after his death, his remains were moved from the Russian cemetery in Paris to the necropolis in the Donskoi Monastery in Moscow.

By the mid-1980s, with encouragement from senior RFE/RL management and explicit endorsement by the directors of the Board for International Broadcasting, the Russian Service added several new programs that dealt exclusively with Christianity: *Beginning of the Day*, *Path and Life*, *Religion in the Modern World*, *Millennium of Christianity*, and *Christian Russia*. Gleb Rahr was the driving force behind this major programming expansion. He relinquished the editorship of *Not by Bread Alone*, passing it on to the Reverend Mikhail Meyerson-Aksenov, and devoted himself to the new programming. In his memoir he claimed that he even had a personal meeting with Frank Shakespeare, former chair of the BIB, who told him that the White House fully supported additional programming on religion and especially the celebration of one thousand years of Russian Orthodox Christianity in 1988.[14]

With his usual enthusiasm, Rahr set about developing an ambitious multiyear plan. At its core was the *Millennium of Christianity*—a thirty-minute weekly program—that presented Russian culture and statehood as indivisible from its Christian roots. Drawing principally on Russian émigré studies of Byzantium and Kyivan Rus, Rahr conveyed a heroic story of the baptism of Prince Vladimir and the people of Kyiv. Not one to parse the finer points of East Slavic culture, with its eventual split into separate Russian, Ukrainian, and Belorussian languages and cultures, Rahr trumpeted the Great Russian narrative that extolled Vladimir's Kyiv as the progenitor of Russian statehood. He even included readings from a conservative historian of the Orthodox Church, Anton Kartashov, who referred to Prince Vladimir as the "father of Russian culture," an epithet that would have puzzled the Viking warlord. Drawing heavily on materials prepared by Russian émigrés for the 950th anniversary year in 1938, Rahr presented a wide range of topics, from the architecture of Kyiv to Russian traditions of sainthood and iconography. The overall import of the program was a celebration, an opportunity for Russians to take pride in their culture and to realize that communism was a thin and alien layer in their long and glorious history.

After 1988, the *Millennium of Christianity* was transformed into a new program, *Christian Russia—the Second Millennium*. This program, also under Rahr's editorship, took advantage of glasnost and perestroika in the Soviet Union to address the central question: What would a free Russia look like? Rahr would often cite Soviet publications about religion, but his main focus remained on émigré writers. Many of the broadcasts began with a quotation from Ivan Ilyin to the effect that Russians must comprehend and build their political culture not by means of rational thought or Western theories but through a religious apprehension of the essence of their unique culture. A favorite philosopher of conservative Russians, Ilyin advocated a Christian-based, corporatist Russia that would eschew Western democracy and favor a strong leader (*vozhd*) who would stand above day-to-day politics and rule the country for the greater good of the state.[15] Rahr also explored how a future Russia would draw on its past national culture. In his broadcast of *Christian Russia* on October 13, 1989, he drew on the work of an émigré historian, Nicholas Ross, to tell the story of General Pyotr Wrangel's brief rule in Crimea in 1920. Presented as the "last best hope" to save Russia, the White Army tried to institute legal order, implement Stolypin's land reforms, establish local government, recognize the rights of Ukrainians and other national minorities, form alliances with the United States and European countries, and offer an alternative to Communist rule. That Wrangel eventually lost to the Red Army and had to evacuate over 150,000 Russians to safety in Turkey was presented as one of the great tragedies of Russian history. But this brief period of posttsarist Russia, in Rahr's words, could serve as a model for a new Russia as it emerged from Communist rule and explored new ways of shaping government and society.

In contrast to Rahr's programs, RL's other religious shows—*Path and Life* and *Beginning of the Day*—steered clear of politics but quoted extensively from the Bible and dealt with such topics as Christian family values, active church membership, the meaning of the liturgy, explications of the Old and New Testament, and lives of saints. By the late 1980s one could easily conclude that Radio Liberty—a grantee of the U.S. government funded through congressional appropriations—had become a major religious broadcaster.

Criticism of RL religious broadcasting focused primarily on the conservative Orthodoxy exhibited by the editors. "Rahr's religious ideology," Lyudmila Alexeyeva noted, "is not so much Christianity per se as romantic nostalgia for the Russian Christian past."[16] She attributed this narrow view of religion to Rahr's adherence to the conservative Russian Orthodox Church Abroad and argued, together with other independent evaluators of the Russian broadcasts, that RL needed a broader, more inclusive view of religious life. After considerable deliberation, RFE/RL management responded by introducing still another program on religion, entitled—*Religion in the Modern World*. Prepared by the Reverend Kirill Fotiev, a member of the more liberal Russian Orthodox Church in America, this program focused on such issues as ethical theology, the pacifist movement, Catholicism, ecumenism, different translations of the Bible, the role of the World Church Council, religion in Eastern Europe, and the tension between science and theology. It was the liberal answer to Rahr's conservative ideology.

As important as *Religion in the Modern World* was in broadening the scope of RL broadcasts, it still left out many important questions about religion in general. In his memoir, Rahr stated that he was criticized for his "excessive Orthodoxy"[17] and defended himself by asserting that he had wanted to develop a program on Islam or, at least, include segments on Islam in some of his broadcasts but was unable to find competent experts who could prepare Russian-language texts. But that was certainly not the case with Judaism. Rahr recalled: "Shortly before the anniversary year, 1988, I had a visit from a writer, Arkady Lvov. He knew about the criticism I was subjected to and suggested that the Thursday slot be given to him to create a program devoted to Judaism. . . . Lvov's programs turned out to be on such a high professional level and of such deep culture that they attracted even Russians who were not particularly interested in questions of Judaism."[18]

Radio Liberty: Jewish Programs

Born in Odessa in 1927, Lvov was best known in the Soviet Union for his novel, *The Courtyard* (*Dvor*), written between 1968 and 1972. Set in Odessa, it drew on the city's rich literary traditions and described the lives of different social classes in a highly realistic style. In the early 1970s Lvov became involved in Jewish causes and was charged by the KGB with the "crime of Zionist activity." No longer allowed to publish in the Soviet Union, he emigrated to the United States in 1976 and shortly afterward started working at Radio Liberty.

In many ways, Lvov's program, *Judaism*, mirrored RL's Christian programs. Its basic mission was to provide moral sustenance to beleaguered Soviet Jews who were experiencing growing anti-Semitism and were eager to learn more about the religion, culture, and customs of their ancestors. Many Jews were caught in the tentacles of Soviet bureaucracy. Jewish quotas and anti-Semitic practices denied them the opportunity to advance in their professions, raise a family, and eke out a normal Soviet existence. But applying to emigrate to Israel resulted in the loss of employment and no guarantee of actually receiving the necessary exit visa. Many Jews ended up in no-man's-land—refuseniks, in the parlance of the day.

Adopting the tone of an empathetic fellow communicant, Lvov crafted programs that explicated the readings from the Torah, related relevant episodes from Jewish history, described Jewish rituals and practices, and offered prayers (sung by famous New York cantors) and traditional music. Like Matlin at VOA, Lvov tried to help Soviet Jews, often very secular, to gain a basic understanding of their religion by including talks by prominent rabbis on religious and ethical questions.

Since the plight of refuseniks and the issue of Soviet anti-Semitism were treated extensively in Radio Liberty's human rights programming, Lvov adhered to a strictly apolitical approach. On occasion, however, he would draw on Russian history to illustrate an important concept in Jewish thought. One such example was his two-part program on the infamous trial of Menahem Mendel Beilis in 1913, an episode that no doubt all his listeners had heard of. A simple worker in Kyiv, Beilis was accused of kidnapping a young boy and committing a ritual murder. In late tsarist rule, the Union of the Russian People and other far-right groups used blood libel as an anti-Semitic canard, accusing Jews of murdering Christian children to use their blood in religious ceremonies. This charge would often lead to vicious pogroms. The Beilis case caused an outcry in Russian society, pitting the liberal intelligentsia against the extremist groups. Rather than simply condemn anti-Semitism, Lvov used the trial to show what he considered to be deeply held Jewish values of open and fair trials, the power of truthful testimony, and the belief that through questioning and evidentiary facts, one could uncover the truth. For Lvov, truth and justice were not relative concepts.

The scales of justice were clearly tilted against Beilis: the jury was comprised of twelve Christians, seven of whom belonged to the arch-conservative Black Hundreds. With the exception of the Rabbi of Moscow, Yaakov Mazeh, all the expert witnesses were Christians, and their task was to explain Jewish religious practice. The prosecution even called on a so-called expert—a Catholic priest, Justinas Pranaitis—who claimed that ritual murders were condoned in the Talmud. As Lvov explained, the key to the Beilis case was the trial itself. When Beilis was still under investigation, he was offered the possibility of a pardon in connection with the tercentenary of the Romanov dynasty, but he refused, insisting that only an open and fair trial could prove his innocence. Lvov showed how Beilis's defense lawyers, among the most prominent in tsarist Russia, questioned Pranaitis, revealing his ignorance of Judaism and inability to provide any evidence for his charges. The lawyers then brought in several experts who were Russian Orthodox but knew Hebrew texts and Jewish traditions, and they explained to the jury the sheer absurdity of the charges. Finally, they gave the floor to Rabbi Mazeh, a brilliant and passionate orator. At the end, the jury acquitted Beilis, and the trial became a symbol of a potentially liberal society emerging in tsarist Russia. But Lvov's intention was not to reexamine the Beilis case or to explore prerevolutionary Russian society but rather to use the trial as a vivid example of fundamental ethical and moral principles of Judaism triumphing over ignorance, deceit, and lies. Lvov's programs were highly professional, thoughtful in their presentation of eternal religious questions, and instructive in their explanation of Judaism. They are among the more exemplary RL broadcasts of the 1980s.

Why Religious Programming?

Russians and Americans who have come of age after the dissolution of the Soviet Union may find it difficult to understand why VOA and RL devoted so much airtime to programming about religion. After all, in today's Russia, the core historical religions—Russian Orthodoxy, Judaism, Islam, and Buddhism—enjoy official status. The Russian Orthodox Church has reclaimed its prerevolutionary preeminence as an ideological arbiter and has accumulated wealth and political power. Judaism is now accepted as an important part of Russian life: there are no longer quotas for admission to top universities; overt anti-Semitism is "politically incorrect"; there is a major museum of Jewish life in Moscow; Russian Jews are free to emigrate; and the Putin government has even carved out a good relationship with Israel. On Muslim holidays, streets in Moscow are blocked for religious processions, and Islam has emerged as the fastest growing religion in the Russian Federation. At major state functions, senior representatives of the four core religions are always present and prominently featured in state-run media. But the political situation in the 1970s and 1980s was diametrically opposite: the Soviet Union viewed religion as its primary ideological enemy and battled it with a vengeance, born of desperation.

During my years in international broadcasting, I participated in many meetings devoted to programming strategy, and the subject of religion frequently came up. Whatever personal religious views senior VOA management or the directors of the BIB may have held, these discussions were strictly secular and strategic in nature. The aim was not to proselytize but to offer VOA and RL listeners an opportunity to learn more about the religious traditions that inform so much of Russian history and culture. Ben Wattenberg and Michael Novak—to cite just two BIB directors—saw religious programming as the most effective way to reach a broad audience of believers and nonbelievers and were highly supportive of the Christian and Jewish broadcasts. Wattenberg paid special attention to our Jewish programming, but he was adamant that we should devote most of our airtime to Orthodoxy. Novak was especially interested in how RL presented the value of freedom of religion and whether it could help our listeners better understand free choice and the essence of capitalism.

Based on anecdotal materials, as well as RFE/RL audience research, we knew that the subject of religion was the soft underbelly of the Soviet regime and that broadcasting Sunday talks, liturgies, and explications of the Torah and the Bible chipped away at the edifice of Marxist ideology. As the number of religious dissidents and Jewish refuseniks grew from year to year, we realized that our programming on religion could provide much needed moral support and even protect individuals from harassment or arrest by the KGB.

In our deliberations, especially at the board level, we also discussed the domestic repercussions of our religious programming. We knew there was strong support in the White House, and through formal and informal channels, we made sure that appropriate officials at the NSC and members of Congress were aware of our religious programs. If many of RL's and VOA's political, historical, and literary programs were high-brow, aimed primarily at well-educated urban elites, our religious programming could appeal to a very broad swath of the Soviet population, and religious ceremonies could be of solace to both urban and rural listeners.

Gorbachev's policy of glasnost proved us right. By 1987 most religious dissidents were freed from the gulag; religious literature could be published and openly sold; and baptisms became the rage. The freedom to explore religion became a hallmark of the late 1980s and early 1990s. According to Levada Center polling, the most authoritative source in post-Communist Russia, by the early 1990s, only 8 percent of Russians thought that religion should not play a role in public life. Roughly 50 percent felt that religion formed the core of public morals and ethics, while a third supported the active involvement of the Orthodox Church and religious organizations in preserving cultural traditions and conducting charitable work. Nearly 60 percent thought that the basics of religion should be taught to all students in middle school.[19] Our strategic deliberations were clearly on target, and VOA and RL can take pride in having played a significant role in this dramatic transformation of Russian society.

8
Glasnost

In early September 1987 the Board for International Broadcasting received a cable from Ambassador Jack Matlock at the U.S. Embassy in Moscow, inquiring if we were interested in testing Gorbachev's policy of glasnost by meeting with Soviet officials to discuss the cessation of jamming of Radio Liberty broadcasts. While the broadcasts of BBC and VOA were periodically not jammed, reflecting shifts in Soviet foreign policy, RL had always been under attack in the Soviet media and its broadcasts heavily jammed. We were initially skeptical that any Soviet official would meet with representatives of RFE/RL or BIB, but after considerable deliberation, the board of directors decided that Matlock's suggestion was worth pursuing and proposed that my colleague, Bruce Porter, and I travel to Moscow to begin initial discussions. As senior federal officials, we carried black diplomatic passports, and the directors felt that this provided at least a modicum of protection from arbitrary actions that could be taken by the Soviet authorities.

The relationship between the Soviet Union and RFE/RL was fraught with danger and intrigue. When I joined RFE/RL in 1982, all employees had to sign an official form indicating that they would not travel to the Soviet Union or any country in the East bloc. We were also warned that we were potential targets for Soviet agents and should be especially careful when traveling outside the United States or Western Europe. In the 1950s several RL broadcasters were assassinated by Soviet agents; in 1981 RFE/RL headquarters in Munich was bombed at the direction of East bloc security services; and in 1986, Oleg Tumanov, a senior editor of the Russian Service, redefected to the Soviet Union and claimed that RFE/RL executives and broadcasters were CIA agents working to destroy the Soviet Union. In a press conference he even said that "Mark Pomar traveled with a diplomatic passport that served as his *krysha* [protection] to collect information about the Soviet Union."[1] While

Gorbachev's policies of opening up to the West were rapidly taking hold, RL continued to be routinely lambasted in the Soviet media and portrayed as a nest of vipers. Until Porter and I submitted our applications for Soviet visas, no one employed at RFE/RL or the BIB had officially requested to travel to the USSR.

As I waited to learn if the Soviet Embassy would grant us visas, I started to prepare for the negotiations by reviewing the effect of glasnost on Soviet media and identifying those aspects of Radio Liberty programming that might be useful in explaining to Soviet officials why jamming was counterproductive. A year and a half earlier, at the 27th Party Congress (February 25, 1986), Gorbachev declared the need for glasnost as an integral part of the transformation of the Soviet Union. He described it as the "further democratization of Soviet society" but also cautioned that it was inextricably tied to the "intensification of socialist self-governance." Initially, glasnost was a limited concept, intended for criticism of government and party actions by trusted establishment figures. But by early 1987, as Alexey Smirnov, a prominent human rights activist, quipped, "Glasnost became a tortoise crawling toward freedom of speech." Two mass-circulation periodicals, *Moskovskie Novosti* and *Ogonek*, now had more liberal editors, Yegor Yakovlev and Vitaly Korotich, who began to publish previously banned literary works and introduced a more conversational style of writing, shorn of the usual Soviet clichés about the decadence of the West and the glories of socialism. Under Korotich's editorship, *Ogonek* was breaking new ground with informative pieces about life in the Soviet Union. As Soviet censorship became laxer, previously banned books such Mikhail Bulgakov's *Heart of a Dog* and Boris Pasternak's *Doctor Zhivago* began to appear in Moscow bookstores, while provocative films such as Tengiz Abuladze's *Repentance*, a semiallegorical critique of Stalinism, were being screened in select cinemas. Among the more hopeful signs was the appearance of the first nongovernmental association of television producers—*Assotsiatsia avtorskogo televideniia*—that promised livelier and less tendentious programming. Even government commissions were being set up to examine the Stalinist terror of the 1930s and 1940s. As potential liberalization gathered strength, I found myself reading the Soviet press with avid interest, trying to glean the latest tidbits of free speech and to anticipate what the next surprise revelation might be. I even joined a glasnost brown-bag lunch group that met once a month at the Center for Strategic and International Studies (CSIS), in Washington DC, where American analysts of Soviet politics would share insights, often based on their latest trip to the USSR. I recall one participant describing how in the underground passage at Pushkin Square he saw a small kiosk selling icons and religious artifacts and another, slightly larger kiosk, just a few yards away, displaying stacks of *Playboy* and *Penthouse* magazines. Could the Soviet Union, he wondered, long survive if its principal ideological bugbears—religion and eroticism—could coexist so publicly in the heart of Moscow.

Like many "Russia hands," I was happy to see new sparks of freedom in the Soviet Union, but as my personal notes from those years reveal, I remained highly skeptical that Gorbachev's campaign would result in any lasting change. It was easy to allow for "controlled criticism," where the all-important guardrails were set up *a priori* to ensure that criticism would not exceed its remit. It was quite another to allow independent voices to report and comment on political and economic developments. My main reason for casting doubt on glasnost and perestroika had to do with the relentless war that the Soviet authorities continued to wage against Western broadcasters, primarily Radio Liberty. Despite proclamations by Gorbachev about a new era of openness, mainstream Soviet media had not changed its tune. In early 1987, in a prominent policy journal, *Mezhdunarodnaya zhizn'* (International affairs), Dmitri Biriukov unleashed an attack on the radios in the Stalinist mode, comparing our work to Nazi propaganda and stating that "Radio Liberty is now trying to cozy up to glasnost."[2] His principal aim was to malign the broadcasters and researchers working at RFE/RL and to imply that they were merely tools of the CIA. Biriukov focused much of his attention on the work of the RFE/RL Audience Research office, even singling out its director, Gene Parta, and providing the exact address of the RFE/RL office in Paris. More troubling were his attacks on individual RL employees, many of whom had relatives in the USSR and were always fearful that such articles in the Soviet press would endanger them, perhaps even leading to their arrest and imprisonment. This purportedly serious policy article was simply a rehashing of old-fashioned diatribes intended to scare our staff and to send a signal to other Soviet publications that glasnost did not extend to such age-old enemies as Radio Liberty.

As for RL programming, Biriukov had little to say. He stated that RL human rights broadcasts simply took materials from Amnesty International, which, he asserted, was "a front organization for the CIA." He also noted the harmful effects of VOA and RL religious broadcasts that were undermining the ideological foundations of the USSR. But his main concern was that RL programs were trying to wean away Soviet youth from communism by sowing doubts about the Soviet system. Even worse, he contended, the radios were inculcating the youth with notions of freedom that can only weaken the foundations of Socialist society. The coda of his screed was the oft-repeated Soviet refrain that the radios were in violation of international law, but this time he added a new twist, stating that their very existence violated the terms of U.S.-USSR treaty, which established diplomatic relations on November 16, 1933. But what caught my eye was Biriukov's description of the BIB as "the screen behind which the CIA pulled all the strings." The implication was clear: we were even more dangerous than the radios. And BIB was the organization I had listed as my employer on the Soviet visa application form.

As I continued to wait to learn if the Soviet Embassy would grant me a visa, I decided to investigate if Biriukov's article was a rogue piece, an expression of anger and frustration by an opponent of Gorbachev's reforms, or if it reflected official Soviet policy toward RFE/RL. The best way to do this was to examine as much of the mainstream Soviet press as I could to determine if other articles adopted a different tone toward the radios, more in keeping with Gorbachev's own rhetoric, or if they hewed to familiar lines of attack. Drawing on the rich resources of RFE/RL's monitoring division, I found forty-four articles about the radios that appeared in just the previous nine months (January to September 1987). Their titles pretty much told the whole story; among the more colorful were "Poisoners of the Airwaves" (*Pravda Vostoka*, February 15,

1987); "Relics of the Cold War" (*Molodezh Estonii*, February 11, 1987); "A Kitchen of Slanderers" (*Soviet Latvia*, August 20, 1987); "Shards of a Crooked Mirror" (*Pravda*, June 29, 1987); "Sabotage—the Music of Heavy Metal" (*Soviet Estonia*, July 7, 1987); "And the Caravan Advances: On the Front Lines of the Ideological Battle" (*Pravda Vostoka*, August 20, 1987); "Pharisees without Masks" (*Sovetskaya molodezh*, September 25, 1987); and "RFE/RL: The Tricks of Gene Pell" (*Krokodil*, March 1987). In tone and substance they all echoed Biriukov's article and reminded me of the hundreds of similar pieces that had been churned out over the decades by the Soviet ideological cottage industry. They all repeated the same tropes—Nazi collaborators, CIA agents, former Soviet ne'er-do-wells.

A few articles about Radio Liberty in 1987, however, did acknowledge Gorbachev's new policies, but rather than exploring the natural commonalities between glasnost and Western broadcasting, they twisted their logic to show that the radios were working against glasnost. In a telling piece entitled "New Recipes, an Old Kitchen: How Radio Liberty Is Fighting against Perestroika" (*Izvestia*, May 22, 1987), the authors, A. Alekseev and V. Valentinov, cited congressional testimony by Steve Forbes, chair of the BIB, noting that Radio Liberty was "interpreting glasnost and perestroika in its own way" and did not follow the official Soviet line. They then posed the question "How did Radio Liberty oppose perestroika?" and proceeded to answer: "All masters of disinformation understand that to attack perestroika frontally is a hopeless task. Their main thesis is that perestroika in the USSR is only a partial measure, that there is no follow-through, and hence Soviet people will not be able to create a successful economy in the Western style without cardinal changes in the Soviet system." This assessment, attributed to RL, suggested that Gorbachev's policies posed a direct threat to the livelihood and even survival of the Soviet ruling class. To inoculate Soviet citizens against RL's assessment of glasnost and perestroika, the *Izvestia* article yet again raised the specter of CIA warfare: "Recently, consultants from the CIA—specialists in social psychology—recommended that RL reorient its programming to appeal to different social groups—religious believers, urban professionals, and, most important, youth. . . . The CIA further instructed the radios to increase their broadcasts to the Soviet nationalities that would inflame anti-Russian sentiments and to activate its ideological call for freedom of religion in the USSR." Going further, the *Izvestia* piece even claimed that current RL programming was resurrecting the initial precepts of psychological warfare first propounded by Allen Dulles, one of the iconic Russophobes in Soviet polemics, by encouraging internal opposition to the state. Much of the article was a rehashing of Soviet clichés, but the frequent references to current "CIA experts" influencing the radio broadcasts was of concern. Since there was no relationship between the CIA and RFE/RL after 1971, I could only surmise that the dangerous "CIA recommendations" the authors were citing were in fact reports I had prepared at the BIB. One of my main responsibilities was to select RFE/RL broadcasts at random and send cassette recordings to independent outside specialists—usually university professors—who would review the tone and content and make recommendations for improvement. This was an open process, and we always sent the complete reports to RFE/RL management and, on occasion, to the National Security Council, the State Department, and appropriate Congressional committees. There was nothing secretive about our work, but given the *Izvestia* article, I could only conclude that the BIB was becoming a target for Soviet ideological warriors.

Curiously, the articles about RFE/RL in the Soviet press ignored an important element of the radio broadcasts: the voices of Russian writers, cultural figures, and major dissidents. The only people the Soviet officials attacked by name were either American executives—most often, Charles Wick and Gene Pell—or mid-level Russian editors and producers and even long-deceased broadcasters. The Soviet articles in 1987 avoided mentioning the very people who formed the core of our programming: Solzhenitsyn, Sakharov, Voinovich, Rostropovich, Nekrasov, Galich, and hundreds of other prominent émigré contributors. In a certain sense, this was understandable because Soviet ideologues did not want to advertise our broadcasts, knowing that there was a thirst among Soviet citizens to learn more about the blank pages of their history.[3] But on a deeper level, they probably understood that the appearance of major Russian artists and writers on the airwaves, many of them ardent patriots, directly undercut their main charge against RL, namely that it was part of an orchestrated Western campaign to weaken the country and to deny Russia its rightful place among the major powers in the world. The ideologues also understood that by 1987 no one could be certain what banned Russian writer or dissident— vilified for years as an enemy of the people—might suddenly be resurrected, brought home from exile, and judged acceptable by the new standards of glasnost. In such chaotic times, it was safer to stay on well-trodden paths, repeating time and again the standard line that RL was the eternal enemy.

Confronting Soviet Jamming

To our surprise, the Soviet Embassy in Washington acted expeditiously and granted us diplomatic visas, allowing Porter and me to travel to Moscow for one week of talks with Soviet officials. On our arrival at Sheremetyevo International Airport in late October 1987, we were met by a U.S. Embassy official and quickly whisked through Soviet passport control. On our way into the city, the official told us that the Security Office at the embassy had determined that it would be dangerous for us to stay in an Intourist hotel, where foreigners were normally housed, and that for our safety we would live in one of the newly built townhouses on the embassy grounds. We were free to go to our meetings and explore Moscow, but were cautioned to be careful and alert to possible "unpleasant incidents."

The next morning, we met with Ambassador Matlock, who presented us with a full schedule of meetings with officials from the Ministry of Foreign Affairs, Gostelradio (state radio), the Central Committee, as well as the U.S.A. Canada Institute, part of the Soviet Academy of Sciences that trained experts on the United States. In addition to that schedule, I had a list of requests from several Russian broadcasters in Munich to visit their relatives and friends from whom they had been cut off. I had greetings to pass on and presents to deliver to elderly parents, adult children from earlier marriages, and friends. Bruce and I decided that we would attend most meetings together and while he would go to others by himself, I would deliver the gifts. To our surprise, every meeting we had on our schedule was cancelled immediately before it was to begin. We would enter the government building, be escorted to the meeting room, and then be told that the official with whom we were to meet had been suddenly called away. After two days, we realized that our visit must have caused such confusion in the Soviet bureaucracy that no one was brave enough to sit down with two representatives of that dangerous radio station. We dutifully went to the scheduled meetings in the naive hope that someone would actually speak with us, but to no avail. Finally, on our last day in Moscow, when we had practically given up hope, a young member of the U.S.A. Canada Institute met with us. He seemed nervous, listened to us describe the work of the radios and why it supported Gorbachev's policy of glasnost, and then ended the meeting without saying a word.

We returned to Washington by way of Munich, where we met with the RL staff and described our experience in Moscow. The tone of the staff meeting was one of deep pessimism. Most RL broadcasters had experienced hardships in the Soviet Union, whether anti-Semitic attacks, arrests, or even years in the gulag. It was hard for them to conceive of a liberalizing Soviet system, and they felt that our visit was just a fluke, the result of a rash decision by an inexperienced bureaucrat. That no one, except for a low-level representative of the U.S.A. Canada Institute, would meet with us was further proof that the system remained intact. Frankly, they concluded, we were lucky to make it out safely and especially to deliver the presents as instructed without getting arrested.

My sense was that our trip was not a fruitless effort and that major changes were underway in the USSR. Not only was the Soviet press more lively and open, but people on the streets and in stores seemed friendlier, more interested in chatting with foreigners, than I had experienced on earlier trips to the USSR in the 1970s. Along with the customary shabbiness of Moscow, there were now splashes of new color—notably on the old Arbat Street, closed to traffic and sporting small cafes—and a definite spirit of hope in the air. Since the concept of glasnost was at the core of RL's mission—indeed the word itself had been used in RL policy guidelines as early as the 1950s—I was convinced that if Gorbachev's policies proved to be a new direction for the country, and not just window dressing, then the Soviet Union would eventually have to stop jamming and engage with international broadcasters. To do otherwise would be to admit to absolute hypocrisy, and by the 1980s, people in the USSR had become too worldly, too eager to see and understand the West to fall prey to another sham campaign. That gave me hope that at some point we would be able to hold the originally scheduled meetings, but only after Gorbachev's policies had worked their way through the thickets of Soviet bureaucracy. To prepare for that eventual day, I adopted a two-track approach. I would spend considerable time listening to RL broadcasts to better understand how they were responding to glasnost and perestroika. Alongside that effort I would parse the Soviet press to see if glasnost had started to alter the official Soviet assessment of RFE/RL and if the Soviet authorities were showing signs of being ready to engage with us on substantive issues.

As a first step, I met with Vladimir Matusevich, the head of the Russian Service, to discuss how RL broadcasts were handling glasnost. Brusque, acerbic, and at times quite opinionated, Matusevich was a tough task master. Few broadcasters liked him, but the entire staff respected him as an exceptionally talented journalist, a witty and trenchant writer, and a superb programming strategist. In the early days of glasnost, Matusevich realized that Gorbachev's policies offered a remarkable opportunity for RL to strengthen its role as a surrogate broadcaster. He understood that glasnost and perestroika, if carried to their logical end, would fundamentally disrupt the well-oiled Soviet bureaucratic machine. To succeed, he reasoned, Gorbachev would have to overcome deep bureaucratic resistance by going over the heads of the various government ministries and official institutions and creating an image that would appeal directly to the population as a whole. For that to happen, he would need all the resources of Soviet media, and especially television, the most popular source of news and information available in virtually every household in the country. Fortuitously, in the mid-1980s, Soviet satellite transmission made Russian television available in Europe in real time, and that meant that RL broadcasters could watch television programs along with their listeners, respond immediately to political changes, and, most important, provide a much needed political context for the programming by explaining what was new and what issues still remained taboo. In Matusevich's conception, RL would become the indispensable complement to Soviet television, the trusted guide who could help Soviet viewers make sense of the dramatic changes underway.

Trained as a film critic, Matusevich took on the task of analyzing Soviet television. "I followed Gorbachev's path as leader through television," he reminisced. "Even under conditions of harsh censorship, television gave me an insight into Gorbachev's character which I could never have gotten from books and newspapers. . . . I vividly remember a moment two or three months after he came to power. There was a meeting in a provincial city, and Gorbachev abruptly broke off the ritual of the five-minute standing ovation for the leader. These Communist rituals may have seemed ridiculous to outsiders, but they were very important to the system. And I realized right then that this guy could destroy everything."[4]

Matusevich's analysis of how Soviet television portrayed Gorbachev inspired a new weekly RL program, *A Review of Soviet Television*, that examined the content and style of the Soviet news broadcasts, as well as the new and daring television programs, such as *Vzgliad* (Viewpoint), *Prozhektor perestroiki* (Searchlight of perestoika), and *Chelovek i zakon* (Man and law). These Soviet television programs were at the cutting edge of glasnost, investigating such previously censored subjects as the gulag camps, émigré writers, environmental degradation, shortages of goods, transportation safety, and unsanctioned gatherings of Soviet citizens protesting local issues. RL programming analyzed these outbursts of free media, often providing additional information that would help Soviet citizens make sense of the story.

RL broadcasters welcomed glasnost and perestroika and applauded the brave Soviet reporters who were breaking new ground, but as well-trained journalists, they probed further, asked more questions, and would not let a pat answer by a government official be the end of the story. As Sergei Dovlatov, a major Russian writer and RL freelance contributor, noted, it was commendable that the Soviet Union was finally allowing the publication of works by Vladimir Nabokov, Osip Mandelshtam, and Anna Akhmatova, but how about the works of many contemporary Russian writers living in the West? Making the works of Solzhenitsyn or Aksyonov or Voinovich freely available would show that glasnost was indeed taking root. "Baby steps," Dovlatov cautioned his listeners, were absolutely necessary, but to be meaningful they had to grow into major adult strides.

Russian Broadcasts (October 1987–November 1988)

To test the efficacy of Matusevich's strategic approach to glasnost and perestroika, I began to listen to many different RL broadcasts from late October 1987, when we were shunned by Soviet officials in Moscow, to November 29, 1988, when all jamming of Radio Liberty ceased. These thirteen months played a critical role in the evolution of glasnost when Soviet officialdom overcame its longstanding opposition to Radio Liberty and reversed its thirty-five-year policy of condemning the radios as "mortal foes" (*smertelnye vragi*) or "enemies of the people" (*vragi naroda*). Because Radio Liberty was the voice of free Russians, how Soviet authorities treated it became a litmus test of glasnost: Would the Soviet Union allow open debate among Russians, or would it continue to circumscribe political discourse? The key words here were *Russian voices*, not those of foreigners who could always be dismissed as Russophobes. Try as they might, Soviet propagandists could not succeed in turning Solzhenitsyn, Sakharov, or many Russian émigrés into the enemies of Russia.

In examining RL's response to glasnost, I was guided by four basic questions: Was RL programming now markedly different? If it was, what were its salient features? Did the changes involve just tone and perspective, or was the content different? And did the RL broadcasters take advantage of the new spirit of openness by inviting Soviet citizens to appear on their programs?

Even a cursory examination of RL broadcasts indicated that glasnost and perestroika were major subjects. Programs such as *Writers at the Microphone* explored the new parameters of censorship and reviewed the publications of previously banned works. *Events and People, Millennium of Christianity*, and *Human Rights* analyzed new political and social developments in Russia, especially as Soviet publications started to raise subjects considered taboo in earlier times. But to gain a deeper understanding of how well Radio Liberty dealt with glasnost, I started with a reexamination of *Russia: Yesterday, Today, Tomorrow* (RYTT), a program that had traditionally focused on pre-Soviet subjects, often reflecting a narrow émigré outlook on Russian history. By the late 1980s *RYTT* was a professionally produced program that reflected different views of recent émigrés, dissidents, and Western historians.

In a May 1988 program, for example, Lyudmila Alexeyeva filed a report on a lecture given by Celestine Bohlen at the Kennan Institute of the Woodrow Wilson International Center in Washington DC. Having just completed a four-year stint as a *Washington Post* correspondent in Moscow, Bohlen described how glasnost was affecting the work of Western journalists in the Soviet Union. Drawing on her in-depth knowledge of the country, she explained how Western journalists were now able to interview even mid-level Soviet officials, attend most public events, interact freely with ordinary Soviet citizens, attend meetings at the Glasnost Club in Moscow, and, on occasion, even travel to previously closed cities. She noted that there was a new camaraderie among journalists and that the editors of popular glasnost publications, notably *Moskovskie Novosti* and *Ogonek*, made a point of welcoming Western reporters. All of these developments pointed to a dramatically different Soviet Union, but Bohlen cautioned her audience that the USSR remained a highly controlled society, still governed by fear. Her observations—candid, truthful, even empathetic—provided Soviet citizens with an all-important context for understanding the dramatic changes taking place in their country. If the Soviet authorities were truly serious about opening up the country to the world, they would have welcomed such RL programs as friendly and objective pictures of their society.

Although a foreigner's perspective on glasnost was useful, RL mostly invited prominent Soviet émigrés to comment on glasnost and perestroika, especially those who could draw on their personal knowledge of Soviet society and had continuing ties with influential figures in their home country. A good example was a program of RYTT (October 5, 1988) devoted to Alexander Zinoviev (1922–2006). An eccentric polymath, satirist, philosopher, and enfant terrible, Zinoviev was interviewed by Vladimir Tolz about the political changes taking place in the Soviet Union. Rather than speak of glasnost as a step in the direction of Western democracy, the usual response of most guests on RL, Zinoviev inveighed against Gorbachev and his associates, describing them as demagogues, hypocrites, and careerists with little knowledge of Soviet communism. He suggested that Gorbachev was building a power base not unlike the one built by Stalin and that real glasnost was not sustainable and would soon peter out. He also spoke disparagingly of the inchoate cooperative market economy and argued that Western democracy and a multiparty system were incompatible with Russian and Soviet values. Although most of the points made by Zinoviev were clearly misguided, RL broadcast the interview in full but did not endorse his views. Matusevich and his senior editors felt that it was imperative for RL, as a surrogate broadcaster, to present its listeners with a broad range of interpretations of glasnost and perestroika and allow them to draw their own conclusions.

A major achievement of RYTT was a two-part series devoted to the well-known Soviet historian Natan Eidelman (1930–89), aired on June 22, 1988 and July 27, 1988. A specialist on eighteenth- and nineteenth-century Russian history, Eidelman was an official Soviet historian. Though not part of the dissident movement, he was nonetheless universally respected as a serious and honest scholar. In June 1988 he was invited by the University of Paris to give a lecture on glasnost and new historical research in the Soviet Union. In a bold move, Fatima Salkazanova, a senior editor in the Paris bureau, approached Eidelman, requesting permission to tape his lecture for broadcast on RL and conduct an in-depth interview with him, focusing on how glasnost was affecting Russian historiography. In a sign of the times, Eidelman agreed and became one of the first Soviet citizens to appear in an RL broadcast, interact with an RL correspondent in a professional and friendly manner, and, most important, return home safely.

An engaging lecturer, Eidelman noted three areas where glasnost was having a profound effect on historiography. The first dealt with the publication of histories, memoirs, and documents that had been banned for years. Eidelman admitted that this was a significant development, but cautioned that many important works, including *The Gulag Archipelago*, remained under lock and key. The second area was Soviet radio and television that were growing bolder in tone and raising probing questions about Soviet history. But the real impact of glasnost, he noted, was taking place in closed seminars and roundtable discussions where historians and writers were examining Soviet archival documents about collectivization, the gulag, and other proscribed subjects. These young historians, Eidelman reminded RL listeners, were no longer afraid to raise thorny questions, probe historical sources, question the role of Lenin, or interpret events without resorting to Marxist theory. If glasnost continued to develop, Eidelman predicted, Russian archives would be open in the 1990s, and new histories of the Soviet Union would be published. In her interview, Salkazanova encouraged Eidelman to project what the Soviet Union might look like in the 1990s, even, she said, if this was a flight of fantasy. While Eidelman did not anticipate the collapse of the USSR, he described a future Russia as a soft authoritarian power with a state-run economy. He placed great hope in the growth of business cooperatives and joint ventures and believed they could evolve into a vibrant market economy, but one limited to small business. Big business, he said quite presciently, would always be in the hands of the state.

Listening to Salkazanova's interview with Eidelman, I could sense the natural flow of the conversation. Eidelman expressed no fear in appearing on Radio Liberty, and his voice was relaxed as he described conditions in the Soviet Union. That he was in Paris as a member of a Soviet delegation meant that he had had to go through the prescribed KGB briefing, warning Soviet travelers to avoid "dangerous émigrés" and to steer clear of anti-Soviet organizations. Yet the fact that Eidelman, who had spent his entire life walking a fine political line, chose to cooperate with Radio Liberty in a forthright manner could only indicate that he knew that the party line had shifted (or would soon shift) and that he would not face disciplinary action on his return. For her part, Salkazanova exemplified professional Western journalism. She knew she had a major story and wanted to make sure that her listeners would hear directly from Eidelman without any commentary or editing on her part. By presenting Eidelman's lecture first, she laid the groundwork for her interview. Knowing the risk that Eidelman was taking, she probed gently. At one point, as Eidelman described the pitfalls of Soviet historiography, she ventured to ask if he had ever had to lie in his works. Eidelman responded that he had always strived to tell the truth but that Soviet ideological constraints made it virtually impossible for historians to tell the full truth. As an example, he cited his extensive research of the Decembrist Revolt of 1825 and his discovery that some of the revolutionaries, accorded heroic status by Soviet ideologues, had in fact cooperated with the tsarist authorities and had even betrayed their fellow rebels. When he wanted to include this nugget in his book, he was cautioned by a senior Soviet historian that it was best to leave out material that challenged ideological icons. The Soviet Union had decreed that the Decembrists were the precursors of the October Revolution, and hence one could not cast aspersions on them. What Soviet historians had to do, Eidelman told Salkazanova, was to fight hard to include as much truthful information as possible, knowing there were red lines they could not cross. This was not an easy task, but, Eidelman noted, the best Russian historians strove to tell the full truth.

Sensing that Eidelman was relaxing and enjoying the interview, Salkazanova asked a more probing question: "Why was there so much literary samizdat of high quality and so little, if any historical samizdat?" Eidelman took slight exception to this assertion and answered that historians in the Soviet Union had many ideological barriers to overcome, first and foremost access to historical archives, books, and Western scholarship. Those barriers were fiercely guarded by ideological watchdogs. But Eidelman remained hopeful that glasnost would soon silence those ideologues and the entire field of history would be "liberated" (*"pri glasnosti raskreposhchaetsia istoriya"*). No longer burdened by ideology, young historians would cite historical facts, question Soviet ideology, and feel free to present new conceptions of Russian history. In conclusion, Eidelman stated his belief in the honesty of the coming generation of Russians, which he termed "*ne pugannoe pokolenie*" (the fearless generation).

The broadcasts of RYTT illustrated the growing significance of glasnost, but they were not the only programs to tackle the burning issues of the day. Another innovative new program, entitled *Over the Barriers* (*Poverkh bar'erov*), was a "political-cultural journal," hosted by RL bureaus in Munich, Paris, and New York. *Over the Barriers* explored new artistic developments under glasnost, the prospects of democracy in Russia, new Soviet ties with the West, and even the emergence of explicit depictions of sex in Russian arts and culture. Sex has always been an entertaining subject for media, but in the case of the Soviet Union, it carried political significance. After a brief period of openness about sexual matters in the 1920s, the Soviet Union adopted a puritanical approach that deemed virtually any public display of physical sex or nudity as pornographic and dangerously Western. Even kissing on stage or in films in the 1940s was seen as provocative. In sharp contrast to twentieth-century Western literature, Soviet writings avoided graphic descriptions of sexual relations. At times, Soviet public prudery even resulted in comical situations. In July 1986, during a telebridge hosted by Vladimir Posner and Phil Donahue, one of the American participants asked if "Soviet television ads were also focused mostly on sex," to which a Russian participant indignantly responded, "We don't have any sex, and we're categorically against it." Her utterance, taken out of context, caused tittering among the Russian audience, and in time entered the Russian lexicon as a popular Soviet meme— "*seksa u nas net.*"

As ideological strictures fell by the wayside, Soviet artists began to address questions of sex, violence, and gender roles. In 1987 Lev Dodin, the director of the Maly Drama Theatre in Moscow, caused a sensation in elite cultural circles when he staged Alexander Galin's play *Stars in the Morning Sky*, a brutal story about four prostitutes who were locked away in a mental institution during the 1980 Olympics so that Moscow would have a "pristine look." The audience was shocked by the nudity and even a scene of sexual coupling. A year later, Vasily Pichul's film *Little Vera* appeared in Soviet theaters and quickly became the most popular film of the year with over fifty-four million viewers. It told the story of a teenage girl who goes to seedy nightclubs, listens to Western pop music, apes the latest Western fashions, venerates Madonna, and lives—in the classic words of Soviet ideologues—a decadent Western life. The success of *Little Vera* was shortly followed by *Intergirl* (*Inter-devochka*), a play on the word *Intourist*, a Soviet travel agency catering exclusively to foreign travelers. It's the story of Tanya, a nurse by day and a high-class prostitute by night, who quite openly declares that she wants a "good life," to own her apartment, drive a nice car, and see the world. In a conversation with her mother, she declared that prostitution was just a trade, an amorality traditionally scorned in Russian culture but popular in 1989. The sexual revolution under glasnost also extended to the printed word, with translations of such works as D. H. Lawrence's *Lady Chatterley's Lover*, as well as the publication of previously banned classics of Russian erotic writing, including Ivan Barkov's "Shameful Odes" and Pushkin's playful "The Gabrieliad." Years of ideological constraints and harsh censorship were disappearing, and Russian society was bursting forth with giddy freedom.

The new sense of freedom was precisely the kind of subject that *Over the Barriers* would tackle because it not only connected Russian arts with Soviet politics but also raised broader questions of eroticism in Western culture, new conceptions of the self, and even evolving gender roles. To grapple with this subject, on November 18, 1988, RL brought together a stalwart group of New York writers—Alexander Genis, Petr Weil, Boris Paramonov, and Sergei Dovlatov—to try to make sense of new cultural developments and provide Russian listeners with a richer context for assessing these radical changes. Weil began by juxtaposing two different views of sex in Soviet arts. On one hand, the youth magazine *Smena* (Change), praised the new eroticism in Russian literature and film while on the other, Valentin Rasputin (1937–2015), a popular "village writer," condemned overt sexual content in the arts, claiming that it was alien to Russian artistic tradition and one more example of Western corruption of the Russian soul. Soon, Rasputin opined, Russia would allow pornography and, even worse, sanction homosexual relations. Given this framework, Paramonov spoke about how the freedom to express sexual matters corelated closely with political structure and human rights. He called the Soviet Union an ideocracy, with the state imposing artificial constraints on natural human activities in the name of an abstract ideal. Genis and Weil, meanwhile, turned the discussion to the literary antecedents of this new sexual awakening, noting the Russian tradition of dividing human behavior into the "higher sphere" of love, ideals, and beliefs and the "lower depths" of physical love and animal instincts. They pointed out that even though classical Russian literature dealt head-on with sexual desire—in *Anna Karenina* and *The Brothers Karamazov*, for example—Russian writers did not develop a literary language to describe the physical aspects of love. But the highlight of the discussion was Sergei Dovlatov's "tongue-in-cheek confession" that it was very difficult for him to write well about sex. The two most challenging subjects for a writer, Dovlatov stated, were diametrical opposites—God and religion on one end; sex and love on the other. He tried to write about both but found the process humbling, with his prose often riddled with clichés. In Dovlatov's opinion, with the exception of James Joyce and William Faulkner, there were few English writers who could write well about sex. Even Hemingway, he quipped, was more successful in describing fishing than in depicting sex. Dovlatov concluded his commentary by noting that Russian artistic attempts at representing sex were understandable and probably necessary for breaking out of the grip of Soviet censorship, but it would take years of freedom and experimentation before Russian literature would develop its own erotic voice.

The tone of *Over the Barriers*—entertaining, reasonable, empathetic—illustrated the most effective way to shape RL programming in the time of glasnost. The aim was to be fully engaged with the dramatic changes taking place in the Soviet Union. The more successful RL programs identified subjects that exposed deep rifts in society, had broad social resonance, and expressed ideas still too raw to be discussed and debated calmly in Soviet media or public space. This approach included interviews with such prominent literary figures as Tatiana Tolstaya,

Efim Etkind, Iuz Aleshkovsky, and Andrei Bitov and the examination of selective censorship, especially of more controversial works. At their best, the Russian broadcasts provided context, explaining how the issues of the day related to broader world trends and helping listeners to understand what was truly new in the Soviet Union.

Soviet Press (October 1987–November 1988)

While Radio Liberty was engaging seriously with glasnost and perestroika and inviting Soviet experts to participate in their broadcasts, the Soviet press continued its familiar drumbeat of attacks. During the period from October 1987 to November 1988, I found thirty-one articles about the Radio Liberty (with only occasional mention of VOA) that repeated the same stories and clichés about the dangerous activities of the two radios. One article, entitled "The Choice—Freedom" (*Sovetskaya kultura*, December 26, 1987), even resorted to Stalinist rhetoric, lambasting prominent RL broadcasters by name and quoting from their private correspondence. Americans were not spared, and Keith Bush, the venerable director of the RL Research Department, came under direct attack. Most articles during this thirteen-month period, however, acknowledged the political changes taking place under Gorbachev but argued that this "new openness" made the USSR more vulnerable to Western influence. A telling piece in *Argumenty i fakty* (April 1988), entitled "The KGB Informs and Comments: What Is behind Strategic Plans?," began with a dire warning about the coordinated efforts of the secret services of the United States, West Germany, and France "to conduct covert operations in the USSR with the aim of forming political opposition groups that would take advantage of perestroika and democratization to destroy the Soviet State and its social order from within."[5] The article further noted that these covert activities would encourage Soviet citizens to call for "independent unions, multiparty elections, public demonstrations," and even the freedom to share "publications hostile to socialism." Waging these activities on behalf of the CIA were various émigré groups, but the most dangerous, the KGB concluded, were those found at RFE/RL and coordinated by three human rights activists: the head of RL News, Edward Kuznetsov, and two frequent contributors—Vladimir Bukovsky and Vladimir Maximov. The article concluded that the gravest danger to the survival of the Soviet state came from RFE/RL.

To further emphasize this point, *Argumenty i fakty* ran a companion piece in the same issue, entitled "Why We Continue Jamming RFE/RL?" The author, N. Panin, sketched out a brief history of the radios and even quoted C. D. Jackson, one of the founders of RFE, that the radios were set up with "the aim of psychological warfare that would provoke domestic instability." Panin asserted that "virtually all management positions at RFE/RL were manned by CIA agents who organize, direct, and coordinate all activities of the radios." Their current tactics "included raising nationality issues, encouraging religious fanaticism, and trying to convince their listeners of the futility of perestroika." But after mounting an attack on RL, Panin could come up with only three examples of harmful programming. His first example was RL's apparent admonition to its listeners to assess current Soviet policies in "a sober way" and "without illusory dreams"; the second cautioned listeners to "pursue legal means in asserting their rights"; while the third acknowledged "that ethnic conflicts within the USSR could bring to an end Soviet tyranny." There was no indication if these snippets were from correspondent reports, comments by guest commentators, or quotes from the Western press. In short, Panin's examples bore no relationship to psychological warfare.

None of the media attacks cited any proof that RL was violating its journalistic code or inciting illegal activity. Some of the articles expressed fear that the nationality services of RL, broadcasting in the languages of Central Asia and the Caucasus, were abetting independence movements, but those assessments simply reflected a growing sense in the USSR that the country was splintering along national lines. At other times, Soviet television tried to resurrect the image of RL as an evil force by interviewing Oleg Tumanov, the former RL editor who had redefected in 1986, but he had nothing new to add and probably had lost whatever credibility he may have initially enjoyed. Indeed, any open-minded Soviet listener would quickly see that RL programming welcomed the political changes underway, expressed empathy for the challenges Soviet citizens were facing, and was supportive of freedom in Russia. But for those Soviet citizens who were fearful of glasnost and opposed Gorbachev's overtures to the West, RL remained a convenient symbol of the "eternal enemy," that conglomerate of émigré activists and secretive CIA agents who were using Gorbachev's openness to destroy the old order. Knowing that it would be difficult to attack glasnost in the Soviet press, the domestic opponents of Gorbachev could use Radio Liberty as its tocsin, sending a warning that an age-old foe was at the front door and that mindless democratic liberals were ready to usher in RL, treating it as a legitimate international broadcaster.

Despite the preponderance of attacks on RL, there were three short articles that presaged a new era. The first was a TASS report, reprinted in *Argumenty i fakty* (February 1988, no. 8), that summarized the 1987 BIB annual report, citing the RFE/RL budget and listing the main programming priorities for the coming year. TASS made no mention of the CIA, avoided commentary, and stated that Radio Liberty was an independent broadcaster funded by the U.S. government. This was the first neutral description of RFE/RL that I found in my extensive research of the Soviet press. The second reference to RFE/RL was in a letter, published in *Izvestia* (June 6, 1988), in which the author confessed that he was a regular listener to RL and often discussed the broadcasts with his friends. He added that with Gorbachev's glasnost in force, there was no need to jam the broadcasts. The third piece appeared in *Argumenty i fakty* (no. 35, 1988) and simply affirmed that Soviet authorities should not fear the radio broadcasts and hence there was no need for jamming. Small as these examples were, they pointed to a struggle within official Soviet circles about how best to deal with an emblematic symbol of the Cold War: Should the USSR continue jamming RL, or should it embrace its new freedom and cease jamming? This question became especially acute as U.S.-Soviet relations began their fitful upswing and the question of jamming was seen by the United States as a major impediment to the improvement of relations.

End of Jamming

Despite continuing Soviet disinformation campaigns in the 1980s, American and Soviet senior officials began to meet frequently, and the tone of those meetings gradually became less confrontational. At the presidential level, Ronald Reagan and Mikhail Gorbachev were developing a close working relationship and on January 1, 1988, exchanged televised New Year's greetings. After years of being vilified by the Soviet media, Reagan was beginning to be viewed by ordinary Russians as a benign figure. As Charles Wick noted, "Reagan's television appearance and interview in *Izvestia* had sparked a full-fledged 'Reagan phenomenon' in the USSR. The U.S. Embassy in Moscow reported that the Soviet public perceived the President as 'sincere, straightforward, and humane,' a 'moderate man and likeable.'"[6] Such warming relations were accompanied by concrete achievements. In January 1988 the Soviet Union ceased jamming VOA broadcasts and the Polish broadcasts of Radio Free Europe. In April, Wick led a delegation of U.S. government and private sector leaders at a broad-ranging meeting with Soviet officials that explored ways of expanding the exchange of books, print journalism, broadcasting, and films.[7] That meeting was followed by the Reagan-Gorbachev Summit in Moscow (May 29–June 2), which raised questions of public diplomacy and communications. As Nicholas Cull noted, "The highlights of the Summit included Reagan's announcement of a new youth exchange initiative. The Soviet press accentuated the positive, reporting the conference as 'truly a landmark,' the beginning of serious nuclear disarmament and the 'dying of the Cold War.'"[8]

At the Board for International Broadcasting, we watched these high-level meetings with keen interest, trying to determine how we could most effectively raise the question of jamming. We decided that our best shot was to join forces with USIA and to secure a seat at the next major round of the U.S.-USSR Bilateral Information Talks, scheduled for September 26–29, 1988, in Moscow. With USIA and White House concurrence, we accompanied Wick and sixty-seven American government and private sector leaders to Moscow for high-level discussions about the free flow of information. This time, Bruce Porter and I were joined by Steve Forbes for whom this was the first trip to the heart of the "evil empire."

The plenary session got off to a shaky start. After the customary exchange of pleasantries, Wick raised the question of Soviet disinformation, stating that it should be deplored by everyone who professes a belief in reform. "Under new thinking," Wick asked, "how could the Soviet side knowingly approve the dissemination of such patently false and misleading stories as the alleged invention of AIDS in a U.S. military laboratory, the alleged invention by the U.S. of an ethnic weapon, or the alleged U.S. responsibility for the Jonestown tragedy?"[9] Soviet disinformation campaigns were a point of contention between the two countries, and it was proper for Wick to raise the issue forcefully. But as other senior USIA officials chimed in with more examples, I thought the Soviet side would object and bring our meeting to a quick close. To my surprise, the back-and-forth continued for quite a while with the American side citing more examples of Soviet disinformation and the Soviet side denying those charges. The plenary session initially sounded like a UN debate with each side speaking past each other, but as the meeting progressed there were momentary flashes of honesty. Leonid Dobrokhotov, the head of the Propaganda Department of the Central Committee, admitted that Soviet scientists had long ago rejected the notion that the United States invented the AIDS virus. Vadim Perfiliev, deputy chief of the Information Department of the Ministry of Foreign Affairs, conceded that there were times his department had issued "incorrect information." Those comments ensured that the session ended on a positive note, and specific plans were drawn up to hold another round of discussions in several months.

The next day, Forbes, Porter, and I met with Valentin Falin, the chair of the Novosti Press Agency and the formal head of the Soviet Information Talks. A long-time Soviet official, who had served in the KGB, in the Ministry of Foreign Affairs, and as ambassador to West Germany, Falin greeted us in a cold and perfunctory manner. There were no pleasantries to exchange, and he seemed visibly uncomfortable sitting down with three representatives of RFE/RL, acting as though he had been sent to deliver a message he did not agree with. His first words caught us by surprise. "We have noticed," he said, taking a long pause, "a distinct improvement in the broadcasts of Radio Liberty." What followed those key words was the usual litany of RL sins: unfair criticism of the Soviet role in Afghanistan, insufficient respect for the democratization of Soviet society, a lack of appreciation for the new freedom of religion in the USSR, encouragement of nationalism in the Soviet republics, wrong data, and incorrect facts. As I listened to Falin's criticism, all standard Soviet fare, I felt that he was simply going through the motions and reading from a list prepared by his staff. He knew the decision to stop jamming RL had already been made at the top, and he was just the messenger. The world that he and his colleagues had strived to build was crumbling before his very eyes. Radio Liberty—vilified for decades, emblematic of a non-Communist Russia—was now being treated in Moscow with respect as an important international broadcaster. How uncomfortable that meeting must have been for him, a party apparatchik and a diehard opponent of glasnost.[10] We dutifully noted his criticism, politely stood our ground regarding specific broadcasts, and promised to relay his specific complaints to RFE/RL management. Toward the end of the meeting, Forbes raised the issue of jamming, reminding Falin that it was a violation of international law and contradicted the spirit of glasnost. There was no response from Falin, and the meeting came to an abrupt end. But as we walked out, we all had a sense of jubilation—we knew we had won. Just by sitting down with us and talking about RL, Falin communicated to us that it was only a matter of time before jamming would cease. Knowing that the Soviet authorities had just approved a VOA news bureau in Moscow, we even wondered if someday RL would be able to open an office as well. It was at that moment that I began to believe that the USSR had indeed embarked on an unprecedented path of reform and no one, least of all senior Soviet officials, knew where it would lead.

On the night of November 21, 1988, roughly two months after our Moscow meeting, George Woodard, the director of engineering at RFE/RL, received a call from the RFE/RL technical monitoring station in Germany, indicating that jamming of RFE and RL broadcasts had abruptly ended. "So unbelievable was this development," Woodard reminisced, "that all my colleagues and I could think of doing was to 'keep listening—it must be a mistake.' Throughout the night, into the next day, and in the days following it was confirmed. . . . RFE/RL programs were clear of jamming noise."[11] Our reading of the meeting with Falin had been correct, and it had simply taken several weeks for the decision to stop jamming to work its way through the many layers of Soviet bureaucracy to the hundreds of actual stations spread across the entire country. Jamming was a large operation in the USSR; engineers at VOA and BBC estimated that the Soviet Union spent between $500 million and $1 billion annually to jam, more than the combined annual operating budgets of the VOA, RFE/RL, the BBC, and Deutsche Welle.[12]

The end of jamming opened up a new era for Radio Liberty. "From that moment on," noted Sofia Berezhkova, a Russian expert on international media, "the gradual rehabilitation of Radio Liberty in the USSR began and changes in its operations were noticeable."[13] One of the first steps taken by the Russian Service was to hire freelance contributors in Moscow and other Russian cities. The initiative came from Savik Shuster, an experienced journalist who had joined RL in 1988 after working for several Western news organizations. "I thought it was absurd that RL did not have any freelancers or stringers in Moscow," Shuster recalled. "This is the very basis of sound journalism. So I started looking for journalists willing to report under their own names. These had to be brave souls."[14] The first stringer Shuster hired, Dmitri Volchek, recalled when he was hired:

I was working at a semilegal, independent journal, *Glasnost*. We had just finished preparing our daily human rights bulletin when the telephone rang—it was Savik Shuster calling from Munich. He explained that he was looking for a Moscow correspondent for a new live radio program.... The first assignment was very simple—to do a survey of the Soviet press. I accepted immediately. The next day I rushed to the nearest kiosk to buy *Pravda*, *Sovetskaya Rossiya*, and others.... That evening, when I heard my voice over the RL airwaves, I didn't know what was greater—sheer terror or absolute joy. What I had done seemed inconceivable—a direct challenge to the entire Soviet government ... and I expected to be arrested the next day ... but nothing happened. The colossus crumbled silently.[15]

Within a short time, Volchek was joined by some of the finest young investigative journalists in the Soviet Union, including Andrei Babitsky, Mark Deich, Karen Agamirov, Mikhail and Maxim Sokolov, and stringers in Leningrad, Kyiv, Riga, Tallinn, and Tbilisi. By 1989 RL was fully engaged as a local news station and was often credited with being the first to scoop other media in presenting quickly evolving political stories.

The cessation of jamming required serious rethinking of RL programming strategy. Samizdat, in its traditional sense, disappeared as Soviet censorship weakened by the day and self-published works could circulate freely. Extensive readings from banned books—long a staple of RL broadcasts—had also outlived their relevance. By 1989 Solzhenitsyn's works began appearing in Moscow and other cities, and in July it was announced that *The Gulag Archipelago* would be published in the USSR. New arrests of political activists were rare, and the dissidents still held in the gulag were gradually being released. Although RL continued to report on violations of human rights, this subject no longer dominated the programming schedule.

With new times came new programs. Along with *Liberty Live* that incorporated direct feeds from freelance correspondents in the USSR, RL started to introduce programming that addressed more complex subjects, now that listeners no longer had to deal with external interference and could follow nuanced interpretations. A good example of this new programming was a half-hour show produced primarily in the New York bureau, called *The Russian Idea (Russkaya ideia)*. Coined by the Russian philosopher Vladimir Soloviev in 1887, the term *Russian idea* was intended to express "the meaning of Russia's existence in world history" and "to embody the Christian transformation of life, built on Russian values of truth, virtue, and beauty." This utopic concept became a prominent part of Russian philosophy in the late nineteenth and early twentieth centuries and was used by many Russian philosophers—among them Evgenii N. Trubetskoi, Vasily V. Rozanov, Semen L. Frank, and Ivan A. Ilyin—to project a nationalist vision of Russia in opposition to Marxism and communism. Before glasnost, Soviet writings about the Russian idea were mostly proscribed, but once censorship ended, there was pent-up interest in exploring this aspect of Russian culture. Radio Liberty had aired programs about the Russian idea in earlier times, but those were primarily reports by RL contributors and readings from texts. Now, with Russian classics of philosophy readily available in bookstores, Soviet writers were beginning to explore age-old Russian ideas, and RL could engage its listeners in a broader discussion of them.

The RL program *The Russian Idea* covered many different subjects, ranging from culturology and utopian beliefs to the works of such seminal Russian thinkers as Georgy Fedotov, Nikolai Berdyaev, and Viacheslav Ivanov. The most interesting programs responded directly to recent publications in the Soviet Union. In the premiere broadcast, on February 19, 1989, Boris Paramonov began with a reference to Andrei Sinyavsky's assertion that the ideological fault lines in the USSR were now between nationalists and liberals and no longer between Communists and anti-Communists. Communism and Marxist theory were passé, Sinyavsky contended, and Russian intellectuals were now either hewing to a conception of Russia as an exceptional country and a unique civilization or seeking to join the Western world. Paramonov then related these notions to a recent three-part article in *Izvestia* by Boris Vasiliev, a Soviet writer, that explored the moral foundations of Russian culture, juxtaposing them with bourgeois principles in the West. After reminding his listeners of the main points in the *Izvestia* articles, Paramonov questioned Vasiliev's conception of Western culture and his ignorance of the moral imperatives of the Protestant ethic. Paramonov engaged Vasiliev in a friendly intra-Russian discussion of key points about Russian history and traditions. This was not a foreign voice telling Russians what they should do, but rather Russians talking among themselves about their traditions, their civilization, and the path ahead for the country.

Another example of RL's direct engagement with topical issues of the day was a lengthy interview on May 11, 1989, in *Over the Barriers* with Vasily Belov, the acclaimed Soviet *derevenshchik* (village prose writer) who managed to be idolized both by far-right Russian nationalists and the Soviet Communist establishment. The author of over sixty books—among them *Privichnoe delo* (Business as usual), *Kanuny* (Eves), and

God velikogo pereloma (The year of the great break)—Belov was a harsh critic of Soviet collectivization, which he asserted had been devised by cosmopolitan bureaucrats to destroy the Russian people and their national identity. In his conspiratorial writings, he saw Stalin as a victim of Jewish-Masonic forces within the Soviet government led by Iakov Iakovlev, the chair of the All-Union Commission on Collectivization. These views, more often expressed through anti-Semitic "dog whistles," did not prevent Belov from being hailed as the "conscience of Russia" by the ultranationalist organization Pamiat' or from receiving the highest accolades from the Communist Party, including the USSR State Prize (1981), Order of the Red Banner of Labor (1982), and the Order of Lenin (1984). Belov also enjoyed public prominence as a member of the Supreme Soviet of the USSR (1989–91). After the Soviet Union collapsed, he retained his Communist Party membership, but that did not preclude his receiving the Order of the Venerable Sergius of Radonezh (2002) and the Order for the Merit to the Fatherland (2003). An ardent nationalist, Belov devoted himself to preserving Russian historical monuments and, upon his death in 2012, was honored by Patriarch Kirill.

Belov was a major figure in Russian culture and Soviet politics and a worthy subject for an in-depth interview. But to provide a proper context, Vladimir Matusevich first reminded listeners of Belov's anti-Semitic views, his reliance on conspiracies, and his unfair criticism of Radio Liberty. Only then did he turn to Mikhailo Mikhailov, a prominent Yugoslav writer and human rights activist, to conduct the interview. In the finer traditions of Western journalism, Mikhailov posed probing questions without resorting to sarcasm. He began by referencing Igor Vinogradov's recent critique of Belov's anti-Semitic views. Mikhailov then asked why Belov believed in conspiracies and why he thought a relatively low-level bureaucrat like Iakov Iakovlev[16] could determine national policy. When Belov hemmed and hawed about Iakovlev's role, insisting that the Soviet bureaucracy "broke the back of the peasantry," Mikhailov agreed that Stalin's so-called second revolution and resulting famines, especially in Ukraine, were national tragedies, but he didn't let Belov off the hook, questioning why he fell so easily for pat explanations. The more Mikhailov probed, the more uncertain and evasive were Belov's answers. By the end of the interview, one could sense that Belov had basically discredited himself and kept insisting that until all historical documents from the 1930s were declassified, Russians could not know for sure how decisions about collectivization were taken. Having conducted an interview that would resonate with Russian listeners, Mikhailov gladly conceded that last point.

With each month of unhindered radio transmission, RL gained greater public stature, and that opened up new programming opportunities. A growing network of freelance journalists in different Soviet cities and republics allowed RL to report on local events and review the regional press, making their stories accessible to the entire country. The program, *The Soviet Union and the Nationality Question*, provided regular reports about developments in different republics, including discussions by Western experts on how other societies in the world coped with the complexities of a multiethnic population. The nationality question was further supplemented by such programs as *The Baltic Journal* and *Jewish Culture and Social Life*. On the cultural front, RL introduced *Ex Libris*, which presented works by promising writers. Among the more memorable broadcasts was a dramatization of Alexander Kabakov's controversial screenplay, *The Defector*, and Sergei Kaledin's short novel *The Construction Battalion*. The new programs were further enhanced by the presence of popular Soviet cultural figures, including the well-known Soviet writer Anatoly Strelyany, who prepared humorous and highly entertaining radio sketches about the impact of perestroika on life in the Soviet hinterlands. In 1989 RL conducted interviews with many leading figures in the country, including Boris Yeltsin, Andrei Sakharov, Roald Sagdeev, Yuri Lyubimov, Andrei Voznesensky, and Anatoly Rybakov. In 1990 the Russian Service aired an interview with Svetlana Alexievich about her recent book, *Zinky Boys*, a collection of first-hand accounts of the war in Afghanistan. In the interview, the future Nobel laureate described how the Soviet military had attacked her work, how she was scorned by the authorities for revealing the true side of the war, and how she detested the retrograde Soviet bureaucracy. In keeping with its core mission, RL offered her the opportunity to speak "over the heads of those bureaucrats" and reach her growing readership. As Ivan Tolstoy has noted, virtually every famous (and not so famous) writer in the Soviet Union wanted to appear in RL broadcasts, and those programs contain their fresh and unfiltered voices as they responded to the new freedoms ushered in by Gorbachev's reforms.

During 1990 and 1991 RL continued to develop its innovative programming, introducing new shows that took advantage of untrammeled access to Soviet listeners. The New York bureau produced a lively, twice-weekly program, entitled *Broadway 1775*, which communicated the dynamism of American life through interviews with Soviet tourists and visitors, reviews of the American press, and timely discussions of political and economic issues of interest to the Soviet audience. Another program, *Aspects*, summed up the main news of the week and discussed the many letters that RL was now receiving from listeners across the USSR. But the biggest achievement of those years was the systematic building of a unique stringer network that numbered over one hundred freelance journalists reporting from all the main cities of the country. Most of the reports were filed in Russian, but some of the journalists were also able to provide on-the-ground reporting in one of the twelve nationality languages of Radio Liberty. This network made the Russian broadcasts an all-union news service, an accomplishment that would have seemed inconceivable to the founders of RFE/RL.

Radio Liberty as National Hero

Despite the end of jamming and the growth of the freelance network in the Soviet Union, RFE/RL continued to be a polarizing factor in Soviet politics, as reflected in the Soviet press. To raise doubts about the decision to stop jamming RL or to remind Soviet citizens of the initial CIA funding of the radios was a politically safe way to question Gorbachev's reforms and the negative effects of glasnost. It was not surprising that Nina Andreyeva began her infamous assault on glasnost and perestroika in *Sovetskaya Rossiya* by singling out the baleful influence of international broadcasters on Soviet youth and the "ideologically weak." International broadcasting, she stated, was infecting her country and destroying the very principles of communism and the

Socialist way of life.[17] In contrast, to write positively about RL in the Soviet press or to participate in the Russian-language broadcasts was to signal a ready acceptance of democratic norms and a more open Russian society.

Six weeks after jamming ceased, *Pravda*, the official newspaper of the Communist Party of the Soviet Union, published a front-page article, entitled "A Conversation without Dictaphones: A Report from the Headquarters of Radio Liberty" (January 16, 1989). Natalya Larionova, a special *Pravda* correspondent, began her exposé in the style of a mystery novel. With just a hint of intrigue, she described being led by a Radio Liberty staffer to the Washington bureau and seeing many security cameras. After describing the offices and listing the names of the RL correspondents, Larionova rehashed RL history, noting its goal of liberating Russia from communism. She stated that RL served three functions: propaganda, subversive activities, and espionage. So detailed was her presentation that she even quoted William Donovan, the legendary head of the OSS in World War II and founder of the CIA, about the "use of propaganda as an instrument of war." Her aim was to draw a direct line between RFE/RL and the CIA by accusing RL of sowing hatred among the peoples of the USSR, undermining public trust in the Soviet government and the Communist Party of the Soviet Union (CPSU), spreading disinformation about the economic and military might of the USSR, and describing the advantages of a Western lifestyle, including the system of free enterprise. In conclusion, she mused that "it would seem that my views of Radio Liberty would not be to the taste of the journalists with whom I am meeting."

Up to this point, Soviet readers would have recognized common Soviet clichés about RFE/RL. Perhaps the only difference was that Larionova did not engage in ad hominem attacks on individual RL broadcasters. But having established the standard Soviet narrative, she abruptly changed her tone and invited the RL broadcasters to have their say. "Actually, we were the forerunners of glasnost and perestroika in your country," Larissa Silnitskaya, the head of the Washington office, told Larionova. "What we have been broadcasting for many years, you are now able to say openly as well. You, Soviet journalists, should be thankful to us for setting in motion glasnost. But unfortunately the Soviet press still has to contend with many taboos so our task is to give our listeners the full picture and to provide thoughtful commentary. This is much easier for us to do since we have neither censorship from above nor self-censorship." Having presented RL's views openly and honestly—an unprecedented step for an authoritative official Soviet publication—Larionova returned to her critical stance by accusing RL of trying to wean away Soviet youth from communism. To illustrate RL's hostile intentions, she quoted from a recent RL broadcast: "Everyone knows that in the USSR there is a divide between the proponents of official ideology and Soviet youth who see ideology as hypocrisy and social injustice." Having listened to RL broadcasts in preparation for writing her article, Larionova apparently could cite only this bland truism as proof of RL's aggressive intentions. In the boisterous 1980s this comment would have scarcely caused a ripple in Soviet society. It certainly would not have supported Larionova's criticism of RL. Indeed, after beginning with a negative assessment of RL, Larionova ended her article on a positive note: "To be fair," she concluded, "reports about my visit to the RL news bureau in Washington were aired several times and everything that was said was completely correct and objective."[18]

Compared to the press articles in Eastern Europe, which described RFE/RL in laudatory terms, Larionova's piece was a curious soviet hybrid, an attempt both to appease the hardline opponents of democratic change and, at the same time, to acknowledge Gorbachev's glasnost by openly quoting RL broadcasters. And yet, even this half-hearted step of recognizing Radio Liberty as a legitimate international broadcaster was not welcomed by Soviet ideologues. Roughly two months later, Larionova made amends by rewriting her initial article for a sister publication, *Pravda Ukrainy* (March 3, 1989), in which she radically changed her tone and assessment of RL. In the first piece she wrote warmly about the young staffer who escorted her to the RL office; in the second article she described him as a traitor to his homeland. She not only repeated the same claims about CIA ties to the radios but also added names of individual RL broadcasters, accusing several of being Nazi collaborators. She also excised Larissa Silnitskaya's eloquent description of RL's mission and concluded that RL was the "eternal enemy." Several days later, another mainstream Soviet publication, *Komsomolskaya Pravda* (March 5, 1989), reprised a familiar attack on Radio Liberty, this time singling out Steve Forbes, Gene Pell, and Vladimir Matusevich. The author, R. Guseinov, accused RL of psychological warfare and stated that Soviet bureaucracy had made a grave mistake when it stopped jamming RFE/RL. Although Guseinov acknowledged that glasnost was forcing RL to change its tactics, he reiterated the common refrain that RL's goal was to destroy the USSR.

For roughly sixteen months after the cessation of jamming, the Russian broadcasts existed in two separate Soviet worlds. In one, RFE/RL was seen as a professional broadcaster that was steadily expanding its freelance network, sending its researchers to conduct on-the-ground studies, and interviewing prominent Soviet writers and politicians. The BIB senior staff was also able to travel freely to the USSR and engage in serious discussions about the opening of full-fledged news bureaus in Moscow and Kyiv. In a parallel Soviet world, RL was still viewed as a pariah and a dangerous enemy of the state. An article in *Sovetskii patriot* (May 24, 1989) even called the Russian Service a "wolf pack of gangsters" and claimed that RFE/RL managers "were dangerous killers."

Soviet media in 1989 and 1990 reflected a schizophrenic approach to Radio Liberty. In sharp contrast to *Komsomolskaya Pravda* and *Sovetskii patriot*, which cast the Russian Service as the eternal enemy, *Novoe vremia* (*New Times*) published a thoughtful piece by Vladimir Ostrogorsky that welcomed the cessation of jamming as a sign of democratization and a willingness to engage in a dialogue with the West. "Of course, much of what was written about international radio broadcasts [in the Soviet press] was sheer rubbish," Ostrogorsky boldly asserted. "The 'radio voices' did not spread lies, slander, or engage in subversive activities. Their staff was not comprised of Nazi-sympathizers; indeed, the radios employed some of the best writers who had emigrated."[19] Having categorically rejected nearly forty years of Soviet attacks on the radios, Ostrogorsky reminded his readers that alongside preserving Russian national culture, RFE/RL tried "to embed Western thinking among the Soviet people as the only right one." He saw nothing wrong with that approach and noted that Radio Moscow was engaged in the same type "influence peddling," trying to promote Marxist thinking in the West. The solution, Ostrogorsky contended, was not to jam international broadcasters or to vilify them, but to urge all international broadcasters to adhere to "responsible programming" and to build bridges between the Soviet world and the West.

Ostrogorsky's cautious approach to the radios was a significant step toward a more balanced assessment of Radio Liberty and other international broadcasters. For the most part, the Soviet mainstream press gradually dispensed with Soviet caricatures of the radios but resisted outright praise for the programming, settling on what could be called the "interview approach." This format allowed Soviet journalists to repeat standard cliches about the evil nature of RFE/RL, thus pleasing the hardliners, but at the same time to pose questions to the RL staff and, most important, publish their answers in full, without either endorsing or criticizing them. In this way, the interviewees could speak freely and express their views, and the readers could draw their own conclusions. This was politically safe journalism because in the late 1980s no one in the Soviet Union could be certain who would emerge on top—the democrats or the neo-Stalinists.

In August 1989 a popular Soviet publication featured an interview with Vladimir Matusevich, the head of the Russian Service, entitled "Information or Propaganda?"[20] The interviewer began with a frank question: "Isn't RL simply old-fashioned propaganda?" Matusevich responded that propaganda had many different definitions, but the one he preferred defined it as the willful distortion of the full story, when a reporter ignored certain key facts and overemphasized others. RL did not practice that kind of journalism, Matusevich stated categorically. To further elucidate his conception of news reporting, he added that RL adopted the Anglo-Saxon principle of separating straight news from commentary. News items always required at least two independent sources and were presented in a straightforward, unemotional manner. However, commentaries, labelled as such, could express the personal views of the author but always aimed to be balanced and fair. The subsequent questions posed by the Soviet journalist ranged from hostile ones—about the aggressive programming of the 1950s and stories of espionage at RFE/RL—to friendly ones about RL's plans to open a news bureau in Moscow. In each case, Matusevich handled them with aplomb, and the article as a whole conveyed a positive image of RFE/RL.

The significance of this publication lay not so much in what Matusevich said but in the fact that the head of the Russian Service, a person repeatedly attacked in the Soviet press and called a traitor, was given a public forum to present his vision of RFE/RL. His interview in a widely distributed publication prompted two responses, published two months later in *Sobesednik* (October 1989). One was by Vladimir Ostrogorsky, who had earlier penned a relatively positive review of RL programming (*New Times*, May 1989). In this short piece, entitled "What Voices Do We Hear?," Ostrogosrky used the Matusevich interview as a hook to speak more openly about the achievements of Radio Liberty and to note the continuing weaknesses of Soviet media. "Radio Liberty, of course, is the most interesting international broadcaster," Ostrogorsky stated boldly. "Its relatively small staff and wide network of freelancers include many talented journalists and even brave people, many of whom were famous fighters for freedom and human rights. The spiritual connection between them and our life in the Soviet Union has not frayed. . . . But the popularity of RL broadcasts is not only their singular achievement but also the result of our deficiencies as journalists."[21] Decrying the stifling censorship and administrative chaos of Soviet radio, Ostrogorsky lamented, "Why is it that to hear radio essays by Anatoly Strelyany, or learn about informal groups in the Soviet Union, or become acquainted with our latest literary works, we need to tune in to a foreign radio station?" The cessation of jamming, Ostrogorsky concluded, was just the first step in developing true glasnost. Now the challenge for Soviet domestic media was to create worthy competitors to Radio Liberty.

The companion piece in *Sobesednik* was an essay by a well-known conservative Russian writer, Anatoly Salutsky. A member of the Communist Party and the Union of Soviet Writers, Salutsky wrote primarily about the Russian countryside, supported an imperial Soviet Union, and embraced strident nationalism after the collapse of communism.

While on a visit to New York, he received a call from Boris Paramonov, inviting him for an interview. "We know your point of view is at odds with ours," Salutsky recalled Paramonov's words, "but we're ready to offer you the opportunity to be on our show. We'll have a dialogue. Maybe even an argument." Salutsky readily accepted, but as he was entering the New York bureau, he experienced a sense of dread, recalling that "from my earliest days I considered RL the refuge of all that was anti-Soviet, the poisoner of our nationalist spirit and the holy springs of our historical memory." That vilification of RL, however, had also piqued his curiosity about this "prominent symbol of the Cold War." Despite his initial hesitation, Salutsky proceeded to meet the RL staff, tour the offices, and sit down with Paramonov in the RL studio for a lengthy discussion.

What is remarkable about Salutsky's article is his measured tone and the absence of Soviet clichés about the radios. Admitting that he was a longtime listener, Salutsky spoke about the variety of voices in the Russian Service, reflecting what he considered to be different attitudes toward political developments in the Soviet Union. "This was most readily apparent in the depth of the analytical programs," he noted, "as well as in the degree of empathy in the assessments of our political process." The forty-minute interview turned into a long discussion about Russia, which "at times, became heated, but was always genuine and honest." Salutsky was amazed by the keen interest RL staff showed in the minutiae of Soviet life and by their "deep desire not just to highlight some negative aspect [of the Soviet Union] but to thoroughly understand the complex political process of perestroika." That led him to conclude that "RL journalists were highly professional Sovietologists who read the Soviet press from morning to night, but to grasp the sharp divide between the rhetoric of perestroika and its actual realization, they needed to spend time in the country." Salutsky singled out RL's adherence to journalistic ethics and the professional manner in which the interview was conducted. "Unlike our Soviet journalists," he noted, "Paramonov did not try to trip me up with some nasty questions but led our discussion in a calm and professional manner, allowing me the opportunity to express my point of view, thus demonstrating his journalistic objectivity." Although at the end of his piece, Salutsky took issue with some earlier RL broadcasts from Munich, he offered Soviet readers a radically new portrait of the radios. Gone were the ugly cartoon descriptions of Nazi collaborators and CIA epigones who wanted to destroy Russia; in their place were well-meaning, friendly professional journalists. Salutsky spoke warmly of the "radio voices" and especially about Yuri Handler, the much beloved head of the RL bureau in New York, noting that he did not exhibit any "confrontational bitterness [toward the Soviet Union] but rather tried very hard in a friendly way to understand what was taking place in Russia." As a prominent Soviet writer, Salutsky was able to reach a broad segment of the Soviet population with an honest portrayal of Radio Liberty that set a new standard for subsequent public assessments of RFE/RL.

Shortly after the publication of Salutsky's article, *Komsomolskaya Pravda*, a popular newspaper, published a lengthy piece, entitled "The ABC's of Glasnost . . . from Munich" (October 21, 1989) that further humanized the image of RFE/RL. "The stereotypes and ideological clichés about RL are receding into the past," V. Rakhlyavichus and G. Vainauskus noted, "but for many Soviet citizens the very names— Radio Free Europe and Radio Liberty—are still associated with Stalinist propaganda: CIA stations, saboteurs of the airwaves, voices of imperialism."[22] The article then gave a straightforward historical sketch of the radios and asked two experienced RL broadcasters, Lev Roitman and Giovanni Bensi, to explain how the Russian Service operated and why it was a strong proponent of democratic change in the USSR. The questions from the authors were not aggressive, and the overall tone of the article was calm and professional. Indeed, by late October 1989, approximately one year after the cessation of jamming, official Soviet press began to treat RL as a respectable international broadcaster. Among the emerging "democratic publications," RL was frequently singled out for its professional coverage of domestic political events. *Atmoda*, the newspaper of the Latvian National Front, even regularly printed the complete schedule of the RL Russian broadcasts, at the request of its many readers.[23]

The crowning moment in Soviet revisionism was a lengthy article by Leonid Shinkarev in *Izvestia*, entitled "Above the Borders" (March 31, 1990). Forgoing conventional Soviet descriptions of the radios, Shinkarev began by stating that RL was a strong supporter of glasnost and Gorbachev's policies. He noted that in the past RL was staffed by many major Russian cultural figures—among them Gaito Gazdanov and Alexander Bakhrakh—and the goal of the broadcasts was to preserve and communicate Russian culture. "In the silent years of our isolation from the world," Shinkarev wrote, "it was the RL broadcasters—émigrés labelled traitors and cosmopolitans—who brought us the voices of Sakharov and Solzhenitsyn, who day after day reported on the human rights movement, who read on air underground samizdat works. What we talk about today, they talked about twenty or even thirty years ago."[24] On his tour of the Munich headquarters, Shinkarev was astounded by the extent to which the broadcasters continued to "live Russian lives" listening to Soviet radio, watching Soviet television, and avidly reading the press. He noted that he had heard the word *perestroika* mentioned more often in Munich than in Moscow. But what he found most remarkable was that RL broadcasters held "a wide range of political views, from monarchist to left-liberal and that the staff divided into radicals, liberals, and conservatives." He proceeded to describe some of the more colorful programmers, including Lev Predtechevsky, who hosted a show on military issues, and Evgeny Kushev, whose program—*Siberian Fates*—explored the different ethnic, historical, and political movements specific to Siberia. But in concluding his laudatory piece, Shinkarev sounded a cautionary note, warning his readers that the dramatic changes underway in the USSR could still be reversed and then Radio Liberty would be needed more than ever.

Shinkarev's article heralded a new era for Radio Liberty. With only a few minor exceptions, subsequent articles in the Soviet press about RL were straightforward and professional. More important, RFE/RL broadcasters and researchers were now able to publish their own articles in the Soviet press. Here are just a few examples: Alexander Rahr, a young researcher, published a long analytical piece on Gorbachev's policies (*Atmoda*, April 3, 1990); Victor Fedoseyev, a longtime senior editor, wrote a series of articles on democracy for *Sovetskaya molodezh* (Soviet youth, April–May 1990); Rachel Fedoseyeva penned a provocative piece, "Political Prisoners in the USSR: Yesterday, Today . . . and Tomorrow?" (*Atmoda*, May 14, 1990); Sergei Dovlatov gave an interview to *Ogonek* (no. 24, 1990); and Vadim Belotserkovsky, our "house leftist," was able to present his Socialist economic views in *Novoe vremia* (November 24, 1990).

With every month, RL broadcasters were coming home, primarily in word and spirit, though occasionally even in person. After eighteen years abroad, Julian Panich returned in triumph to Leningrad in January 1991. A well-known actor of stage and screen before his emigration, Panich appeared in a special performance, *Three Lives*, in Leningrad that portrayed his life as a Soviet actor and RL broadcaster. He began with an homage to Alexander Galich that included recordings of Galich's RL programs. The evening concluded with a celebration of RL cultural programming, with most of the Soviet audience indicating their preference for RL over official Soviet radio. Afterward, in an interview on Soviet television, Panich described the work of the radios in a friendly setting. "I have been in the theater all my life," Panich recalled after returning to Munich, "but those days in Leningrad represented the crowning achievement of my career."[25]

The August Putsch

The Soviet coup d'état attempt (August 19–21, 1991), or the August Putsch, as it is commonly referred to in Russia, presented Radio Liberty with its greatest challenge and marked its most notable triumph. Fearful that Gorbachev would sign the New Union Treaty, making the Soviet Union a federation of independent republics with only a common president, foreign policy, and military, a small group of high-level hardline Communist officials declared a state of emergency at the crack of dawn on August 19. They formed the State Committee on the State of Emergency (in Russian, known as the GKChP) and issued orders to isolate Gorbachev, cutting all his lines of communication. They also took control of all Soviet media, including the fledgling private radio station Echo of Moscow and moved tank divisions and paratroopers into Moscow. On hearing the news, Boris Yeltsin, then president of the Russian Federative Socialist Republic (RSFSR, currently named the Russian Federation), arrived at the White House, the Russian Government Building, early on August 19. Together with Ivan Silayev (prime minister of the RSFSR) and Ruslan Khasbulatov (chair of the Supreme Soviet), Yeltsin condemned the GKChP's actions as an unconstitutional coup, urging the military not to take part, and called for the return of Gorbachev, who was under house arrest. For the next thirty-six hours there was a tense standoff, as the coup leaders brought in military forces and tried to gauge whether they had broad support in the country. Meanwhile, ordinary Muscovites gathered at the White House, built barricades of trolleybuses and street-cleaning vehicles, and prepared for the onslaught. As the tense hours dragged on, hundreds of thousands of Russians came out in solidarity and resisted the return to totalitarian rule.

Shortly after midnight on the twenty-first, infantry fighting vehicles began to move toward the White House, and the people sheltering with Yeltsin expected an imminent attack and considerable bloodshed. But the Muscovites who had gathered to protect the White House bravely stood in the way of the tanks. At one point, shooting broke out, and three young men were killed. According to eyewitnesses, those deaths so horrified the Russian troops and the elite military divisions that instead of continuing to move toward the White House, they stopped dead in their tracks. As night hours passed, the troops began to side with their own people, who were standing resolutely for constitutional order. By eight in the morning on the twenty-first, the committee lost its will, and the troops started heading back to their barracks.

The last desperate attempt by the Soviet hardliners to hold on to power came to an ignominious end. On the twenty-second of August, Gorbachev returned to Moscow; Vladimir Kryuchkov, Dmitry Yazov, and Alexandr Tizyakov—the principal conspirators—were arrested; and Boris Pugo, the minister of the interior and coup participant, committed suicide, together with his wife. Within days, Gorbachev resigned as CPSU general secretary (but remained president), and Yeltsin decreed the termination of all Communist Party activities on

Russian soil, closing the Central Committee building. The coup failure set in motion a series of steps that had been brewing for many months. On the twenty-fourth of August the Verkhovna Rada in Kyiv adopted the Declaration of Independence of Ukraine; on the twenty-fifth the Byelorussian Soviet Socialist Republic declared its independence, renaming itself the Republic of Belarus. In December, Yeltsin, Leonid Kravchuk (Ukraine), and Stanislav Shushkevich (Belarus) met outside of Minsk and signed the Belavezha Accords, which declared that the Soviet Union had ceased to exist as a subject of international law and geopolitical reality.

The failed Soviet coup was RL's moment to draw on its professionalism and serve as an independent Russian voice. As soon as the coup was declared, RL dropped most of its regular programming, focusing its attention on the fast-breaking events in Moscow. Each hour began with an extensive update of what was happening in the country. Drawing on its extensive network of freelance contributors, RL was able to assign five stringers just to the events in Moscow. Two were stationed in the White House itself throughout the ordeal and were provided with an open telephone line to the Munich office. Two other freelancers reported on the crowds gathering outside the White House and described the reactions of ordinary citizens to the coup attempt. A fifth correspondent worked closely with Soviet news media that had been shuttered, sending reports from Soviet journalists who could not publish them in their own papers. RL not only broadcast Yeltsin's appeals to the nation but also conducted interviews with key political figures, including Anatoly Sobchak (mayor of Saint Petersburg), Eduard Shevardnadze (former USSR foreign minister), Alexander Yakovlev (member of the Politburo), Yuri Afanasiev (cofounder of Democratic Russia movement), and virtually all the ministers of the Russian Republic government. RL also broadcast several exclusive interviews with Nikolai Vorontsov, USSR minister of the environment, who gave a minute-by-minute account of the crucial August 19 extraordinary session of the USSR cabinet ministers at which the coup was hatched; Sergei Stankevich, RSFSR state secretary who provided a detailed account of the arrest and detention of Gorbachev; General Konstantin Kobets, deputy chief of the Soviet General Staff, who assessed the military situation in the capital in the first two days of the coup; Vladimir Lysenko, RSFSR parliamentarian, who gave a detailed account of the arrests of two coup plotters, Vladimir Kryuchkov and Gennady Yanayev; and Valery Stepanenko, RSFSR prosecutor general, who discussed the ongoing investigation of the coup and the role of the KGB. Further enhancing RL's unique coverage of the coup were reports filed from outlying areas of the Russian Republic (Chelyabinsk, Tambov, Sverdlovsk, Khabarovsk, Siberia), in addition to reports from Ukraine, the Caucasus, Moldova, and the Baltic States. As a professional news organization, RL also reported on groups and organizations that supported or sympathized with the coup leaders, including interviews with Viktor Alksnis, the "Black Colonel" and cochair of the Party Soyuz; Vladimir Zhirinovsky, head of the Liberal Democratic Party (LDPR); and Alfred Rubiks, first secretary of the Latvian Communist Party. Taken together, the RL reports and interviews formed the only comprehensive national coverage of events in the USSR. At a time of crisis and potential chaos, RL was able to hold the country together through accurate, up-to-date information and analysis.

Listening to the broadcasts about the coup some thirty years later, I was struck by the steely professionalism of the Munich anchors, notably Savik Shuster and Irina Khenkina, who maintained a calm and reassuring tone when no one knew how the events in Moscow would unfold. Vladimir Matusevich, not one to wax sentimental, became emotional in his editorial comments about the heroic work Gorbachev had done. It was a *"chudo"* (miracle), he said, that Gorbachev, a product of the system, could destroy the core of the Soviet Union so effectively. Not knowing at the time if Gorbachev was alive, Matusevich ended his remarks with a phrase of deep significance in Russian culture: "*Prostite*, Mikhail Sergeyevich (forgive us, Mikhail Sergeyevich), for not fully understanding and appreciating your true accomplishments." But the heroes of the day were RL's freelancers. Mark Deich, Mikhail Sokolov, Andrei Babitsky, Dmitri Volchek, and many others were models of grace under pressure. Their on-the-ground reports and interviews will remain an indispensable firsthand source of information for historians of the August Putsch.

Accolades for RL's coverage poured in quickly. Upon his return from Crimea, Gorbachev declared that RL and BBC were his best sources of information. In his more emotive way, Boris Yeltsin immediately expressed his gratitude by issuing an unprecedented ukase (decree) on August 24, 1991, which praised RFE/RL for "its role in objectively informing the citizens of the Russian Republic and the world [about] the democratic processes in Russia ... and the legal leadership of the Russian Republic during the coup d'état in the USSR."[26] The decree also called for RFE/RL to open a news bureau in Moscow and to set up offices throughout the country. At a subsequent press conference, Yeltsin added, "During the coup, RL was one of the few channels through which it was possible to send messages to the whole world and, most important, to all of Russia, because virtually every family in Russia [was] listening to Radio Liberty." Praise for RL also came from Russian journalists. Sergei Timofeyev, the director of All-Russian State TV and Radio, spoke for many when he thanked RL and its "coverage of the tragic events of August 19–21." "Millions of Soviet people," he told RL, "deprived of the possibility of receiving information through Russian media, have listened to your free voice. It strengthened their faith and their determination to combat dictatorship."[27] After years of being maligned as traitors, RL was now basking in the public recognition of its heroic role. This boosted morale at the station and helped us to explain to U.S. policymakers and members of Congress why RL was such a vital U.S. investment. But the most moving tribute to Radio Liberty came from Elena Bonner, the human rights activist and widow of Andrei Sakharov, who acknowledged the brave professional freelance reporters: "Boys, during those days, you were on the barricades with us."

In the last four years of the Soviet regime, Radio Liberty's public image shifted from that of a dangerous enemy to a celebrated national hero. In October 1987 I could not secure a single meeting with senior Soviet officials to discuss the jamming of Radio Liberty. In October 1991, I had collegial meetings with senior officials in the Russian White House who praised RL programming. During those fateful four years, RL responded to political changes in the Soviet Union, reassessed its feature programming, introduced new shows, and continued to adhere to fact-based reporting. It welcomed glasnost and perestroika, but its mission and values remained the same as they had been for decades. What changed was the Soviet Union itself. In effect, Radio Liberty functioned as a barometer of political change. When repression held sway, Radio Liberty broadcasts were jammed and its journalists vilified. As the Soviet Union steadily grew more democratic, jamming ceased, and the broadcasters were welcomed back home. When the Soviet regime finally collapsed, Radio Liberty was publicly acknowledged for what it had always been: a free media voice in an independent and pluralistic Russian society.

9

Victory Lap

In one of his frequent conversations with President George H. W. Bush, Vaclav Havel, the revered dissident and playwright turned president of independent Czechoslovakia, raised the question of RFE/RL's future, asking Bush to meet with his foreign minister, Jiri Dienstbier, to discuss the continuing need for broadcasts. "I understand the Congress may cut funding for RFE," Havel told the president. "I hope it will be possible to give support to this institution. It is very important."[1] Bush was pleased that Havel had raised the question of the future of RFE and welcomed Dienstbier's views on the radios. He also assured Havel that no decision had been taken to close the services. "The reason why we want RFE open," Havel continued, "is that, although our radio is free, our journalists are not experienced enough. RFE is an educational institution for us. We need to learn from it." Just three days after this telephone call, Bush addressed the National Association of Broadcasters Convention, noting the critical importance RFE/RL had played in the political changes in the East bloc: "Last year Vaclav Havel came to the White House and told me that he and others used to listen to Radio Free Europe and the Voice of America. And President Havel credited those broadcasts with helping to launch the Velvet Revolution and turn a totalitarian society into a democratic one.... Free and accessible media strengthen and help to build democracy."[2]

The Bush-Havel conversation summed up the key issues facing RFE/RL (and to a lesser degree, VOA) in the late 1980s and early 1990s, as Central and East European countries were gaining their full independence and the Soviet Union was hurtling toward its demise. Havel raised a fundamental question facing U.S. policymakers and members of Congress: Did free media in the former East bloc countries render RFE/RL obsolete? And if so, could the language services be closed and the budget savings be proclaimed a peace dividend? Although Congress was ready to make cuts in the BIB (RFE/RL) budget, the Bush administration resisted any rash decisions and wanted to examine the future of RFE/RL within the framework of a new U.S. foreign policy strategy. Several months after the fall of the Berlin Wall and the proclamation of newly independent countries in Central and Eastern Europe, the NSC initiated a major reassessment of international broadcasting—"National Security Review 24"—that directed the major foreign policy agencies—including the Board for International Broadcasting and USIA—"to consider the future role of U.S. government broadcasting at a time when many, but not all, parts of the world enjoy an increasingly free flow of information, including indigenous free media." This study "should cover planning, programming, and resource implications, including the allocation of limited resources to various regions, countries, and languages."[3] The directive called on all broadcast entities to address the central question: "What should be the role of surrogate radio broadcasting (RFE/RL) to areas increasingly open to media and the exchange of ideas?" At the time of the Havel-Bush telephone conversation (April 1991), this major study was still underway, in large part because the political situation on the ground was changing so rapidly. But Havel's request for more support for RFE/RL did not surprise Bush since he had been hearing the same message from other newly elected democratic leaders in Eastern Europe. The key point for Bush was Havel's succinct description of RFE/RL's new role as an educational institution that would share its knowledge, experience, and journalistic resources with emerging free media in the former East bloc. Havel understood that as democratic institutions gained strength and as domestic media became more professional, RFE would no longer be needed. But that day was still far in the future; in the meantime, the fledgling democracies of Central Europe relied on U.S. international broadcasting.

The political changes taking place in Central and Eastern Europe and the Soviet Union presented starkly different challenges to the two U.S. broadcasters. In the case of VOA, its future was taken for granted since the Bush administration and Congress understood that there would always be a need to tell America's story to the world and explain U.S. policy. In a rapidly changing political world, however, VOA would have to realign its priorities, shift resources from Central Europe to other parts of the world, and redesign its programming to complement the emerging free press in former Communist countries. The Presidential Task Force on International Broadcasting—an august body of outside media experts—endorsed this vision of VOA, suggesting that it "take on more of an educational role [of explaining] the workings of the free market system, the banking system, the free press, and such other instruments of democracy which are fairly new to these countries."[4] VOA broadcasts adopted this approach by developing radio bridges that brought Russian and American experts together to explore the challenges facing Russia in building a vibrant market economy. VOA was also able to place its programs on local Russian radio stations, thereby significantly increasing its audience reach, and to establish successful training programs for young journalists, helping them to acquire new skills as independent journalists.

In contrast, the growth of independent professional media and democratic institutions in Eastern Europe and the Soviet Union posed an existential threat to RFE/RL's operations. From its earliest days, radio management knew that someday the two radios would no longer be needed, but it felt that it could ignore that eventuality. The Soviet Union appeared firmly entrenched, showing no signs of liberalizing its internal political system or decolonizing Eastern Europe. Indeed, most Western experts were convinced that the Soviet Union was a permanent member of the world community. But with Gorbachev's glasnost and perestroika gaining momentum in the late 1980s and East European countries asserting their independence, the BIB began to look more critically at the future of the radios. Even before the Soviet Union ceased jamming RFE/RL, we set up a Committee on Long-Range Planning, charged with establishing metrics that could be useful in reallocating resources and planning for the possible phase-out of certain language services.

To develop its strategy, the BIB drew on the expertise at RFE/RL. Gene Parta, the director of the Audience Research Department, gave several presentations to the board of directors, citing data culled from interviews with émigrés and travelers. The BIB also invited outside experts to board meetings to share their unique personal perspectives on changes within the East bloc. During 1987 and 1988, the board was addressed by such distinguished figures as Slava Rostropovich, the renowned cellist and human rights advocate; Mark Palmer, the U.S. ambassador to Hungary; Richard Perle, the former assistant secretary of defense; Senator Richard Lugar; Robert Gates, the deputy director of the NSC; and Natan Sharansky, the former Soviet dissident and advocate for Soviet Jewry. In 1989 we were joined by Ronald Reagan at a festive board dinner, where the ex-president shared his views on the role of international broadcasting and commended us for bringing hope, democracy, and freedom to people in Eastern Europe and the Soviet Union. These talks were supplemented by outside scholarly forums that explored systematic ways of gauging the longer-term need for RFE/RL broadcasts. In May 1987, for example, the BIB directors attended a symposium organized by RFE/RL at which Peter Reddaway, secretary of the Kennan Institute; Robert Conquest, of the Hoover Institution; Vladimir Bukovsky, a prominent Russian dissident; and several other experts suggested ways of assessing the impact of our broadcasts.

After the cessation of jamming in November 1988, the BIB implemented a two-track approach. At the director level, we would seek out opportunities to travel to the broadcast region and set up meetings with newly elected leaders, democratic activists, and journalists. At the working level, I (as the BIB executive director) joined a senior interagency committee on international broadcasting, headed by the deputy NSC director, Robert Gates, and coordinated by Nancy Bearg Dyke. The interagency group met regularly in Washington to share information and establish metrics needed for an eventual presidential decision on broadcasting budgets and priorities. Our working group also held meetings in Eastern Europe and the Soviet Union, where we discussed the future of surrogate broadcasting with U.S. ambassadors and embassy specialists, as well as with a broad range of experts on the ground.

While the BIB was engaged in policy issues, the management of RFE/RL sought out opportunities to enhance its news-gathering operations. Their initial forays into Eastern and Central Europe showed that the new democratic leaders wanted closer ties with RFE/RL broadcasters. The first country to make a bold move was Hungary. On July 3, 1989, RFE/RL opened a full-time news bureau in Budapest, its first in the East bloc. Several days later, on an official visit to Hungary, President Bush referred to RFE in his speech at Karl Marx University: "The creative genius of the Hungarian people, long suppressed, is again flourishing in your schools, your businesses, your churches. . . . Voices stifled are being heard again. An independent daily newspaper is now sold on the streets. And Radio Free Europe is opening its first Eastern European bureau right here in Budapest."[5] Buoyed by positive developments in Hungary, the BIB and RFE/RL started seeking out more opportunities to expand RFE/RL presence in-country and acquire a deeper understanding of the underlying political processes that would help shape a new broadcasting strategy.

As a first step, in September 1989 Kenneth Tomlinson, a member of the board, A. Ross Johnson, director of RFE, and I traveled to Poland, where we met with Polish officials and Solidarity members, including Lech Walesa, Bronislaw Geremek, and Adam Michnik. Everyone we spoke with acknowledged RFE's role in bringing democratic change to Poland and encouraged us to establish a strong presence in Poland. When we asked Walesa about the significance of RFE broadcasts, he responded, "Can you imagine the earth without the sun?" a quip that gained currency and was often cited by U.S. politicians. Later, when we met with Jacek Ambroziak, the chief assistant to Prime Minister Tadeusz Mazowiecki, he welcomed our visit, noting that "if RFE applies for accreditation, the answer will be affirmative."[6]

Taking advantage of opportunities to expand its coverage of Central Europe, RFE/RL opened news bureaus in Warsaw and Prague in early 1990. Each bureau became the hub of a network of locally hired freelance journalists who acquired professional experience working for a Western news organization. Their contributions significantly improved the immediacy, depth, and variety of RFE's programming. In the case of Czechoslovakia, RFE even gained access to four powerful medium-wave transmitters, letting listeners tune in programs on ordinary AM radios at home or in their cars. These new bureaus also allowed correspondents from other RFE/RL language services to travel freely to Central Europe and file their reports, expanding one of RFE/RL's core strengths—cross-reporting, or the sharing of news and information across Eastern Europe and the Soviet Union. In a sign of the times, when a TASS correspondent asked Alexander Yakovlev, Gorbachev's senior adviser and a Politburo member, at a Prague news conference how he assessed Soviet media coverage of Eastern Europe, Yakovlev complained about a lack of objectivity and said Radio Liberty provided an impartial and useful perspective. "We can always learn details of what bad or negative event has happened in, say, Czechoslovakia," he noted, "but we learn about the consequences from Radio Liberty's news."[7]

At the grand openings of the news bureaus, the newly elected democratic leaders called on RFE/RL to help explain the challenges of building stable democracies and a market economy on the ruins of Communist rule. The most effective way to achieve this, in the words of Polish prime minister Tadeuz Mazowiecki, was for RFE "to continue to serve as a reliable source of information and discerning commentary."[8] In a similar vein, Hungarian prime minister József Antall expressed gratitude for forty years of RFE broadcasts but stressed that in the immediate future, RFE "can help the strengthening of democracy in Hungary in many ways. . . . Although our press is freed from censorship, it still must learn how to live with this freedom. RFE can provide a standard for quality and balance, in healthy competition with our own journalists."[9] Antall's words were echoed by one of the heroes of the Polish Solidarity movement. "In all the countries of Eastern Europe, dictatorship has lost and freedom has won," Adam Michnik stated, "but that does not mean that democracy has won. Democracy means the institutionalization of freedom. We don't have democratic order, and that is why our freedom is so fragile and so shaky."[10]

As advice, testimonials, and accolades poured in from East European leaders, we realized that the new political order required us to refine our strategic approach to programming. Every democratically elected leader we spoke with wanted RFE/RL to continue playing the role of a national broadcaster. Often, leaders would mention the emergence of free elections and urged RFE/RL to devote more airtime to explaining their significance because under Communist rule voting had been a public charade. As an independent news broadcaster, RFE/RL could maintain strict nonpartisanship and, at the same time, encourage turnout by helping voters to understand new and often complex election procedures. As part of domestic media, but independent of party factions, RFE/RL could analyze election procedures, give voice to serious candidates, and contribute to political stability by providing realistic and credible appraisals of candidates and issues.

To broaden its understanding of the political changes in Eastern Europe, the BIB sought out the views of former RFE/RL broadcasters who were now able to visit their home countries and provide firsthand assessments of the political situation. As prominent national figures, the former broadcasters had remarkable access to the new political leadership and everyday listeners. Jan Nowak, the former director of the Polish Service, returned to a hero's welcome in Warsaw after an absence of forty-five years. Invited to Poland by Lech Walesa, Nowak was greeted by banner headlines in major Polish newspapers. Upon returning to the United States, he wrote to the BIB: "I was aware of RFE's contribution over the past 37 years but I never realized that its role was so universally appreciated by the people of Poland.... Wherever I went I was thanked profusely by my former listeners.... In all the private homes which I visited, radio receivers were tuned permanently to the RFE frequencies.... Prominent individuals told me that they would not go to sleep before tuning in RFE's *Night Package*."[11] In a similar vein, George Urban, a former director of RFE, traveled to his native Hungary after a long absence and provided powerful testimony about the impact of the RFE broadcasts: "My talks with ordinary citizens, with Budapest radicals, with members of the Democratic Forum and Populist writers and intellectuals left me with the clear impression that RFE is the single most important arbiter in the life of the nation.... RFE is an educator of morals, loyalties, and tastes, as well as a source of information.... RFE has defined the intellectual context and the language in which the national debate is now conducted."[12]

Statements of support by the democratic leadership in Eastern Europe were indispensable as the BIB prepared materials for the Presidential Task Force on International Broadcasting and testimony in Congress. The directors, however, were eager to visit the countries to which we were broadcasting and speak directly with its leaders, members of the political opposition, and everyday listeners. Given the openness of Hungary at the time, the BIB decided to hold its first official board meeting in a former Communist country in Budapest (September 18-19, 1990). After concluding the formal part of the meeting, the directors, RFE/RL management, and senior staff met with Hungarian journalists to discuss the relevance of RFE broadcasts. Afterward, we attended a private meeting with Prime Minister Antall, at which he explained the invaluable role of RFE as a source of news and information independent of domestic politics. The highlight of our trip was an invitation to attend a session of the Hungarian Parliament. We were escorted to a place of honor and the head of the parliament formally thanked the Board for International Broadcasting and Radio Free Europe for the many years of broadcasting to Hungary. Then, to our astonishment, all the parliamentarians rose and enthusiastically applauded us for our contributions to Hungarian freedom. We felt pride in the American leadership of the radios over the decades and especially in the work of the émigré broadcasters who had never given up hope that freedom would eventually come to their homeland. Despite the criticism leveled by Communist authorities and occasionally by Americans, the radios had stood their ground and fulfilled their mission, and now we were publicly honored by democratically elected representatives of Hungary.

Heartened by the reception in Budapest, the BIB made plans to hold working meetings in other parts of our broadcast region. In December 1990, together with senior RFE/RL executives, we traveled to Moscow to open an office and attend a reception at Spaso House—the residence of the U.S. ambassador—where we were greeted by several hundred leading Russian political figures, parliamentarians, and journalists. Although we did not have any meetings with Kremlin officials, we met privately with the democratically elected mayor of Moscow, Gavriil Popov, and discussed the further expansion of RL's presence in the city. Following the Moscow visit, the BIB traveled to Warsaw, where we met with representatives of the new Polish government. In the evening, President Lech Walesa invited us to a formal dinner at the Belvedere Palace, one of the official residences of the Polish president and the state guest house. As we entered the building, Walesa greeted each of us warmly, but when he saw Lane Kirkland, he stopped, gave him a bear hug, and said, "It's because of you that Poland is free and that I am here." As one of our prominent Democratic Board directors, Kirkland was not only a staunch supporter of international broadcasting and democracy promotion overseas but also a major public voice that members of Congress would heed. As the president of the American Federation of Labor–Congress of Industrial Organizations (AFL-CIO), Kirkland had funneled support to the Solidarity movement through the 1980s, keeping the free union movement alive when many Western governments had come to accept the Jaruzelski regime as inevitable. Both the AFL-CIO and RFE had remained committed to a free Poland. Walesa expressed that sense of solidarity in a subsequent letter to the RFE Polish Service, noting that "when a democratic opposition emerged in Poland, RFE accompanied us every step of the way—during the explosion of August 1980, the unhappy days of December 1981, and all the subsequent months of our struggle. It was our radio station. But not only a radio station. Presenting works that were 'on the red censorship list,' it was our ministry of culture. Exposing absurd economic policies, it was our ministry of economics. Reacting to events promptly and pertinently, but above all, truthfully, it was our ministry of information."[13] Eloquently stated, these words encapsulated the essence of the RFE/RL mission.

After Warsaw, the BIB traveled to Prague and met with Vaclav Klaus, then the finance minister, to discuss the economic changes underway in Czechoslovakia. Although unable to meet with Vaclav Havel because of schedule conflicts, we saw his close advisers, who assured us of Havel's strong support for our work. In a letter to RFE, Havel noted, "In the nascent pluralism of our information media, your station continues to occupy an irreplaceable position. We are too often absorbed by our own problems and lack sufficient detachment necessary for an objective evaluation of events. We need your professionalism and your ability to see events from a broad perspective."[14] We rounded out our visit with a meeting with U.S. ambassador Shirley Temple Black and attended a major exhibition at the National Technical Museum, entitled *Radio in the Service of Liberty*, commemorating forty years of RFE broadcasts to Czechoslovakia.

The trips to Prague, Warsaw, and Budapest and meetings with presidents and prime ministers were glamorous, and the BIB and RFE/RL management enjoyed the status of heroes. These trips, however, also carried symbolic significance that Communist rule had come to an end and that a new and hopeful era was beginning. For people across the entire East bloc, our physical presence in their countries was proof of tectonic political change. After all, RFE/RL was the public face of the Cold War, maligned for decades in the official press, scorned by Communist leaders, and even attacked by their secret services. Now we were welcomed as honored guests. No longer the enemy of the people, we were now seen publicly, standing side by side with their freely elected leadership, ready to help the former Communist countries to integrate into the free world. These were heady times, and we were acutely aware that our trips were playing a positive role by helping to advance democracy. As we pondered where we should go next, I suggested to Steve Forbes that Kyiv would be an ideal venue for a future board meeting. I had recently returned from the opening of our fledgling news office, colocated with Ukrinform, the official Ukrainian news service, and was pleased to hear strong support for RL broadcasts voiced by leading Ukrainian journalists.

In early June 1992 BIB directors and RFE/RL management traveled to Kyiv, where we were greeted warmly by President Leonid Kravchuk, who underscored the vital role Radio Liberty Ukrainian broadcasts had played in the development of Ukrainian democracy. The director of the Ukrainian National News Agency, Vitaly Vozianov, acknowledged the continuing importance of RL broadcasts, especially our role in helping to raise journalistic standards in the country. To take full advantage of our presence in Ukraine, we held a reception attended by over two hundred prominent Ukrainian cabinet ministers, defense officials, former opposition figures, and leading church prelates. Although the Kyiv visit was a celebratory occasion, a "planting of the flag" on former Soviet soil, we also had in-depth presentations about emerging Ukrainian statehood and learned about the horrors of Soviet rule, including a tour of a Cheka prison where hundreds of thousands of Ukrainians had been executed during Stalin's rule.

Looking back at the years 1990 to 1992 from today's vantage point, one might find it hard to believe how warmly welcomed the United States was in the former Communist countries. The West in general, and the United States in particular, were greeted as liberators, as forces of good that had saved people from the misery of Communist rule. Wherever we traveled, we were thanked for standing with ordinary people, for helping to preserve their culture and religion when they were under threat. Even Germany, which had always looked askance at RFE/RL operations on its soil, joined in the celebrations by awarding the Grand Cross of the Order of Merit of the Federal Republic of Germany, the highest distinction the German government bestows on a foreign citizen, to the RFE/RL president, Gene Pell. Exuberance and inflated expectations were everywhere, and even though we understood that this euphoria would not last, especially as economic hardships grew, we basked in this glorious unreality. To be associated with RFE/RL was to be a hero, a fighter for freedom and human dignity. Indicative of that unique moment in history was the formal nomination of RFE/RL— initially a covert CIA operation—for the Nobel Peace Prize, put forth by Lennart Meri, foreign minister of Estonia (and later, president) on behalf of newly elected democratic leaders. In his nominating letter, Meri noted, "There is abundant evidence—including statements by the freely elected leaders of Czechoslovakia, Hungary, Poland, and Bulgaria—that Radio Free Europe and Radio Liberty have made, and continue to make, a unique contribution to the rebirth of democracy in our region of the world, upon which lasting peace depends."[15]

The sense of heady unreality continued through 1992 and reached its apex in March 1993. As Gene Sosin reminisced, "If a soothsayer had predicted at the birth of Radio Liberty in 1953 that forty years later we would celebrate our anniversary in Moscow with the blessings of the democratic government of Russia, he would have been ridiculed as a madman. But there we were, a small contingent of Radio staff . . . BIB members . . . joined by the cultural and political elite of Moscow at the landmark Central House of Writers for a gala celebration."[16] Under the direction of Melissa Fleming, the RFE/RL director of public relations, RFE/RL mounted an exhibit of old photographs, RL microphones, Soviet cartoons attacking our broadcasts, excerpts from the Communist press, and representative programs in one of the most famous mansions of Moscow, used by Tolstoy as the Rostov residence in *War and Peace*. For one unforgettable night that mansion was the home of Radio Liberty.

To walk among the hundreds of guests at the reception was to be surrounded by the who's who of the Russian cultural and political elite. President Yeltsin had accepted our invitation but at the last moment had to bow out because of pressing business and sent his formal greetings and best wishes. Sergey Kovalev, one of the most prominent human rights advocates who had spent years in the gulag, came to express his gratitude for RL broadcasts. Bulat Okudzhava, one of the most revered bards in the Soviet Union, whose songs RL had played for years, came and sang a song in honor of Radio Liberty. Other well-known cultural figures included Veronika Dolina, a popular poet and singer; Innokenty Smoktunovsky, one of the most acclaimed actors of the Soviet Union; Zinovy Gerdt, a famous actor; and Andrei Voznesensky, a beloved poet. Even Oleg Kalugin, the former KGB general, showed up, now that he was a firm supporter of Boris Yeltsin and able to sport his democratic bona fides. But the true star of the evening was Mikhail Gorbachev. Now an ex-president, he was not accompanied by an entourage and slipped into the reception hall almost unnoticed. Once we saw him, everyone rushed to greet him, snapping pictures and trying to shake his hand. Gorbachev was in good spirits and gladly addressed the gathering. He lauded RL broadcasts for their contribution to Russian culture, their coverage of the attempted coup d'état, and especially their support of glasnost and perestroika. After his formal remarks, Gorbachev agreed to meet with just the BIB directors and senior RFE/RL executives for a private chat about the radios and their role in the monumental political changes that had taken place. I had the privilege of being Gorbachev's interpreter that evening and recall how relaxed and open our conversation was. Gone were the slings and arrows of Cold War rhetoric, the competition of economic systems, and the militarized state of the world. Here we were—several Americans and the former CPSU general secretary—talking about what was most important for Russia as it struggled to build a market economy and an open society. As I jotted down in my notes, Gorbachev at one point said, "I could have continued as head of the Soviet Union for decades, but I understood that the whole system was flawed and that sooner or later, it would collapse. I just sped up that process." In turn, we reminded him that Radio Liberty was never anti-Russian and that our singular aim was to help Russia in its transition to democracy. We parted on warm terms with Gorbachev reiterating his strong belief that Radio Liberty was critically needed and even promising to come to our fiftieth anniversary.

10

Reflections

To write this book, I listened to hundreds of hours of VOA and RL Russian-language broadcasts spanning different periods of the Cold War and examined nearly one thousand individual programs. This work gave me a nuanced understanding of how VOA and RFE/RL sought to communicate with their listeners, a deep appreciation for the professionalism of the Russian-language broadcasters, and a heightened awareness of the challenges of broadcasting to a closed society. In conclusion, I would like to share some personal reflections and offer a general assessment of what the Russian broadcasts sought to achieve.

I would begin with the essence of radio—the "voice." Like music, radio is sound—immediate, ethereal, evanescent. There is no text to reread, no picture to watch. All you have are syllables strung together to convey information, evoke feelings, and explain ideas. With short-wave broadcasting, often jammed, you have the added sense of sounds emanating from a fleeting and ghostly distant world.

In sharp contrast to Soviet news media that strived for a standard homogenized sound, VOA and Radio Liberty gloried in the voice and language of a free society, with its individuality, personality, and diversity. As I listened to the broadcasts, I could easily identify the individual voices on air—people I had known during my years at the two radio stations—because they spoke the way they were, with their quirks, idiosyncrasies, and verbal tics. Some, like Julian Panich at Radio Liberty or Alexey Kovalev at VOA, had been professional actors in the Soviet Union and read their texts with professional polish unmatched by other broadcasters. They were the go-to readers for texts that required the right intonation and gravitas to convey the message. Others, notably Irina Khenkina and Vladimir Matusevich at RL or Ludmila Foster at VOA, spoke directly to their listeners, betraying their attitudes and occasional biases simply through their manner of speech. Just by hearing their voices, you would know exactly what they thought of the material they were reading, and that gave their programs an authenticity and a loyal following. In contrast, we had self-effacing broadcasters—Yuri von Schlippe (RL) and Nik Sorokin (VOA) come to mind—who were exceptionally talented readers able to engage the listeners without calling attention to themselves. There were also sexy voices. Molly Gordin at RL received love letters from her avid listeners, as I am sure Zhanna Vladimirskaya at VOA did as well. We were proud to have non-Russians on air who had learned the language to an astoundingly high level, among them Mario Corti and Giovanni Bensi at RL and William McGuire, Jack Murphy, and Bill Skundrich at VOA. Their voices confirmed that Russian was a world language, known and loved by people of different ethnic backgrounds. Finally, we had prominent Russian writers and cultural figures—Yuri Lyubimov, Alexandr Solzhenitsyn, Vladimir Voinovich, among many others—who said exactly what they thought in their own unique way. Taken together, our broadcasters created a polyphony of voices, capturing the full richness of the Russian language as spoken by recent Soviet émigrés, children of the first and second emigrations, and non-Russians. We didn't sound like Radio Mayak or Radio Moscow and didn't want to. I resisted advice from outside radio experts who told us that we needed to sound more modern and hew closely to the Russian language spoken on Soviet television. I felt that would be a travesty because it would strip VOA and RFE/RL of one of the most precious gifts we could give our listeners—the sound of vivid, highly individual broadcasters who not only spoke of freedom but also lived that freedom in their voices.

The word *freedom* best characterizes the Russian broadcasts. The founders of the Russian broadcasts of RFE/RL created an independent Russian world not beholden to the dictates of the Communist Party or the Kremlin. It was free to explore, interpret, and engage with the traditions of Russian culture, as well as with the West. In our expansive Russian world there were no prohibited topics or censorship from above; broadcasters and radio guests were free to argue and debate, so long as they adhered to accepted Western norms of decorum and relied on fact-based information. In all the programs

I listened to, I never came across any instances of rumors, empty chatter, or vituperation. Except for a few programs in the 1950s that openly derided communism, I didn't hear gratuitous insults, sneers, or degrading comments about the Soviet leadership. At times, guests on RFE/RL and VOA would express sharp criticism of the Soviet regime, but the overall tone of the broadcasts was calm and professional. An examination of the entire corpus of Cold War programming, from the late 1940s to 1992, would reveal a vibrant and rich Russian culture, including conservative traditions, liberalism, and even socialism. We tried to give voice to many different strands of Russian culture, confident that our listeners would appreciate the diversity of views. Though often attacked in the Soviet press as enemies of the people, VOA and RL were never anti-Russian. The programs challenged the basic precepts of communism and exposed the crimes of Soviet rule, but the broadcasters at both radio stations had the deepest respect, if not outright love, for Russian culture and believed that their programming existed to enrich that very culture.

Looking back at the Cold War years, I would identify three basic strategic challenges facing the Russian Services of both VOA and Radio Liberty. The first was to pierce Soviet censorship by giving voice to Russians, both inside the USSR and in emigration, who were arbitrarily cut off from their own country and people. This meant inviting artists, writers, philosophers, historians, and human rights activists whose names had been excised from Soviet publications to participate in the programs and speak directly to their compatriots. We would often begin our weekly strategy meetings by analyzing the latest Soviet attacks on individual Russians and then discuss how best to present their stories in our programming. Our intention was to give voice to the voiceless and fill the glaring lacunae in Soviet coverage of Russian culture writ large. For that reason, broadcasting the works of Solzhenitsyn on VOA or the works of virtually every contemporary writer on RL was fundamental to our overall mission. At the core of our strategy was the belief that by overcoming Soviet censorship we were expressing the fundamental values of democracy and freedom and contributing to an open Russian society.

The second challenge was to present American and Western life in a way that our Soviet listeners could understand and appreciate. We were mindful of the advice proffered by Ambassador Bedell Smith in 1948, namely that presenting problems and scandals in the United States in the same way that American media painted them was to reinforce the anti-American propaganda that our listeners were already subjected to every day. Yet we understood that we had to present U.S. policies and American life in a critical way, ensuring that all responsible views were aired and that the warts and injustices in Western society were not glossed over. This required nuance and context. For this reason, merely translating or adapting an article from the *New York Times*, the *Washington Post*, or the VOA Central News Desk could not convey the texture of Western life that would be understandable to our listeners. Whenever possible, we tried to include Russians (or Westerners deeply steeped in Russian culture) who could serve as cultural translators. At RL, this was an easier task since Russian editors prepared all the feature programming and could draw on a growing number of highly educated émigrés. At VOA, this posed a greater challenge since many senior executives preferred uniformity across language services and at times insisted that a VOA report in English could be simply translated into Russian. I would often take issue with this approach, explaining to VOA management that what American journalists thought was a great story could easily fall on deaf ears in the Soviet Union or, worse, paint a distorted picture of the United States. I argued that VOA's features, often dubbed "Americana," without a Russian cultural context, were at best a waste of airtime. For this reason, whenever possible, I would seek out Russians capable of explaining American life in a way that made sense to our listeners. In 1984, for example, I invited Vasily Aksyonov to be the color commentator for the Democratic and Republican Party conventions and the presidential elections, knowing that his remarks not only would be highly entertaining but also would give Russian listeners a far better understanding of the American political process and how it protected basic American freedom.

The third challenge, and perhaps the most important during the Cold War, was to confront the Soviet Union by exposing its distortions of Russian history and culture; rejection of religion; subjugation of Ukraine, Georgia, and other nations within its empire; and worldwide disinformation campaigns. We were on the frontlines of the Cold War, and we came to work every day ready to challenge the Soviet Union. During my years at RL and VOA, we spent most of our time discussing and debating how we could fashion programs that would be fair in judgment, scrupulously researched, and, at the same time, strike the Soviet Union where it was most vulnerable. At RL, every feature program challenged the Soviet Union, from human rights, Orthodoxy, and Judaism to nationality issues and the crimes of Stalin's regime. Every day, RL programs offered its listeners new ways to see their own country and to understand its role in the world. As a general rule, VOA took a less confrontational approach, but in the Reagan years, the VOA Russian Service was often the equal of RL. As we saw in earlier chapters, VOA broadcast Russian literature that was banned in the USSR; aired extensive reports on Soviet abuses of human rights, often employing the same writers as RL; and developed first-rate programs on religion. VOA's Orthodox and Judaism broadcasts—very much in the spirit of surrogate programming—were among the major strategic achievements of the Russian Service.

The Russian Services of VOA and RL were born of the Cold War. They were conceived not only as weapons to confront the Soviet Union but also as bridges for mutual understanding with the Russian people and repositories of independent Russian culture. These strategic aims formed a daunting task, especially since the two highly complex organizations were constantly buffeted by political demands from American management and staffed by talented but temperamental émigré broadcasters who often had differing conceptions of what constituted highly effective programming. To add to this volatile mix, the VOA and RL Russian Services would be occasionally attacked by various Russian émigré organizations that had their own agenda for opposing the Soviet Union and by American politicians, journalists, or academics who relied on a distorted picture of the actual broadcasts. In addition, there was the unending stream of Soviet press attacks on the two Russian Services, with their shameless pillorying of journalists and outright lies about the programming. Through it all, year after year, the Russian Services of VOA and RL carried on, producing professional programs that have withstood the test of time. Many Russian programs, if rebroadcast today, would be of relevance and interest to anyone trying to understand the latter decades of Soviet rule. For historians of Russian literature and culture, the Cold War, or U.S.-Soviet relations, the VOA and RL Russian broadcasts will remain an unrivaled treasure trove of unique and indispensable resources.

A NOTE ON SOURCES

Although international broadcasting played an important role during the Cold War, VOA and RFE/RL have received little attention from historians of the twentieth century and scholars of Russian and Eastern European studies. There have been major studies of RFE/RL, primarily by A. Ross Johnson, R. Eugene Parta, and Arch Puddington, but few have examined in any detail the actual programming or placed the broadcasts in a historical and cultural context. VOA has been especially poorly served. While Holly Cowan Shulman produced an admirable study of the early years of VOA, focusing on the French broadcasts, the other major studies of VOA, primarily by Robert Pirsein and Alan Heil, have provided only a broad picture of the radio station.

The major drawback has been the difficulty of accessing the broadcasts, especially in the original language. For reasons that are hard to understand, the Russian Service of VOA did not retain copies of its feature programs, making it difficult to acquire an in-depth understanding of the broadcasts during the Cold War. Fortunately, several VOA broadcasters kept cassette recordings of their programs and were willing to share them with me. I am especially grateful to the Rev. Victor Potapov, Vladimir Matlin, and Alexey Kovalev, who were eager to discuss their programs with me, some thirty years after we worked together at VOA, and directed me to sites where I could listen to their broadcasts. When I left VOA, Marina Oeltjen, the chief producer, gave me several cassette recordings of significant broadcasts, including the entire cycle of Solzhenitsyn's reading from *August 1914*. Those broadcasts were indispensable for revisiting the highlights of Russian programming in the 1980s. I will donate copies of all these materials to the Hoover Institution and make them available to all researchers.

RFE/RL has done a far better job of maintaining archives and recordings of their significant broadcasts, and that made it possible for me to examine the Russian programs in greater detail. Thanks to the Vera and Donald Blinkin Open Society Archives (https://www.osaarchivum .org), I was able to listen to hundreds of hours of broadcasts spanning the entire Cold War. These broadcasts are online and can be accessed by anyone interested in hearing exactly what went on the air. I also had the opportunity to listen to Ivan Tolstoy's magisterial fifty-hour series of broadcasts highlighting the most significant programs from 1953 to 2003 (https://archive.svoboda.org). These programs are not only instructive but also highly entertaining. In addition, Columbia University has made available online sixty-nine interviews that RL conducted in the 1960s with prominent Russian émigrés who witnessed the 1917 Revolution. This is a unique and invaluable source of information about the actual events in 1917. See https://blogs.cul .columbia.edu/rbml/2020/11/17/radio-liberty-oral-history-project -newly-available-to-the-public/.

The Woodrow Wilson Center digital archives, accessible online, contain many recently declassified U.S. government documents that pertain to the early history of VOA and RFE/RL. Thanks to the work of Ross Johnson, we are now able to access these documents and learn how the CIA utilized the skills and knowledge of displaced persons in developing the Russian broadcasts. See https://digitalarchive.wilsoncenter.org.

The Hoover Institution at Stanford University contains the BIB and corporate RFE/RL documents, including policy-guidance memos, internal correspondence, and short descriptions of the broadcasts.

NOTES

Preface

1. Kenneth L. Adelman, "Speaking of America: Public Diplomacy in Our Time," *Foreign Affairs*, Spring 1981, 4.
2. Ronald Reagan, "Address at Commencement Exercises at the University of Notre Dame" (speech), May 17, 1981, https://www.reaganlibrary.gov /archives/speech/address-commencement-exercises-university-notre -dame.
3. Alan L. Heil, *Voice of America: A History* (New York: Columbia University Press, 2003), 176.

Introduction

1. George F. Kennan, "The Inauguration of Organized Political Warfare," memorandum, April 30, 1948, redacted version, Wilson Center Digital Archive, document 114320, https://digitalarchive.wilsoncenter.org /document/114320.
2. Kennan, "Inauguration of Organized Political Warfare."
3. See Alister Miskimmon, Ben O'Loughlin, and Laura Roselle, *Forging the World: Strategic Narratives and International Relations* (Ann Arbor: University of Michigan Press, 2017).
4. George Urban, *Radio Free Europe: My War within the Cold War* (New Haven CT: Yale University Press, 1997), 1.
5. A. Ross Johnson, *Radio Free Europe and Radio Liberty: The CIA Years and Beyond* (Redwood City CA: Stanford University Press, 2010), 6.
6. Urban, *Radio Free Europe*, 10.
7. The term *propaganda* generally refers to information or ideas spread by an organized group or government to influence people's opinions, especially by not giving all the facts or by secretly emphasizing only one way of looking at the fact. See *Cambridge Academic Content Dictionary* (Cambridge: Cambridge University Press, 2008).
8. Arch Puddington, *Broadcasting Freedom: The Cold War Triumph of Radio Free Europe and Radio Liberty* (Lexington: University of Kentucky Press, 2000), 4.

9. Puddington, *Broadcasting Freedom*, 11.

10. John F. Kennedy, "Address on the 20th Anniversary of the Voice of America," speech, Health, Education, and Welfare Building, February 26, 1962, Washington DC, https://www.americanrhetoric.com/speeches/jfkvoiceofamerica.htm.

1. Setting the Stage

1. Holly Cowan Shulman, *The Voice of America: Propaganda and Democracy, 1941-1945* (Madison: University of Wisconsin Press, 1990), 3.

2. Steven L. Herman, "The Evolution of U.S. Government-Funded External Broadcasting: From the Dawn of Broadcasting to 1948" (working paper, Mountain State University, February 2011), https://www.academia.edu/542000.

3. Herman, "Evolution of U.S. Government-Funded External Broadcasting," 9.

4. See Robert William Pirsein, *The Voice of America: A History of the International Broadcasting Activities of the U.S. Government, 1940-1962* (New York: Arno Press, 1979).

5. "Calls Lindbergh a Nazi," *New York Times*, December 12, 1940, https://www.nytimes.com/1940/12/12/archives/calls-lindbergh-a-nazi.html.

6. Harriet Hyman Alonso, *Robert E. Sherwood: The Playwright in Peace and War* (Amherst: University of Massachusetts Press, 2007), 88-91.

7. Robert E. Sherwood, *There Shall Be No Night* (Whitefish MT: Kessinger Publishing, 2005), 153.

8. Shulman, *Voice of America: Propaganda and Democracy*, 18.

9. Shulman, *Voice of America: Propaganda and Democracy*, 18.

10. Shulman, *Voice of America: Propaganda and Democracy*, 18.

11. Shulman, *Voice of America: Propaganda and Democracy*, 19.

12. Shulman, *Voice of America: Propaganda and Democracy*, 19.

13. Ted Lipien, "Stalin Prize-Winning Chief Writer of Voice of America News," Tadeusz Lipien (website), March 12, 2019, https://www.tadeuszlipien.com/stalin-prize-winning-chief-writer-of-voice-of-america-news/.

14. Shulman, *Voice of America: Propaganda and Democracy*, 13.

15. Pirsein, *Voice of America: History of International Broadcasting*, 76.

16. Heil, *Voice of America*, 39.

17. Shulman, *Voice of America: Propaganda and Democracy*, 53.

18. Pirsein, *Voice of America: History of International Broadcasting*, 14.

19. Heil, *Voice of America*, 32. For a detailed examination of the first broadcasts of VOA, see Ted Lipien, "Different Names of the Voice of America," Cold War Radio Museum, December 3, 2020, https://www .coldwarradiomuseum.com/the-voice-of-the-united-states-of-america.

20. Heil, *Voice of America*, 35.

21. Heil, *Voice of America*, 44.

22. James P. Warburg, *The Isolationist Illusion and World Peace* (New York: Farrar and Rinehart, 1941), 24.

23. Franklin Roosevelt, "State of the Union Address," January 6, 1941, Miller Center of Public Affairs, University of Virginia, transcript and MP3 audio, 36:18, https://millercenter.org/the-presidency/presidential-speeches /january-6-1941-state-union-four-freedoms.

24. Shulman, *Voice of America: Propaganda and Democracy*, 76.

25. Shulman, *Voice of America: Propaganda and Democracy*, 80.

26. Heil, *Voice of America*, 42.

27. Shulman, *Voice of America: Propaganda and Democracy*, 82.

28. Heil, *Voice of America*, 45.

29. "Mission," Who We Are, U.S. Agency for Global Media, https://www .usagm.gov/who-we-are/mission/.

30. Shulman, *Voice of America: Propaganda and Democracy*, 181.

31. Shulman, *Voice of America: Propaganda and Democracy*, 185.

32. Heil, *Voice of America*, 46.

33. Shulman, *Voice of America: Propaganda and Democracy*, 185.

34. Nicholas J. Cull, *The Cold War and the United States Information Agency: American Propaganda and Public Diplomacy, 1945-1989* (Cambridge: Cambridge University Press, 2008), 29.

35. George Kennan to George Marshall, telegram ["Long Telegram"], February 22, 1946, Harry S. Truman Administration File, Elsey Papers. See https://digitalarchive.wilsoncenter.org/document/116178.pdf.

36. Alban Webb, *London Calling: Britain, the BBC and the Cold War* (London: Bloomsbury, 2014), 35.

37. Kennan to Marshall, telegram, February 22, 1946.

38. Heil, *Voice of America*, 47.

39. Webb, *London Calling*, 7.

40. Webb, *London Calling*, 36-37.

41. Michael Nelson, *War of the Black Heavens: The Battles of Western Broadcasting in the Cold War* (Syracuse NY: Syracuse University Press, 1997), 10-11.

42. Webb, *London Calling*, 56.

43. Webb, *London Calling*, 62.

44. Christopher Mayhew, *A War of Words: A Cold War Witness*, ed. Lynn Smith (London: I. B. Tauris, 1998), 22.

45. Webb, *London Calling*, 58.

46. Webb, *London Calling*, 57.

47. Webb, *London Calling*, 61.

48. Nelson, *War of Black Heavens*, 16–17.

49. Cull, *Cold War*, 30–31.

50. Cull, *Cold War*, 32–33.

51. Cull, *Cold War*, 32–33.

52. See *Foreign Relations of the United States, 1947* (*FRUS, 1947*), vol. 4, *Eastern Europe; the Soviet Union* (Washington DC: Government Printing Office, 1972), 520.

53. Cull, *Cold War*, 11.

54. Puddington, *Broadcasting Freedom*, 15.

55. *FRUS, 1947*, 4:517–18.

56. *FRUS, 1947*, 4:531–32.

57. *FRUS, 1947*, 4:533–34.

58. The Ambassador in the Soviet Union to the Secretary of State, February 27, 1947, in *FRUS, 1947*, 4:537–38.

59. *FRUS, 1947*, 4:537–38.

60. The Ambassador in the Soviet Union to the Secretary of State, March 1, 1947, in *FRUS, 1947*, 4:541–42.

61. The Ambassador in the Soviet Union to the Secretary of State, March 16, 1947, in *FRUS, 1947*, 4:545–46.

62. *FRUS, 1947*, 4:557.

63. *FRUS, 1947*, 4:557. Samuil Marshak (1887–1964), an ardent Anglophile and a noted translator of English poetry, was a beloved writer of children's literature.

64. *FRUS, 1947*, 4:559.

65. *FRUS, 1947*, 4:559.

66. See Charge in the Soviet Union (Durbrow) to the Secretary of State, *FRUS, 1947*, 4:569. The embassy insisted on the word *censored* because all U.S. correspondent reports had to be sent through official Soviet channels.

67. *FRUS, 1947*, 4:588.

68. Boris Gorbatov (1908–54) was a Russian writer and journalist who received two Stalin Prizes (1946, 1952). He was honored in 2018 with a "postage stamp" issued by the so-called Donbas Peoples Republic.

69. *FRUS, 1947*, 4:595.

70. *FRUS, 1948*, 4:832.

71. *FRUS, 1948*, 4:832.

72. *FRUS, 1949*, 4:653.

73. Cull, *Cold War*, 31.

74. Cull, *Cold War*, 34.

75. Cull, *Cold War*, 37.

76. Pirsein, *Voice of America: History of International Broadcasting*, 117–18.

77. National Security Document on Coordination of Foreign Information Measures, 4, December 17, 1947, https://irp.fas.org/offdocs/nsc-hst/nsc-4.htm.

78. National Security Document 4.

79. Cull, *Cold War*, 39.

80. Alan L. Heil, "The Voice of America: A Brief Cold War History," in *Cold War Broadcasting: Impact on the Soviet Union and Eastern Europe*, eds. A. Ross Johnson and R. Eugene Parta (Budapest, Hungary: Central European University Press, 2010), 30–31.

81. *FRUS, 1951*, vol. 4, *Europe: Political and Economic Developments*, pt. 2, no. 786, https://history.state.gov/historicaldocuments/frus1951v04p2/d321.

82. Cull, *Cold War*, 49.

83. Memorandum, "Voice of America Russian Broadcasting Guidelines," May 1, 1958, document 115021, Wilson Center Digital Archive, https://digitalarchive.wilsoncenter.org/document/115021.

84. Cull, *Cold War*, 46–47.

85. Ludmila Flam, in discussion with the author, February 22, 2019.

86. Flam, discussion.

87. Flam, discussion.

88. See Victor Franzusoff, *Talking to Russians: Glimpses of History by a VOA Pioneer* (Santa Barbara CA: Fithian Press, 1998). The Russian sound is a theme of the entire book.

89. Heil, *Voice of America*, 63.

90. Franzusoff, *Talking to Russians*, 141.

91. Nik Sorokin, in discussion with the author, January 11, 2019.

92. Franzusoff, *Talking to Russians*, 146.

93. Puddington, *Broadcasting Freedom*, 204.

94. Heil, "Voice of America: A Brief Cold War History," 37.

95. Puddington, *Broadcasting Freedom*, 205.

96. See Lyudmila Alexeyeva, *U.S. Broadcasting to the Soviet Union* (New York: Helsinki Watch Report, September 1986), 101–2.

97. Alexandr Solzhenitsyn, *Publitsistika: Stat'i i rechi* (Paris: YMCA Press, 1981), 332–33.

98. Nelson, *War of Black Heavens*, 39.

99. Kennan, "Inauguration of Organized Political Warfare."

100. Johnson, *Radio Free Europe and Radio Liberty*, 26.

101. Sig Mickelson, *America's Other Voice: The Story of Radio Free Europe and Radio Liberty* (New York: Praeger, 1983), 19.

102. Harry S. Truman, *Off the Record: The Private Papers of Harry S Truman*, ed. Robert H. Ferrell (New York: Harper & Row, 1980), 79–80.

103. Paul B. Henze, "RFE's Early Years: Evolution of Broadcast Policy and Evidence of Broadcast Impact," in Johnson and Parta, *Cold War Broadcasting*, 5.

104. Harry S. Truman, "Fight False Propaganda with Truth" (speech), April 20, 1950, Washington DC, quoted in Puddington, *Broadcasting Freedom*, 11.

105. Memorandum, "Radio Liberty Broadcasting Policy," March 28, 1952, document 114376, Wilson Center Digital Archive, http://digitalarchive.wilsoncenter.org/document/114376.

106. Mickelson, *America's Other Voice*, 41.

107. "US Government Policy for Radio Free Europe and Radio Liberty," July 22, 1954, document 114487, Wilson Center Digital Archive, http://digitalarchive.wilsoncenter.org/document/114487.

108. Memorandum, "Radio Liberty Broadcasting Policy."

109. Memorandum, "Radio Policy Paper," January 22, 1953, document 114471, Wilson Center Digital Archive, http://digitalarchive.wilsoncenter.org/document/114471.

110. Frank Wisner to Robert Joyce, memorandum, June 2, 1952, document 114386, Wilson Center Digital Archive, https://digitalarchive.wilsoncenter.org/docuent/114386. The document was released to A. Ross Johnson in March 2009 and quoted in Johnson, *Radio Free Europe and Radio Liberty*, 39.

111. A. Ross Johnson, "Managing Media Influence Operations: Lessons from Radio Free Europe and Radio Liberty," *International Journal of Intelligence and Counter Intelligence* 31, no. 4 (2018): 8.

112. Mickelson, *America's Other Voice*, 60.

113. Robert F. Kelley, "Recommendations on Utilization of the Russian Emigration," memorandum, April 26, 1950, document 114336, Wilson Center Digital Archive, https://digitalarchive.wilsoncenter.org/document/114336.

114. Johnson, *Radio Free Europe and Radio Liberty*, 28.

115. Johnson, *Radio Free Europe and Radio Liberty*, 33.

116. Johnson, *Radio Free Europe and Radio Liberty*, 33.

117. Mickelson, *America's Other Voice*, 90.

118. Gene Sosin, *Sparks of Liberty: An Insider's Memoir of Radio Liberty* (University Park: Pennsylvania State University Press, 1999), 17–18.

119. Gene Sosin, "Goals of Radio Liberty," in Johnson and Parta, *Cold War Broadcasting*, 19.

120. Ivan Tolstoy, *Polveka v efire*, March 24, 2011, CD-ROM, author's collection.

121. Kimberly Springer, "Radio Liberty Oral History Project Newly Available to the Public," *News from Columbia's Rare Book & Manuscript Library* (blog), Columbia University Libraries, November 17, 2020, https://blogs.cul.columbia.edu/rbml/2020/11/17/radio-liberty-oral-history-project-newly-available-to-the-public/.

122. Sosin, *Sparks of Liberty*, 4–5.

123. Sosin, *Sparks of Liberty*, 5.

124. Natalie von Meyer Clarkson, *As I Remember* (Terra Alta WV: Headline Books, 2017), 88.

125. Nicholas Bethell, *The Last Secret: The Delivery to Stalin of Over Two Million Russians by Britain and the United States* (New York: Basic Books, 1974).

126. Memorandum, "Radio Policy Paper."

127. For a detailed examination of the second emigration in postwar Germany, see Elena Kuhlin, "Sud'ba russkikh peremeshchenykh lits v amerikanskoi zone okkupatsii v Bavarii," *Novyi zhurnal* (New review) 295 (2019): 288–344.

128. Ivan Tolstoy, *Polveka v efire*.

129. See Catherine Andreyev, *Vlasov and the Russian Liberation Movement: Soviet Reality and Émigré Theories* (Cambridge: Cambridge University Press, 1987).

130. Lyudmila Lunina, "Novo Diveevo: Lest We Forget," Russkiy Mir Foundation, n.d., https://russkiymir.ru/en/magazines/article/144491/.

131. Sosin, *Sparks of Liberty*, 71.

132. Kelley, "Recommendations on Utilization of Russian Emigration."

133. Sosin, *Sparks of Liberty*, 5.

134. Alexeyeva, *U.S. Broadcasting*, 86.

135. Puddington, *Broadcasting Freedom*, 274.

136. Puddington, *Broadcasting Freedom*, 236.

137. Ksenia Kirillova, "Spy's Wife: How a Soviet Dissident Turned Out to Be an Involuntary Ally of the Most Successful KGB Agent in America," *Forum Daily*, November 30, 2021. Svetlana Tumanova was Oleg's widow.

138. See, among other works, Solzhenitsyn, *Publitsistika*.

139. Llewellyn Thompson and Anatoly Fedorovich Dobrynin, "Soviet Ambassador Dobrynin on Radio Liberty," memorandum, October 23, 1963, document 115062, Wilson Center Digital Archive, https://digitalarchive.wilsoncenter.org/document/115062.

140. Henry Kissinger to Richard Nixon, "Nixon Approves Continuation of Radio Liberty," memorandum, December 29, 1969, document 115128, Wilson Center Digital Archive, http://digitalarchive.wilsoncenter.org/document/115128.

141. Mickelson, *America's Other Voice*, 130–31.

142. Mickelson, *America's Other Voice*, 136.

143. Sosin, *Sparks of Liberty*, 136.

144. "Saving Free Voices," editorial, *New York Times*, February 21, 1972, https://www.nytimes.com/1972/02/21/archives/saving-free-voices.html.

145. Sosin, *Sparks of Liberty*, 141.

146. Sosin, *Sparks of Liberty*, 141.

147. "US Government Policy for Radio Free Europe and Radio Liberty."

148. Cull, *Cold War*, 487.

149. Sosin, *Sparks of Liberty*, 73.

150. R. Eugene Parta, "The Audience to Western Broadcasts to the USSR during the Cold War: An External Perspective," in Johnson and Parta, *Cold War Broadcasting*, 68.

151. Parta, "Audience to Western Broadcasts," 70.

152. George W. Woodard, "Cold War Radio Jamming," in Johnson and Parta, *Cold War Broadcasting*, 53.

153. Elena Bashkirova, "The Foreign Radio Audience in the USSR during the Cold War: An Internal Perspective," in Johnson and Parta, *Cold War Broadcasting*, 104.

154. Vladimir Tolz, "Soviet Reactions to Foreign Broadcasting in the 1950s," in Johnson and Parta, *Cold War Broadcasting*, 282.

155. Tolz, "Soviet Reactions," 284.

156. Tolz, "Soviet Reactions," 285.

2. The Reagan Revolution

1. H. W. Brands, *Reagan: A Life* (New York: Doubleday, 2015), 123.

2. George Eckel, "Freedom Crusade Will Begin Sept. 4," *New York Times*, July 28, 1950, https://www.nytimes.com/1950/07/28/archives/freedom -crusade-will-begin-sept-4-eisenhower-broadcast-to-open.html.

3. "Text of Eisenhower's Radio Speech for the Crusade of Freedom," *New York Times*, November 12, 1952, https://timesmachine.nytimes.com /timesmachine/1952/11/12/84366105.html.

4. Richard H. Cummings, "Rising above Partisan Politics: Fighting the 'Big Lie' with the 'Big Truth' in 1952," *Cold War Radios* (blog), November 3, 2011 http://coldwarradios.blogspot.com/2011/11/rising-above-partisan -politics-fighting.html (site discontinued).

5. Henry Ford II, "Crusade for Freedom," memorandum, November 11, 1952, author's collection.

6. Richard Cummings, *Radio Free Europe's Crusade for Freedom: Rallying Americans behind Cold War Broadcasting* (Jefferson NC: McFarland, 2010), 2–3.

7. Ronald Reagan, "Crusade for Freedom" (commercial), ca. 1952, at "Ronald Reagan 1950s Crusade for Freedom Commercial Soliciting Funds for Radio Free Europe," YouTube video, 0:53, posted by Levan Ramishvili, July 2, 2013, https://www.youtube.com/watch?v=SVy1K_xX5pg.

8. "Reagan, in Direct Attack, Assails Ford," *New York Times*, March 5, 1976.

9. Francis H. Marlo, *Planning Reagan's War: Conservative Strategists and America's Cold War Victory* (Washington DC: Potomac Books, 2012), 16.

10. Marlo, *Planning Reagan's War*, 13.

11. Ronald Regan, *An American Life* (New York: Pocket Books, 1990), 265.

12. Marlo, *Planning Reagan's War*, 41.

13. Donnie Radcliffe, "Fond Farewells at the White House," *Washington Post*, November 17, 1988.

14. Kenneth L. Adelman, "Speaking of America: Public Diplomacy in Our Time," *Foreign Affairs*, Spring 1981.

15. Cull, *Cold War*, 399.

16. Cull, *Cold War*, 399.

17. Cull, *Cold War*, 399.

18. Cull, *Cold War*, 400.

19. Central Intelligence Agency, NSDD 11-82, https://www.cia.gov /readingroom/docs/CIA-RDP85M00363R000200290004-9.pdf.

20. Marlo, *Planning Reagan's War*, 33.

21. Marlo, *Planning Reagan's War*, 33.

22. Central Intelligence Agency, NSDD 11-82.

23. Heil, *Voice of America*, 201.

24. Heil, *Voice of America*, 210.

25. Heil, *Voice of America*, 200.

26. Nicolaides to Conkling, memorandum, September 21, 1981, author's collection.

27. Heil, *Voice of America*, 206–9.

28. Board for International Broadcasting, *1976 Annual Report*, 1977.

29. Sosin, *Sparks of Liberty*, 174.

30. Mickelson, *America's Other Voice*, 207.

31. Urban, *Radio Free Europe*, 77.

32. Puddington, *Broadcasting Freedom*, 262.

33. Frank Shakespeare, interview by Abbott Washburn, Ike and USIA: A Symposium, Washington DC, October 11, 1990, manuscript, 55–56, https://tile.loc.gov/storage-services/service/mss/mfdip/2004/2004eis01/2004eis01.pdf.

34. James L. Buckley, *Gleanings from an Unplanned Life* (Wilmington DE: ISI Books, 2006), 212.

35. Josef Joffe and Dmitri Simes, "How America Backs Critics of Freedom," *Washington Post*, September 25, 1983.

36. Puddington, *Broadcasting Freedom*, 254.

37. Sosin, *Sparks of Liberty*, 179.

38. Sosin, *Sparks of Liberty*, 179.

39. Joffe and Simes, "How America Backs Critics."

3. Human Rights

1. Andrei Amalrik, *Will the Soviet Union Survive until 1984?* (New York: Harper and Row, 1970), 1.

2. Vladimir Bukovsky, *To Build a Castle: My Life as a Dissenter* (New York: Viking, 1979), 141.

3. Harold Berman, *Soviet Criminal Law and Procedure: The RSFSR Codes* (Cambridge MA: Harvard University Press, 1972), 81–83.

4. Puddington, *Broadcasting Freedom*, 171.

5. The *White Book* (facsimile of the original samizdat publication) is available online (https://imwerden.de/publ-1582.html).

6. See Ivan Tolstoy's series—*Polveka v efire*, god 66, at https://archive.svoboda.org/50/.

7. See Tolstoy, *Polveka v efire*, god 66.

8. Mario Corti, "The Year 1968 in the History of Samizdat" (paper presented at the conference of the Center for the Study of East European History, Levico Terme, Italy, November 23-24, 2018). Corti was the

head of RFE/RL samizdat unit and is a renowned expert on the dissident movement.

9. Peter Reddaway, *The Dissidents: A Memoir of Working with the Resistance in Russia, 1960-1990* (Washington DC: Brookings Institution Press, 2020), 72.

10. "Natalya Gorbanevskaya: Soviet Dissident and Poet, Dies at 77," *New York Times*, December 1, 2013.

11. Reddaway, *Dissidents*, 71.

12. Reddaway, *Dissidents*, 77.

13. The operation is also known as the Dymshits-Kuznetsov hijacking affair.

14. Kuznetsov was the author of three novels: *Prison Diary* (1973), *Mordovian Marathon* (1979)—both written secretly in prison and smuggled abroad— and *Russian Romance* (1984).

15. Lyudmila Alexeyeva, *The History of the Dissident Movement in the USSR* (Vilnius, Lithuania: Vest Publishers, 1992).

16. Edward Kuznetsov, *Documents and People*, December 15, 1983, radio broadcast, Open Society Archives, MP3 format, 29:22, https://catalog.osaarchivum.org/catalog/osa:c39ad8e4-26df-4560-af56 -4a88326afdf4.

17. Anatoly Marchenko, *My Testimony* (London: Pall Mall Press, 1969), 25. See also Anatolii Marchenko, *Zhivi kak vse* (Moskva: Vest', 1993).

18. Anatoly Shcharansky, "The Limits of Glasnost" (speech), December 12, 1986, Heritage Foundation, transcript, https://www.heritage.org/node /10242/print-display.

19. Michael Cotey Morgan, *The Final Act: The Helsinki Accords and the Trans-formation of the Cold War* (Princeton NJ: Princeton University Press, 2018), 176.

20. Morgan, *Final Act*, 169-206.

21. Morgan, *Final Act*, 221.

22. Morgan, *Final Act*, 180.

23. Morgan, *Final Act*, 188.

24. Morgan, *Final Act*, 222-23.

25. Morgan, *Final Act*, 223.

26. Morgan, *Final Act*, 231.

27. Doug Underwood, *From Yahweh to Yahoo: Religious Roots of the Secular Press* (Urbana: University of Illinois Press, 2002), 22.

28. Puddington, *Broadcasting Freedom*, 160.

29. Alexey Retivov, "Zvukovye Bar'ery Radioveshchaniya," *Kontinent*, no. 9 (1976): https://vtoraya-literatura.com/pdf/kontinent_009_1976_text.pdf.

30. Retivov, *Kontinent*, no. 9 (1976).

31. Cull, *Cold War*, 330.

32. James Keough to Representative Robert L. F. Sikes, March 5, 1974, in Heil, "Voice of America: A Brief Cold War History," 36.

33. Cull, *Cold War*, 330.

34. Minutes of U.S. Information Agency, July 28, 1976, author's collection. This was confirmed by Lucy Obolensky Flam, in discussion with the author, February 10, 2020.

35. Nikolai Mesyatsev to CPSU Central Committee, "Ideological Subversion on the Airwaves of Foreign Radio Stations Broadcasting in the Russian Language," memorandum, April 14, 1967, document 121515, Wilson Center Digital Archive, http://digitalarchive.wilsoncenter.org/document /121515.

36. Minutes, U.S. Information Agency, July 28, 1976.

37. Minutes, U.S. Information Agency, July 28, 1976.

38. Minutes, U.S. Information Agency, July 28, 1976.

39. Minutes, U.S. Information Agency, July 28, 1976.

40. Minutes, U.S. Information Agency, July 28, 1976.

41. Lucy Obolensky Flam to Director of USSR Division, memorandum, March 11, 1977, author's collection.

42. Alexeyeva, *U.S. Broadcasting*, 82–83.

4. Culture and the Arts

1. Cull, *Cold War*, 278–79.

2. See Douglas Smith, *Former People: The Final Days of the Russian Aristocracy* (New York: Farrar, Straus, and Giroux, 2012).

3. See *Sovetskii Entsyklopedicheskii slovar'* (Moskva: Sovetskaya entsyklopedia, 1980), 1153.

4. Mstislav Rostropovich, in discussion with the author, November 25, 1983. Excerpts from the interview were broadcast in the following VOA Russian programs: *Panorama, Events and Opinions, Night Owl,* and *Breakfast Show.* The full interview was broadcast in the *Performing Arts Show.*

5. Barry Farber, Syndicated Features, to Kenneth Tomlinson, November 21, 1983, author's collection.

6. Galina Vishnevskaya, *Galina: A Russian Story* (New York: Harcourt, Brace, Jovanovich, 1984).

7. Galina Vishnevskaya, in discussion with the author, March 20, 1984.

8. Tatiana Retivov, in discussion with the author, January 28, 2020.

9. Broadcast of Jelagin's book began on December 8, 1986, and continued for several consecutive weeks.

10. Juri Jelagin, *Ukroshchenie iskusstv* (New York: Izdatelstvo imeni Chekhova, 1952), 228.

11. Vasily Aksyonov, *Say Cheese!*, read by the author, July 8, 1986, radio broadcast, Voice of America, *Literary Readings*, audio cassettes, author's collection.

12. Ivan Tolstoy, email message to author, February 16, 2020. Tolstoy is a prominent Russian writer and senior editor of RL in Prague.

13. "In Memory of Vysotsky," October 17, 1981, radio broadcast, Open Society Archives, MP3 format, 50:48, https://catalog.osaarchivum.org /catalog/osa:5f6eb549-2f7f-4661-8cbd-a349ecab53ab.

5. History

1. Urban, *Radio Free Europe*, 113.

2. Radio Free Europe/Radio Liberty Corporate Records, box 2265, folder 2, Hoover Institution Library and Archives, Stanford University, Stanford CA.

3. Sosin, *Sparks of Liberty*, 176–77; Puddington, *Broadcasting Freedom*, 275–76.

4. *Russia: Yesterday, Today, and Tomorrow*, May 21, 1980, radio broadcast, Open Society Archives, https://catalog.osaarchivum.org/catalog/osa: 154d801e-d680-4e9e-a42f-840ae13c02e1.

5. Sosin, *Sparks of Liberty*, 176.

6. Josef Joffe and Dimitri Simes, "Our Propaganda Isn't Always Democratic," *Washington Post*, September 25, 1983. Also see Russ Braley, "The Assault on Radio Liberty," *Human Events*, June 22, 1985.

7. William Korey, "Flouting American Ideals: How RFE/RL Broadcast a Message Insensitive to Jews and Democratic Ideas in the Name of Fighting Communism," Radio Free Europe/Radio Liberty Corporate Records, box 2265, folder 2, Hoover Institution Library and Archives, Stanford University, Stanford CA.

8. Rahr published his memoirs in post-Communist Russia: G. A. Rahr, *I budet nashe pokolenie davat' istorii otchet: vospominaniia* (Moskva: Russkii put', 2011).

9. Marc Raeff, "Review of Novopokolentsy by Boris Prianishnikoff" *Slavic Review* (Summer 1989): 305–6.

10. Lyudmila Alexeyeva, *U.S. Broadcasting to the Soviet Union* (New York: Human Rights Watch, September 1986), 26.

11. Alexeyeva, *U.S. Broadcasting*, 28–29.

12. Richard Pipes, *Russia under the Old Regime* (New York: Penguin Books, 1974), 294.

13. Pipes, *Russia under Old Regime*, 306–7.
14. "Misconceptions about Russia Are a Threat to America," *Foreign Affairs* 58, no. 4 (Spring 1980): 797–834.
15. "Solzhenitsyn to Reagan: Spasibo, Nyet" *Washington Post*, May 16, 1982.
16. Boris Nemtsov, "Pioneering Land Reform," *Moscow Times*, September 29, 1995.
17. Gordon Hahn, "Putin Is No Stolypin," Russian & Eurasian Politics (website), September 14, 2015, https://gordonhahn.com/2015/09/14/putin-is-no-stolypin/.
18. Most Western historians have a mixed picture of Stolypin. See Alexander Yanov, "Russian Prime Minister Pyotr Stolypin: In Anticipation of a Monument," Institute of Modern Russia, June 7, 2012, https://imrussia.org/en/nation/247-russian-prime-minister-pyotr-stolypin-in-anticipation-of-a-monument.

6. Solzhenitsyn

1. Alexandr Solzhenitsyn, in discussion with the author, May 15, 1984, author's collection.
2. *Vremya* (Russian news program), "Vstrecha Putina s Solzhenitsynym" (A meeting of Putin and Solzhenitsyn), aired September 20, 2000, on Russian TV First Channel, https://lenta.ru/news/2000/09/21/putin/.
3. Alexandr Solzhenitsyn, *Krasnoe koleso: Uzel 1. Avgust Chetyrnadtsogo* (Paris: YMCA Press, 1983), 209.
4. Solzhenitsyn, *Krasnoe koleso: Uzel 1*, 249.
5. Alexeyeva, *U.S. Broadcasting*, 87–89.
6. Alexeyeva, *U.S. Broadcasting*, 89–90.
7. Joanne Omang, "Version of Solzhenitsyn Novel, Broadcast by VOA, Causes Flap," *Washington Post*, February 4, 1985.

7. Religion

1. Vladimir Lenin to Molotov for Politburo members, March 19, 1922, quoted in Richard Pipes, ed., *The Unknown Lenin: From the Secret Archive* (New Haven CT: Yale University Press, 1996), 152–55.
2. Douglas Smith, *The Russian Job: The Forgotten Story of How America Saved the Soviet Union from Ruin* (New York: Farrar, Straus and Giroux, 2019), 126–27.
3. Board for International Broadcasting, *1985 Annual Report*, 1986, 20; Board for International Broadcasting, *1986 Annual Report*, 1987, 19–20.
4. Alexeyeva, *U.S. Broadcasting*, 40.

5. Victor Potapov, in discussion with the author, July 2019.

6. Father Victor Potapov's programs are available on YouTube.

7. The episode of *Religion in Our Life* aired on August 18, 1979.

8. The episode of *Religion in Our Life* aired on September 18, 1982.

9. Vladimir Matlin, in discussion with the author, July 9, 2019.

10. Vladimir Matlin, "Evreiskii golos 'Golosa Ameriki,'" *Ierusalimskii Russko-Evreiskii Vestnik*, no. 3, 1998, 32–33.

11. Vladimir Matlin, email message to author, July 2019.

12. Alexeyeva, *U.S. Broadcasting*, 50.

13. James Critchlow to directors of the Board for International Broadcasting, memorandum, RFE/RL Corporate Records, box 2265, folder 2, Hoover Institution Library and Archives, Stanford University, Stanford CA.

14. Gleb Rahr, *Vospominania* (Moskva: Russkii put', 2011), 491.

15. Timothy Snyder, "Ivan Ilyin, Putin's Philosopher of Russian Fascism," *New York Review of Books*, March 16, 2018, https://www.nybooks.com /daily/2018/03/16/ivan-ilyin-putins-philosopher-of-russian-fascism/.

16. Alexeyeva, *U.S. Broadcasting*, 50.

17. Rahr, *Vospominania*, 493.

18. Rahr, *Vospominania*, 493.

19. Levada Center, "Church and State," press release, January 19, 2022, https://www.levada.ru/2022/01/19/tserkov-i-gosudarstvo-3/.

8. Glasnost

1. "Na volne psikhologicheskoi voiny: Pravda o korporatsii Lzhy," *Argumenty i fakty*, no. 25, 1986; Sosin, *Sparks of Liberty*, 33.

2. D. Biriukov, "Diversanty iz chernoi propagandy," *Mezhdunarodnaya zhizn'*, January 1987, 124.

3. R. Eugene Parta, "Audience to Western Broadcasts," 67–121.

4. Puddington, *Broadcasting Freedom*, 285.

5. "The KGB Informs and Comments: What Is behind Strategic Plans?" *Argumenty I fakty*, no. 17, April 23–29, 1988.

6. Cull, *Cold War*, 474.

7. Cull, *Cold War*, 475.

8. Cull, *Cold War*, 476.

9. USIA, "Memorandum of Conversation," September 26, 1988, author's collection.

10. For more on Falin's opposition to glasnost, see Valentin Falin to Mikhail Gorbachev, memorandum, April 18, 1990, excerpts, History Foundation (website), http://historyfoundation.ru/doc16/.

11. George W. Woodard, "Cold War Jamming," 51.

12. Sosin, *Sparks of Liberty*, 203.

13. Sosin, *Sparks of Liberty*, 230.

14. Ivan Tolstoi, *Polveka v efire*, god 1989.

15. Ivan Tolstoi, *Polveka v efire*, god 1988.

16. Iakov Arkadievich Iakovlev (surname Epstein), born in 1896, was the chair of the All-Union Commission on Collectivization from 1931 to 1937 and oversaw the Holodomor in Ukraine. He was shot on July 29, 1938.

17. Nina Andreeva, "Ne mogu postupatsia printsipami," *Sovetskaya Rossiya*, March 13, 1988.

18. N. Larionova, "Razgovor bez diktafonov," *Pravda*, January 16, 1989.

19. Vladimir Ostrogosrky, "Eto prisyv k otvetstvennosti," *Novoe vremya*, no. 19, May 1989.

20. *Sobesednik*, "Svobodnyi mikrofon," August 1989.

21. Vladimir Ostrogorsky, "What Voices Do We Hear?," *Sobesednik*, October 1989.

22. V. Rakhlyavichus and G. Vainauskas, *Komsomolnaya Pravda*, "Azbuka glasnosti . . . iz Miunkhena," October 21, 1989.

23. *Atmoda*, "Peredachi radio Svoboda," March 12, 1990.

24. Leonid Shinkarev, "Poverkh granits," *Izvestia*, March 31, 1990; Puddington, *Broadcasting Freedom*, 305.

25. Sosin, *Sparks of Liberty*, 213.

26. Sosin, *Sparks of Liberty*, 219.

27. Sergei Timofyeyev, "Interview to Radio Liberty," Board for International Broadcasting, *1992 Annual Report*, 1993, 26.

9. Victory Lap

1. Memorandum, "Telephone Conversation with President Vaclav Havel," April 12, 1991, 9:13–9:40 a.m., George H. W. Bush Presidential Library & Museum, https://bush41library.tamu.edu/files/memcons-telcons/1991 -04-12--Havel.pdf.

2. George H. W. Bush, "Remarks to the National Association of Broadcasters Convention" (speech), April 15, 1991, George H. W. Bush Presidential Library & Museum, https://bush41library.tamu.edu/archives/public -papers/2873.

3. Memorandum, "National Security Review 24," March 28, 1990, George H. W. Bush Presidential Library & Museum, https://bush41library.tamu .edu/files/nsr/nsr24.pdf.

4. *Report of the President's Task Force on U.S. Government International Broadcasting: Hearings before the H.R. Subcomm. on International Operations of the Comm. on Foreign Affairs*, 102nd Cong. (February 4, 1992), at 3, https://babel.hathitrust.org/cgi/pt?id=uc1.31210014954232&view=1up&seq=4.

5. Board for International Broadcasting, *1990 Annual Report*, 1991, 1.

6. Board for International Broadcasting, *1990 Annual Report*, 2.

7. *Hearings on U.S. Public Diplomacy in Eastern Europe and the Soviet Union before the Subcomm. on International Operations*, 102nd Cong., at 56–58 (July 30, 1991) (statement of Mark Pomar).

8. Board for International Broadcasting, *1990 Annual Report*, 2.

9. Board for International Broadcasting, *1990 Annual Report*, 2.

10. *Hearings on U.S. Public Diplomacy*, at 56–58 (Pomar).

11. Board for International Broadcasting, *1990 Annual Report*, 4.

12. Board for International Broadcasting, *1990 Annual Report*, 5.

13. Board for International Broadcasting, *1992 Annual Report*, 5.

14. Board for International Broadcasting, *1991 Annual Report*, 1992, 8.

15. Board for International Broadcasting, *1992 Annual Report*, 4.

16. Sosin, *Sparks of Liberty*, 237.

SELECTED BIBLIOGRAPHY

Abshire, David M. *International Broadcasting: A New Dimension of Western Diplomacy.* The Washington Papers 35. Beverly Hills CA: Sage Publications, 1976.

Alexeyeva, Lyudmila. *U.S. Broadcasting to the Soviet Union.* New York: Human Rights Watch, 1986.

Clarkson, Natalie von Meyer. *As I Remember.* Terra Alta WV: Headline Books, 2017.

Critchlow, James. *Radio Hole-in-the Head: An Insider's Story of Cold War Broadcasting.* Washington DC: American University Press, 1995.

Cull, Nicholas J. *The Cold War and the United States Information Agency: American Propaganda and Public Diplomacy, 1945-1989.* Cambridge: Cambridge University Press, 2008.

Cummings, Richard H. *Cold War Radio: The Dangerous History of American Broadcasting in Europe, 1950-1989.* Jefferson NC: McFarland, 2010.

Franzusoff, Victor. *Talking to the Russians: Glimpses of History by a Voice of America Pioneer.* Santa Barbara CA: Fithian Press, 1998.

Heil, Alan L. *Voice of America: A History.* New York: Columbia University Press, 2003.

Johnson, A. Ross. *Radio Free Europe and Radio Liberty: The CIA Years and Beyond.* Stanford CA: Stanford University Press, 2010.

Johnson, A. Ross, and R. Eugene Parta, eds. *Cold War Broadcasting: Impact on the Soviet Union and Eastern Europe.* Budapest, Hungary: Central European University Press, 2010.

Kounalakis, Markos. *Spin Wars & Spy Games: Global Media and Intelligence Gathering.* Stanford CA: Hoover Institution Press, 2018.

Mickelson, Sig. *America's Other Voice: The Story of Radio Free Europe and Radio Liberty.* New York: Praeger, 1983.

Nelson, Michael. *War of the Black Heavens: The Battles of Western Broadcasting in the Cold War.* Syracuse NY: Syracuse University Press, 1997.

Parta, R. Eugene. *Discovering the Hidden Listener: An Assessment of Radio Liberty and Western Broadcasting to the USSR during the Cold War; A Study*

Based on Audience Research Findings. 1970–1991. Stanford CA: Hoover Institution Press, 2007.

Pirsein, Robert William. *The Voice of America: An History of the International Broadcasting Activities of the United States Government, 1940-1962.* New York: Arno Press, 1979.

Puddington, Arch. *Broadcasting Freedom: The Cold War Triumph of Radio Free Europe and Radio Liberty.* Lexington: University of Kentucky Press, 2000.

Short, K. R. M., ed. *Western Broadcasting over the Iron Curtain.* London: Croom Helm, 1986.

Shulman, Holly Cowan. *The Voice of America: Propaganda and Democracy, 1941-1945.* Madison: University of Wisconsin Press, 1990.

Sosin, Gene. *Sparks of Liberty: An Insider's Memoir of Radio Liberty.* University Park: Pennsylvania State University Press, 1999.

Urban, George R. *Radio Free Europe and the Pursuit of Democracy: My War within the Cold War.* New Haven CT: Yale University Press, 1997.

Webb, Alban. *London Calling: Britain, the BBC World Service and the Cold War.* London: Bloomsbury, 2014.

INDEX

arts and culture broadcasting. *See* culture and the arts broadcasting of Radio Liberty; culture and the arts broadcasting of Voice of America

Aspects, 232

Assotsiatsia avtorskogo televideniia, 204

atheism, 50, 181, 182

Atmoda, 239, 240, 241

audience research, 62–64, 183, 201, 249

August 1914 (Solzhenitsyn): conclusions on VOA reading of, 178–80; first chapter VOA reading of, 169–70; second chapter VOA reading of, 170–74; third chapter VOA reading of, 174–75, 176; VOA broadcasting controversy of, 175–78, 179

August Putsch, 241–45

avtorskaya pesnya, 140–41, 258

Babii Yar, 144

Babitsky, Andrei, 228, 244

Baez, Joan, 96

Bailey, George, 82, 147

The Baltic Journal, 231

bard songs, 140–41, 258

Barmine, Alexander, 37

Barnes, Joseph F., 12, 13, 14, 15, 17

Baryshnikov, Mikhail, 121, 126

Bashkirova, Elena, 65

Basic Judaism (Steinberg), 190

Basket III of Helsinki Final Act, 105, 106

BBC (British Broadcasting Corporation), 9, 13, 22–23, 25, 63, 66, 245

Beckett, Samuel, 133

Beginning of the Day, 195, 197

Beilis, Menahem Mendel, 199–200

Belarus, 46, 243

Belotserkovsky, Vadim, 241

Belov, Vasily, 229–31

Bensi, Giovanni, 239, 262

Benton, William, 19–21, 23–25, 32–33, 36

Berezhkova, Sofia, 227

Beria, Lavrenty, 65, 93

Berlin, Isaiah, 154

Berukshtis, Igor, 138

BIB (Board for International Broadcasting). *See* Board for International Broadcasting (BIB)

Biriukov, Dmitri, 205–7

Black Hundreds, 178, 199

Board for International Broadcasting (BIB): about, xii, 60, 64; détente and, 79–80; Eastern Europe and, 253–54; glasnost and, 208, 224; post–Soviet collapse and, 248, 249–50; during Reagan administration, 81–82; religious broadcasting and, 195, 201; Soviet criticism of, 206

Bock, Siegfried, 105

Bogomol'e (Shmelev), 194, 195

Bogoraz, Larissa, 95, 96

Bogrov, Dmitri, 159, 168, 169–70, 174, 176, 177–78

Bohlen, Celestine, 214

Bolshoi Theatre, 122, 124

Bonner, Elena, x, 94, 245

Books and People, 132, 175

Both Sides of the Ocean (Nekrasov), 144

Breton, André, 13

Brezhnev, Leonid, 105, 131

British Broadcasting Corporation (BBC), 9, 13, 22–23, 25, 63, 66, 245
British Foreign Office, 22
Britten, Benjamin, 123
Broadway, 132
Broadway 1775, 232
Brodsky, Joseph, 39, 71, 91–92, 103, 126
Brown, James F., 83
Buckley, James, 82–83
Bukovsky, Vladimir, 89, 90, 162, 221, 250
Bulgakov, Mikhail, 93, 204
Bunin, Ivan, 143–44
Bush, George H. W., 247–48, 251
Bush, Keith, 221
Byelorussian Soviet Socialist Republic, 243

Campaign for Truth, 34
capitalism, 20, 81
Carroll, Wallace, 17
Case, Clifford, 59–60, 72
Catherman, Terence, 37–38
CBS, 10, 68, 135
censorship, Soviet: Alexandr Solzhenitsyn and, 168; background and overview of, 4, 22; glasnost and, 204–5, 212, 213–14, 216, 221; overcoming, 263; Soviet easing of, 88, 93
censorship, U.S., 110
Center for Strategic and International Studies (CSIS), 205
Central Intelligence Agency (CIA). *See* CIA (Central Intelligence Agency)
Chalidze, Valery, 94
Chalidze Publications, 40

Chamberlin, William Henry, 46
Charter 77, 106
"The Choice-Freedom," 221
Christian Committee for the Defense of the Rights of Believers, 188
Christian Missionary Service, 9
Christian Russia, 195
Christian Russia—the Second Millennium, 196–97
Chronicle of Current Events, 40, 94, 95
Church, Frank, 60
Churchill, Winston, 21, 29
CIA (Central Intelligence Agency): funding by, xiii, 59, 68–69; glasnost and, 206, 207–8, 221–22, 223, 239; international broadcasting and, 42, 43, 45–46; RL impact study of, 59; Soviet media and, 233; Vlasovites and, 54
Clarkson, Natalie, 51, 125, 179
Clay, Lucius, 3, 41
clergy executions, 182
Cohen, Pamela Brown, 191
Cold War beginnings, 20–22
Cold War policy. *See* foreign policy, U.S.
collectivization, 157, 159, 230–31
Cominform, 32
commercial broadcasting, 9–10, 19, 126
Commission on Security and Cooperation in Europe (CSCE), 105–7
Committee for Social Self-Defense (KOR), 106
Committee on Human Rights in the USSR, 94
Committee on Long-Range Planning, 249
Committee on Russian Policy, UK, 22

communism: August Putsch and, 242–43; containing, 42–43; détente and, 61; glasnost and, 229; history broadcasts and, 157–58, 163, 164; power and, 20; programming and, 263; religion and, 185; Ronald Reagan and, xi, 71, 73; Soviet youth and, 234; VOA sympathy for, 12

Communist Youth League, 139

Congress, U.S., 2, 19–20, 59–60, 176, 247–48

Conkling, James, 77

Conover, Willis, ix, 132

Conquest, Robert, 154, 156, 250

conservatism, Russian, 150, 151, 152, 154

The Construction Battalion (Kaledin), 231

"A Conversation without Dicta-phones" (Larionova), 233–34

Coordinating Center of the Anti-Bolshevik Struggle, 47

corporatism, 151

Corti, Mario, 96, 262, 278n8

counterculture movement, Soviet, 131

Country Music, 132

The Courtyard (Lvov), 198

Critchlow, James, 147–50, 163, 195

Crusade for Freedom, ix, 67–69

Cull, Nicholas, 24, 33, 72–73, 109, 191, 224

Culture and Politics, 142–45

culture and the arts broadcasting of Radio Liberty, 137–46; back-ground and overview of, 137, 145–46; comedy and, 137–38; *Culture and Politics* and, 142–45; music and, 138–42

culture and the arts broadcasting of Voice of America, 115–37; artists and, 125–26; Galina Vishnevskaya and, 117, 122–25; Juri Jelagin and, 116–17, 126–30; *Literary Readings* and, 126–30; Mstislav Rostropo-vich and, 117–22; music and, 132–33, 134–36; quality of, 126; Russian liberation interviews and, 136–37; theater and, 133–34; variety of, 132; Vasily Aksyonov and, 130–32. *See also specific programs*

Cummings, Richard, 68

Cummins, Barbara, 125

current affairs programming, 35, 78, 132

Czechoslovakia, 95, 247, 251, 255–56

Czechoslovak Service, 42

Daniel, Yuli, 89–93, 94

Davydov, Egor, 101

Decembrist Revolt, 217

defection, 35–36, 88, 93, 99, 136

The Defector (Kabakov), 231

Deich, Mark, 228, 244

democracy, 15–18, 62, 73–74, 85, 158, 252

democratic liberalism, 16, 62

détente: impact on RL/RFE and VOA of, 58–62, 79–81; purist program-ming and, 5; Ronald Reagan and, 70, 72; VOA and, 40, 76, 77, 108–12

Dialogue, 116

Dienstbier, Jiri, 247

disinformation, 80, 224–25, 264–65

dissidents, Soviet: Final Act and, 105, 106; movement of, 90, 94–95; religious, 187–88, 202; RL and,

Ford, Gerald, 70, 106
Ford, Henry, II, 68
Foreign Affairs, 71–72, 155–56, 157, 166
Foreign Broadcast Information Service, 63
foreign policy, U.S., xi, 3, 5, 32–34, 41, 73–75
Foster, Ludmila, 261–62
Fotiev, Kirill, 197
Frank, Victor, 50
Franzusoff, Victor, 24, 37
freedom, 4, 16, 67–69, 72, 87, 120, 252, 262–63
Free Europe Committee, 67
freelance contributors, 227–28, 231, 232, 237, 243, 244, 251
Frenkley, Alexander, 35
Friedberg, Maurice, 143–44
Frumkin, Vladimir, 139–40
Fulbright, J. William, 5–6, 59–60, 61
funding of international broadcasting, 20, 42, 59, 60, 64, 80, 83–84
Fund to Aid Political Prisoners, 165
Fyodorov, Boris, 161

Galanskov, Yuri, 90, 97
Galich, Alexander, 126, 140, 142, 208, 241
Galin, Alexander, 218–19
Gardner, Ivan, 187
Gasparov, Boris, 162
Gates, Robert, 250
Gazdanov, Gaito, 90–91, 240
General Electric Theater, 67
Genis, Alexander, 219, 220
Gerdt, Zinovy, 258
German Auslandsrundfunk, 9
Gershwin, George, 138
Giddens, Kenneth, 111

Ginzburg, Alexander, 40, 90–92, 94, 110, 165
Ginzburg, Yevgenia, 110, 130
GKChP (State Committee on the State of Emergency), 241–42
Glad, John, 177
Gladilin, Anatoly, 143–44
glasnost, 203–41; about, 89, 99, 204–5; history broadcasting and, 162; jamming and, 203, 204, 209–11, 223–24, 225–27; religion and, 202; RL programming post-jamming, 228–32; RL Russian broadcasts and, 213–21; Soviet criticism of RL and, 203, 205–9; Soviet media and, 221–23, 232–41; Soviet television and, 211–12
Gogol, Nikolai, 93
Goldberg, Anatol, 23
Golos Ameriki (Lavrenev), 31
Gorbachev, Mikhail, 6; amnesties of, 188; August Putsch and, 241–42, 244–45; glasnost and, 211–12, 215; RL reception and, 258–59; Ronald Reagan and, 224
Gorbanevskaya, Natalia, 94, 95–96
Gorbatov, Boris, 30, 272n68
Gordin, Molly, 262
Gordon, Ernest, 186
Grafton, Samuel, 17
Gratitude Fund, 101
Great Reforms of 1860s, 155
The Great Terror (Conquest), 156
Greene, Hugh Carleton, 22
Gronouski, John, 80
Gudok, 30
Gul, Roman, 50
The Gulag Archipelago (Solzhenitsyn), 39, 62, 84, 109, 165, 216, 228

Guseinov, R., 235

Haig, Alexander, 39
Hair, 138-39
Handler, Yuri, 239
The Happy Station Show, 9
Harriman, Averell, 33
Havel, Vaclav, 247, 248, 255
Heart of a Dog (Bulgakov), 204
Heil, Alan, 37, 75-77, 191
Helsinki Accords, 105-7
Helsinki Commission on Security
    and Cooperation in Europe
    (CSCE), 105-7
Helsinki Final Act, 105-7
Henze, Paul, 43
history broadcasting, 147-64; back-
    ground and overview of, 147,
    153-54; criticism of, 147-48, 149-
    50, 152; glasnost and, 214, 215-18;
    Gleb Rahr and, 150-53, 156-61,
    162, 163-64; May 21, 1980, pro-
    gram of, 148-49, 150; Richard
    Pipes and, 154-58, 162; Vladimir
    Tolz and, 161-63, 164. *See also*
    specific programs
Horowitz, Vladimir, 134-36
Houseman, John, 12-14, 15, 17
Hughes, Olga Raevsky, 52
human rights, 87-113; religion and,
    183; Ronald Reagan and, 71; sam-
    izdat and, 89-90, 92, 93, 94, 96-
    98; show trials and, 89-93, 94;
    Soviet movement of, 88-93, 94-
    96, 108, 278n8; UDHR and, 87. *See*
    also human rights broadcasting
Human Rights, 214
human rights broadcasting: back-
    ground and overview of, 87-88,

98-99; Helsinki Final Act and,
    105, 106-7; samizdat and, 97-98;
    Soviet dissidents and, 101-4;
    Soviet emigration and, 99, 100-
    101; Soviet Union criticism of,
    206; VOA and, 40, 108-13; VOA
    and RL comparison of, 108; *White*
    Book and, 90-91. *See also specific*
    programs
Hungary, 21, 158, 251, 252, 253, 254
hunger strikes, 95, 101

Iakovlev, Iakov, 230, 284n16
I Chose Freedom (Kravchenko), 88
Ilyin, Ivan, 151, 163, 196, 228
Imperial Wireless Chain, 9
industrialization, 148-49, 152, 173
"Information or Propaganda?,"
    236-37
Intergirl, 219
Interim International Information
    Service (IIIS), 19
International Broadcasting Founda-
    tion, 32
international law, 31, 206, 243
interview approach programming,
    236
interviews of first émigrés, 49-50
interviews of second émigrés, 53
Into the Whirlwind (Ginzburg), 110
Intourist, 209, 219
Isayevich, Alexandr. *See* Solzhenit-
    syn, Alexandr
Islam, 198, 200
The Isolationist Illusion and World
    Peace (Warburg), 15-16
It Happens in Russia (Petrov), 88
Ivanova, Darya Alexandrovna, 125
Izvestia, 207-8, 223, 224, 229, 240

Smoktunovsky, Innokenty, 258

Sobesednik, 237

Sokolov, Maxim, 228

Sokolov, Mikhail, 228, 244

Solidarity movement, 81, 120, 255

Soloviev, Vladimir, 147, 228

Solzhenitsyn, Alexandr: about, xi, xiv; Alexander Schmemann and, 51; author's interview with, 165–69; in *Foreign Affairs*, 155–56, 157, 166; Galina Vishnevskaya and, 122, 123–24; *The Gulag Archipelago*, 39, 62, 84, 109, 165, 216, 228; history broadcasting and, 148, 149, 151; *Letter to the Soviet Leaders*, 149; *One Day in the Life of Ivan Denisovichy*, 89; *The Red Wheel*, 167–69, 178, 179; on RFE/RL and VOA, ix–x, 40; Richard Pipes and, 154, 155–57; Ronald Reagan and, 70, 71, 156; Russian nationalism and, 57, 58; Taiwan speech of, 85. See also *August 1914* (Solzhenitsyn); Voice of America (VOA) and Alexandr Solzhenitsyn

Solzhenitsyn, Natalia Dmitrievna, 165–66, 167

Sorokin, Nik, 38, 262

Sosin, Gene, 50, 54–55, 61–62, 63, 149, 257–58

Sovetskaya kultura, 221

Sovetskaya molodezh, 207, 241

Sovetskaya Rossiya, 227, 232–33

Sovetskii patriot, 235

Soviet Area Audience and Opinion Research division, 64

Soviet émigré project, 41

Soviet media: August Putsch and, 241; glasnost and, 211–12, 221–23, 232–41; propaganda campaign and, 28–29, 30, 39; RL and VOA and, 181, 205–9, 265–66

Soviet Union: anti-Americanism and, 24–25; counterculture movement in, 131; expulsions by, xi–xii, 49, 109, 120–21, 122, 144; foreign broadcasting as a threat to, 65–66; radio in, 122, 139, 216, 237, 241; religion and, 181–83; RL and, 203, 205–9; ruling elite of, 65–66, 73; show trials in, 89–93, 94–95, 99, 102–3, 182, 199–200; television in, 204, 211–12, 222; theatrical life in, 127–30; threat of, 20–22, 43. See also Soviet media

The Soviet Union and the Nationality Question, 231

Stalin, Joseph: criticism of, 88–89, 230; death of, 51, 65–66; history broadcasts and, 148; jamming and, 31; religion and, 182; *The Russian Question* and, 29

Stalin International Peace Prize, 12

Stalin Prize, 31, 118, 272n68

Stankevich, Sergei, 243

Stars in the Morning Sky (Galin), 218–19

State Committee on the State of Emergency (GKChP), 241–42

State Department, U.S.: bureaucratic infighting and, 17, 18; détente impact and, 60; IIIS and, 19; VOA and, xiii, 24–30, 32, 108, 109, 112, 113, 115

Steinberg, Milton, 190

Stepanenko, Valery, 244

Stevenson, Adlai, 67–68

Stilwell, Joseph, 15